D0913425

Up to Date

Language as SOCIAL ACTION

Howard Giles
General Editor

Vol. 24

The Language as Social Action series
is part of the Peter Lang Media and Communication list.
Every volume is peer reviewed and meets
the highest quality standards for content and production.

PETER LANG
New York • Bern • Berlin
Brussels • Vienna • Oxford • Warsaw

Stephanie Tom Tong
and Brandon Van Der Heide

Up to Date

Communication and Technology
in Romantic Relationships

PETER LANG
New York • Bern • Berlin
Brussels • Vienna • Oxford • Warsaw

Library of Congress Cataloging-in-Publication Data

Names: Tong, Stephanie Tom, author. | Van Der Heide, Brandon, author.
Title: Up to date: communication and technology in romantic relationships /
Stephanie Tom Tong and Brandon Van Der Heide.
Description: New York: Peter Lang, 2022.
Series: Language as social action; vol. 24 | ISSN 1529-2436
Includes bibliographical references and index.
Identifiers: LCCN 2021026316 (print) | LCCN 2021026317 (ebook)
ISBN 978-1-4331-4653-4 (hardback) | ISBN 978-1-4331-4654-1 (paperback)
ISBN 978-1-4331-4655-8 (ebook pdf) | ISBN 978-1-4331-4656-5 (epub)
Subjects: LCSH: Online dating. | Dating (Social customs) |
Dating services. | Internet—Social aspects.
Classification: LCC HQ801.82 T66 2022 (print) | LCC HQ801.82 (ebook) |
DDC 306.730285—dc23
LC record available at https://lccn.loc.gov/2021026316
LC ebook record available at https://lccn.loc.gov/2021026317
DOI 10.3726/b18758

Bibliographic information published by **Die Deutsche Nationalbibliothek.**
Die Deutsche Nationalbibliothek lists this publication in the "Deutsche
Nationalbibliografie"; detailed bibliographic data are available
on the Internet at http://dnb.d-nb.de/.

© 2022 Peter Lang Publishing, Inc., New York
80 Broad Street, 5th floor, New York, NY 10004
www.peterlang.com

Dedication

Stephanie: I dedicate this book to Daniel Cook, who not only let me use him as an example in several chapters, but has also been my constant champion and supporter for the last 18 years. Just as he lovingly proofread every sentence of this book in an effort to help me improve my writing, so he continues to enrich my everyday life. To my parents for setting a strong example of a relationship, upon which to build. Finally, of course, to Ison.

Brandon: I dedicate this book to Jen VanDerHeide. Jen routinely tolerates me and puts up with my machinations, and has done so without unwarranted frustration for the past 20 years. Also, to my son Liam, who has most likely shaped Jen and me into better partners to one another and has most definitely forced us to be present as we think about the relationship we display to him.

Contents

List of Figures

List of Tables

Acknowledgments

We want to thank the many researchers whose work on computer-mediated communication, romantic relationships, social media, mobile and Internet technology we have cited. Several of these researchers are people we are lucky enough to call friends and colleagues.

First, we wish to thank our editor Howie Giles who has proven to be among the most encouraging, thoughtful, and (above all) patient humans on the planet.

We thank David DeAndrea and Caleb Carr for providing encouragement, challenges, camaraderie, and intellectual stimulation for the better part of the past two decades. Special thanks to our students who have been such important contributors in our research teams and labs for many years: David Beyea, William Cooper, Elena Corriero, Nancy Dai, Kelsey Earle, Allison Elam, Sean Kolhoff, Ben Lennemann, Adam Mason, Robert Matheny, Benjamin Prchal, Rachelle Prince, Annisa Rochadiat, Soo Yun Shin, Kunto Wibowo, and Chad Van De Wiele.

Finally, both of us thank Dr. Joseph B. Walther for his ongoing mentorship, friendship, and support. Without Joe, this project would never have happened; his habit of helping us organize our research has taught us: (1) to look to theory and proceed from what we know, (2) to "listen to the data," and (3) to pursue compelling and counterintuitive ideas. His teaching has forever shaped the way we understand computer-mediated communication and relational research.

1

An Introduction to *Up to Date*

When we sat down together to write the beginnings of what would become the outline of this book, we noted the considerable challenges associated with choosing an audience to whom we would write, a body of literature we would summarize, and a perspective from which to write. Depending on these decisions, we thought, we could end up with about five or six good—but each very different—books. Given this realization, we saw several options. We could write one book that was about as long as six books, we could cram six books into a single book, or—and this is the option we landed on—we could write one of the possible six books but make it the best book possible. To us, this seemed like the option that (a) you would be most likely to want to read and (b) would spare us the most gray hairs writing. Because of this choice, we feel it important, at the outset, to acknowledge our decisions about audience, scope, and perspective because we hope that understanding what we have chosen also helps you to understand this work just a little bit better.

Audience, Scope, and Perspective

Audience. We set out to write this book for curious graduate and undergraduate students and experienced researchers alike. We both believe that, in its purest form, social science is a collaborative invitation. This invitation seeks to draw the reader into active participation in the conversation with and between scholars.

Imagine you arrive at a cocktail party, and you walk into a room where a lively conversation is happening. In this lively conversation you notice several people you like and admire—although they probably do not know you. You saunter over and join their circle. The first thing you might do is listen. After all, you probably want to make a favorable impression on these people you admire and forcing yourself headlong into their conversation might not yield the best results. Instead, what you are likely to do is listen carefully, thoughtfully about what is being said. Probably one of the things you would be most concerned about as a new party to this conversation is that you might say the same things one of the people in your group said just a few minutes before you arrived. Or, perhaps you adopt a point that, although relevant to the conversation, has already been refuted. You are probably concerned that this would reflect poorly on you in front of these people you hope to impress.

These are, we suspect, also the concerns of new scholars seeking to dip their toes into topics for which they have curiosity in abundance but confidence and experience in short supply. We have both been there, and between you and us (if we are being completely honest) we still both feel that way from time to time. We imagine that one of the biggest barriers to entry for budding scholars (of any age or academic rank) is the concern that their contributions to the scholarly conversation may not be novel or smart enough to get them a seat at the cool kids' table. At best, this represents time lost to worry or fear, and at worst, a reputation tarnished. In the high-pressure world of the 21st century, the scholar can afford neither of these things.

With that said, we believe that more voices representing a diverse range of thought benefit social scientific productivity and progress. To summarize, we understand why you might be reticent to join the conversation; nevertheless, we are writing this book to invite you to join researchers in our public conversations about online and mobile romance in all its forms. The ongoing conversations about these topics have become much more complex in recent years, primarily because online and mobile dating holds such an important place in the contemporary relational landscape. Online and mobile dating platforms are now the most common way adults find new romantic connections in the United States

(Rosenfeld, Thomas, & Hausen, 2019); these technologies also play a key role in our ability to develop new relationships, maintain existing bonds, and even manage unwanted relationships. We begin by first bringing you up to date on where the public conversation currently stands with regard to online romance; we also introduce you to the different scholarly approaches to the study of romance, and finally offer our suggestions about where we might go from here.

To be completely transparent, we have also observed many of our scholarly peers who, after their time in graduate school, began to migrate into the study of computer-mediated communication (CMC), social media, and the effects on communicative functions like relating, persuading, and informing. We suspect they, too, even as experienced researchers find that there are barriers to entry into the study of technology's effects on human communication. If you are interested in romantic relationships and the ways that they are mediated, morphed, or molded by technology, no matter what your own perceived level—novice student to seasoned researcher—this book was written to invite you to participate in these ongoing conversations.

Scope. We confess that some of the most significant authorial decisions we made were those regarding the scope of this project. These decisions could have been made differently and thus resulted in very different final products, none of which would be inherently less valuable than the current work. For example, we could have written a book solely about partner selection processes in online and mobile dating—how do we decide when to swipe right? Or, we could have focused solely on apps and websites that compete for a piece of the lucrative online dating industry. These might have been very interesting books (maybe even books that should be written) but they were not what we elected to do.

Instead, we envisioned the scope of this book as scholars of interpersonal and relational communication. Although we will touch on technologies, individual and cultural differences, societal factors, and demographics, we focus primarily on the ways each of these things does or does not affect communication in romantic relationships. With that said, the study of human communication and technology is, and has always been, an intensely interdisciplinary project. Computer scientists, sociologists, linguists, psychologists, communication scholars, scholars of information science, and anthropologists (to name but a few) have meaningfully shaped the dominant social scientific understanding of online behavior. Our work certainly borrows from and addresses these areas, but we integrate such scholarship through the lens of interpersonal communication. Because of this, it probably comes as no surprise to our readers that rather than structuring the book according to technological affordances, online platforms, psychological theories, or sociological demographics, we chose to structure this work according to how technology has the capacity to influence different stages of the modern romantic relationship. As a result, you will find that we rely heavily on multiple disciplines and cite scholars from all different areas—but ultimately, we will always come back to interpersonal communication and romantic relationships as the foundation for our thinking about online and mobile dating.

Perspective. The authors met one another in the fall of 2006, as graduate students under the tutelage of Dr. Joseph B. Walther at Michigan State University. We mention this, because working with Joe had a profound impact on who we would eventually become as scholars and how we thought about CMC and its effects on human relationship *functions*. This idea that people use interaction to fulfill many different *functions*—from relating, to persuading, to information sharing—is at the heart of the *functional orientation on communication* (Burgoon, Buller, & Woodall, 1996; Burgoon & Saine, 1978), which is the foundational perspective of this book. When you start to consider all of the communicative functions involved in relationships, then ask how contemporary dating websites and mobile apps can impact those functions, modern-day mediated romance can become an interesting puzzle to ponder.

One of the first things a reader should know about this text is that the authors were trained to approach CMC as an interesting laboratory for understanding the key principles of nonverbal communication. After all, in its early days CMC was an interesting communication channel because it forced interlocutors to utilize *primarily* (if not exclusively) verbal interaction. One of the key assumptions of those pioneering CMC scholars was that (a) because social information was primarily transmitted by way of text-based "cues" and (b) because CMC users did not have access to physical behaviors, lots of interpersonal processes—like impressions, status, and attraction—could not develop in CMC (see Kiesler, Siegel, & McGuire, 1984). Such thinking made CMC seem like the cold and dark surface of the moon, where interactions were scrubbed of all but the most sterile exchanges. In CMC, the story went, communication was function without flourish. The perspectives on CMC guided by this assumption have become known as the *cues-filtered-out* (CFO) perspective (Culnan & Markus, 1987).

But being the astute communicator that you are, you are thinking to yourself, "*Does CMC filter out social information? Are interpersonal liking and attraction really suppressed online? If that is true, then how are all of these people getting together on Tinder?! If this is true, then this book about online romance is either going to be very short, or there must be some catch.*" You are right—there is a catch.

Not all scholars adopted the CFO perspective on CMC. Walther's *social information processing theory* (1992) was the first to apply a nonverbal functional perspective to the relatively nonverbal-cue-free environment of CMC in the 1980s and 1990s. While the specifics of this and other CMC theories can wait for later in this book, it is important to note the ways that social information processing theory departed from the CFO perspective. Walther's innovation was to suggest that CMC afforded unexpected avenues for interpersonal affect. To be specific, he proposed that people could use text-based messages to creatively accomplish interpersonal affect functions, persuasive functions, and relational maintenance functions usually imagined to demand physical presence. In a recent retelling of these developments, Walther and Ramirez (2014) summarized this point gracefully:

> This [CFO] approach was an intellectual problem for Walther and Ramirez as well as others who had similar training in the area of personal relationships. . .From a functional perspective it was difficult to accept that nonverbal cues alone. . .could bear the entire responsibility for interpersonal affect, online or elsewhere. As if individuals who could not see or hear could have no relationships; as if writing from poetry to pornography, could not arouse. (p. 266)

In this book, we adhere to the *functional orientation*. We believe that people will utilize the tools at their disposal to accomplish communicative functions to which they set their minds. That includes when people make friends in cyberspace (Parks & Floyd, 1996); carefully navigate the relational dissolution process (Tong, 2013); try to determine who to trust online (Van Der Heide & Lim, 2016); or assess whether a person or entity is being truthful to them or not (DeAndrea, 2014), just to name a few. We believe that a functional orientation is a useful way to think about modern-day mediated romance because it helps to generate theories, principles, and propositions that stand the test of time and apply across new technologies as they develop. By following the functional orientation, the ideas we offer in this book should resonate long after Tinder is gone and replaced by a newer, more popular dating app.

We believe that people who use technology to facilitate parts of their romantic relationships are essentially the same as people who have been experiencing love in some form for millions of years. Reeves and Nass (1996) in their important treatise on the connections between human-computer interaction and social psychology, often suggest that humans have "old brains." In other words, the human brain is not wired to respond to technology differently than any other social stimulus. This proposition led Reeves and Nass to a set of findings now considered to be foundational in human-computer interaction—that people respond to computers in much the same way as they respond to people. People do this because their old brains—created over millions of years of evolution— respond to new stuff in old ways.

It is tempting to buy into the narrative that technologies like social media, online dating websites, text messaging, video chat, and mobile dating apps have turned the human experience of love upside down. To be sure, these are all innovations worth investigating; however, we think that the feelings of intense attraction, bonding, occasional conflict, or the processes of impression formation, relational maintenance, and relational termination are largely the same feelings and processes that humans have experienced and engaged in for a very long time. While we do not believe that the introduction of electronic connectedness has altered human biology, we do believe that people are creatively utilizing technology to accomplish many of the same relational functions they have always sought to accomplish. Sometimes people do this in novel, weird, or exciting ways. Sometimes, the ways people use technology to accomplish online what they would have done in person has interesting, often unanticipated, side effects. And sometimes, technology gets people to the exact same place as a FtF conversation. These things, we think, are fascinating and worth investigation.

What is the Functional Orientation and Why Does It Matter?

As noted above, the functional orientation organizes the field of communication differently than typical paradigms. Rather than organizing the study of communication according to the context in which it happens, the functional approach arranges human communication according to the functions that messages perform. Namely, the chief functions of human communication include informing, persuading, organizing, and relating. You may be used to more traditional divisions in the study of communication such as rhetorical studies, interpersonal, organizational, mass media, or communication technology. These divisions are definitely useful; however, there are several ways in which a functional orientation offers a different way to organize associated research questions, as well as the amalgamation of diverse insights beneath a larger theoretical umbrella.

First, the functional orientation *allows for greater cohesion and clarity of associated research questions*. What we mean by this is that by focusing on functions rather than context, scholars can often draw together multiple perspectives, even multiple disciplines, and approach their research questions from a more informed standpoint. For example, imagine that an interpersonal scholar and a mass media scholar each became interested in the question of how people form impressions in social media. Our hypothetical mass media scholar might be concerned with the ways that observers judge news organizations in social media environments, while our hypothetical interpersonal scholar might be most interested in the types of social information an observer gleans from other people's Facebook accounts. Our hypothetical mass media scholar would likely utilize theories of journalistic credibility to inform his or her work. Meanwhile, our hypothetical interpersonal scholar might tap social psychological perspectives on impression management. It is conceivable, even probable, that these two scholars would submit their work to different journal outlets or conferences—and possibly be unfamiliar with one another's work—while their interests are, in fact, probably quite similar.

We fear that scholars like the fictional ones we describe above are not terribly rare in the field of communication. Like ships passing in the night, sometimes scholars of CMC can be unaware of related work simply because that material is written in an unfamiliar dialect—such as that of mass media, interpersonal communication, or organizational communication, whether microtheory or macro-theory. We, too, have been guilty of this kind of siloing, but by organizing the process of communication according to the functions it serves rather than in the contexts it occurs, we think that the functional orientation might help to draw together research questions into more meaningful groups.

Second, the functional orientation *integrates insights from multiple theoretical frameworks beneath a larger theoretical umbrella*. If, instead of choosing theoretical guidance solely from one's own wheelhouse, scholars begin to draw inspiration from diverse, sometimes competing, perspectives, it is often the case that new theoretical innovations are born. Walther and Parks' (2002) warranting theory, for instance, derives a great deal of its inspiration from Stone's (1995) treatise on the effects of technology at the end of the mechanical age. While Stone's ontological and epistemological perspectives diverged dramatically from the one which Walther and Parks espoused, the latter scholars were able to look past these differences to identify that Stone's contributions could be expounded upon to generate testable social scientific propositions. The functional orientation has the capacity to expand the places from which scholars look for theoretical inspiration.

Third, the functional orientation *helps unite scholars from across the discipline of communication*. Brandon once heard a senior scholar in the field make a joke that organizational communication is just interpersonal communication "in a box" (a joke always uttered by interpersonal communication scholars, and never in earshot of organizational communication scholars). Although this is an attempt at academic humor, the joke is funny to interpersonal scholars because it makes them feel good to be able to claim that an entire sub-field is derivative of one's own. Yet this joke—and others uttered by media, organizational, intercultural, or rhetorical scholars (out of earshot of *us*)—are probably misplaced. Surely, many of us tend to care about different communicative functions: relating, organizing, influencing, or informing; yet, we balkanize ourselves against outside influence in order to speak to our "home" academic community. We hope that adopting a functional orientation helps to ameliorate some of our more territorial, dare-we-say arrogant, influences.

At this point you may be wondering why we have spent so much time introducing and explaining the functional orientation. We assure you that it is not without warrant. We care about the functional orientation because it demands that this book be about more than online "dating." While other projects can be and have been written about the technologies that facilitate online dating, the functional orientation suggests that instead we ought to write about the process of online relating. Specifically, what have scholars learned about the process of online relating, and what areas remain undiscovered?

Book and Chapter Structure

You will see that the book is divided into sections that follow the basic process of the relational lifecycle—development, maintenance, and dissolution. Within each of these sections are chapters designed to answer two broad questions: First, "What do we know?" Among the most important things for scholars to be aware of before they throw their hats in the ring and attempt to join the scholarly conversation are the contributions of their forebears. We hope that after reading each chapter, you become aware of the dominant scholarly voices in the area and what those voices are saying. Although this book will not supplant the need to do your own original literature search, after reading each chapter, you should have a firm sense of where the field stands in relation to some of its major questions.

The second question that each chapter answers is, "Where do we go?" In each chapter, we will also propose new directions for future scholarship to expand on what we currently know. While we will likely fall short of instantiating fully formed new theories, we are hopeful that our readers might pick up some of these research loose ends and start to weave themselves into the scholarly conversation.

Selfishly, we confess that this part of our project is just as much for ourselves as it is for our readers. We hope that providing a window into how we utilize the functional orientation on relational communication and CMC will help you to start imagining new research questions in this vein.

Though the online and mobile dating field seems crowded now, in the 1960s, technology was quite rare and it filled daters with a sense of optimism. Computers expanded people's romantic imagination by providing an air of accuracy, control, and precision; but this potential was also shrouded in mystery (in fact, eHarmony still describes their compatibility dimensions as "magic" and OkCupid calls its algorithm "one-of-a-kind"). The mystique of computers loomed large: many online dating sites seemed to say to daters, "You want access to new-fangled romantic imagination filled with unbounded rationality and unending access to new romantic prospects? Then it will cost you a monthly subscription fee." Computing technology was touted as providing advantages for dating that individual people simply could never hope to replicate. Online dating companies housed clandestine kitchens where the secret ingredients of science, technology, psychology, and spiritualism were cooked up and served to hungry singles (Strimpel, 2017, p. 321). Today, upwards of 30 million daters happily give their credit cards up in exchange for a taste of this secret sauce. So what exactly do people get in exchange for $19.95 every month?

We tackle this question and others in the first portion of the book, which examines the current online and mobile dating arena, and discusses how these technologies have impacted romantic dating. In Chapter 2, we review the history of the online and mobile dating industry—we trace its origins and follow its trajectory into contemporary culture. In Chapter 3, we offer an overview of romantic relationships—what theories help us understand how romantic connections develop between people? In Chapter 4, we survey popular sites and apps, catalog the diverse features that they offer to users, and discuss how the sociotechnical design of these various platforms has affected daters' communication behaviors, particularly in the developmental stages of romantic dating. Throughout this book, we also focus on various communication functions that popular dating sites and apps facilitate, including: self-presentation and impression formation (Chapter 5), partner selection and rejection (Chapter 6), and "modality shifts" which describe how daters move from initial online and mobile messaging to FtF meet-ups (Chapter 7). We also explore the growing reach of online dating by examining the different groups of people who use these sites and apps, and how factors like age, race, and gender have affected the ways people search for romance in online and mobile platforms (Chapter 8).

Oddly, dating apps and websites promote their ability to perpetuate lasting romantic relationships, yet many do not actually help people move beyond an initial introduction. The second portion of this book explores what role Internet and mobile technologies play after partners establish a relationship and decide they want it to last. Are there mobile apps that facilitate relational maintenance between established romantic couples? We focus on that question in Chapter 9, followed by an examination of romantic conflict in Chapter 10, which explores the conditions under which mediated communication escalates big fights versus when it helps to ameliorate romantic skirmishes. The final chapter of this section is Chapter 11 where we look at the ways in which technology can influence the dissolution between partners, as well as the more destructive "dark side" of romantic relationships. We look at how separating from romantic partners now requires more than a painful breakup conversation. Today's breakups involve disentangling not just physically, but also each other's shared online, mobile, and physical spaces. This chapter discusses how couples utilize the affordances of technology to navigate breakups, and how they use social media to fulfill functions of termination during the demise of a relationship.

We then turn to an examination of the larger sociological issues created by online dating. After nearly 15 years of swiping, clicking, and searching, do we still believe in the promise of computing technology and its optimistic outlook on the romantic imagination? Or do we now see these apps and sites as purveyors of hollow hype? In Chapter 12, we first examine the nature of online dating fatigue and how all the swiping, selection, and profile updates can make online and mobile dating feel less like a game and more like a part-time job. In examining this laborious side of online dating, we also discuss the various gig industries that have popped up in response to daters' pleas for help with managing the ever-growing workload of online dating. We delve into first-hand accounts from "online dating assistants" to see what their experiences are like, and what role they see themselves playing in the construction of modern romantic relationships. In Chapter 13, we focus on the larger ethical issues that arise from the popularity of dating technology. We take a closer look at the online and mobile dating industry itself by providing some background on the size and scope of the industry, examine the common business models and corporate strategies used by today's most popular companies, as well as how those business models can compromise users' privacy and safety—of both our physical selves and our electronic data. We end the book with a final set of thoughts and conclusions in Chapter 14 that helps us think about the larger body of research regarding relationships and technology, and how we can continue to investigate the role of communication in contemporary romance.

We intend this book to be a review of the landscape of online and mobile dating and modern romantic relationships, from historical background to present-day trends. We also review how technology has impacted the performance of various communication functions, besides shaping our current conceptualization of intimate relationships. You will see that we incorporate all kinds of different materials in this book, including: primary research conducted by scholars from different disciplines, popular press and journalistic reports, and empirical data that we collected in our own experiments and studies. We also include individual anecdotes from people who have used online and mobile dating platforms, social computing systems, and other forms of technology in their personal interactions and relationships with others. In several chapters, we draw from these individuals' accounts to introduce complex theoretical ideas and to show how people perceive and integrate technology into their relational lives. If you allow us, we would like to offer you some ideas about how today's most popular Internet, computing, and mobile technologies might influence how we imagine the future possibilities of romantic communication between people.

References

Burgoon, J. K., & Saine, T. J. (1978). *The unspoken dialogue: An introduction to nonverbal communication.* Houghton-Mifflin.

Burgoon, J. K., Buller, D. B., & Woodall, W. G. (1996). *Nonverbal communication: The unspoken dialogue.* McGraw-Hill.

Culnan, M. J., & Markus, M. L. (1987). Information technologies. In F. M. Jablin, L. L. Putnam, K. H. Roberts, & L. W. Porter (Eds.), *Handbook of organizational communication* (pp. 420–443). Sage.

DeAndrea, D. C. (2014). Advancing warranting theory. *Communication Theory, 24*(2), 186–204. https://doi.org/10.1111/comt.12033

Kiesler, S., Siegel, J., & McGuire, T. W. (1984). Social psychological aspects of computer-mediated communication. *American Psychologist, 39*(10), 1123–1134. https://doi.org/10.1037/0003-066X.39.10.1123

Miller, G. R., & Steinberg, M. (1975). *Between people: A new analysis of interpersonal communication.* Science Research Associates, Inc.

Parks, M. R., & Floyd, K. (1996). Making friends in cyberspace. *Journal of Computer-Mediated Communication, 1*(4). https://doi.org/10.1111/j.1083-6101.1996.tb00176.x

Reeves, B., & Nass, C. (1996). *The media equation: How people treat computers, television, and new media like real people and places.* Cambridge University Press.

Rosenfeld, M. J., Thomas, R. J., & Hausen, S. (2019). Disintermediating your friends: How online dating in the United States displaces other ways of meeting. *Proceedings of the National Academy of Sciences, 116*(36), 17753–17758. https://doi.org/10.1073/pnas.1908630116

Stone, A. R. (1995). *The war of desire and technology at the close of the mechanical age.* MIT Press.

Strimpel, Z. (2017). Computer dating in the 1970s: Dateline and the making of the modern British single. *Contemporary British History, 31*(3), 319–342. https://doi.org/10.1080/13619462.2017.1280401

Tong, S. T. (2013). Facebook use during relationship termination: Uncertainty reduction and surveillance. *Cyberpsychology, Behavior, and Social Networking, 16*(11), 788–793. https://doi.org/10.1089/cyber.2012.0549

Van Der Heide, B., & Lim, Y. (2016). The conditional cueing of credibility heuristics: The case of online influence. *Communication Research, 43*(5), 672–693. https://doi.org/10.1177/0093650214565915

Walther, J. B. (1992). Interpersonal effects in computer-mediated interaction: A relational perspective. *Communication Research, 19*(1), 52–90. https://doi.org/10.1177/009365092019001003

Walther, J. B., & Parks, M. R. (2002). Cues filtered out, cues filtered in: Computer-mediated communication and relationships. In M. L. Knapp & J. A. Daly (Eds.), *The handbook of interpersonal communication* (3rd ed., pp. 529–563). Sage.

Walther, J. B., & Ramirez, A. (2014). New technologies and new directions in online relating. In S. W. Smith & S. R. Wilson (Eds.), *New directions in interpersonal communication research* (pp. 264–284). Sage.

2

A Brief History of Online and Mobile Dating: The Role of Technology in the Contemporary Romantic Imagination

From an early age, romance captures the attention, if not the interest, of children. Many narratives children view in popular movies or television shows portray the development of romantic relationships. Parents and guardians both explicitly and implicitly communicate their values when it comes to romance through modeling and direct conversation. Children watch kind acts of service, observe squabbles, and bemoan good-night kisses between their parents. Moreover, children mimic these behaviors. When Brandon's son Liam was in daycare at age three, he had no fewer than three (simultaneous) "girlfriends." Of course, these were not girlfriends in any particular developed sense, but these kids, left to their own devices, modeled the relational tropes they had observed in the world. One particularly ardent suitor had to be restrained when, observing Liam share a popsicle with her romantic rival, she lashed out in jealousy.

We were interested in the narratives kids can generate about how romance plays out in a modern date. One of the best ways to do this, we reasoned, was by asking an 11-year-old to describe one. This was his response:

> "Well, the first thing that happens is that a person has to ask the other person out. But, the other person has to say, 'Yes.' You can't just drag someone along on a date. Usually there's a place that they choose—usually it's a restaurant and they

get dinner together. And what happens is that the people sit across from each other, they don't sit on the same side of the table—because it's more formal to sit across than on the same side. Then they order food and they try to talk to each other and start a conversation. For the rest of the night they try to talk to each other and be nice to each other. They then try to figure out if they *LIKE* like the other person. But you wouldn't ask the other person if they LIKE like you, you have to kind of stay passive aggressive because if you don't it gets awkward."

How do you know if a person LIKE likes you?

"I don't know, my mom says the other person sometimes gives you a specific look. But on TV shows it says that you, like, get a feeling."

What do you think the feeling might be?

"I don't know, maybe like comfort. Like the feeling you get when you just ate your mom's homemade grilled cheese and now you're just relaxed."

Are you mostly trying to figure out if THEY like you, or if YOU like them?

"I'd say it's a little bit of both. But you're also trying to just have fun, so you're trying to balance out the three things: Figuring out if they LIKE like you, figuring out if you LIKE like them, and trying to have fun."

So what happens after dinner?

"One person drives the other person back to their apartment and in the parking lot usually one person says that they had a good time and that they should do this again. Then the other person says something nice and says goodbye. And it kinda doesn't matter if you actually LIKE like the other person or not, that's the way this conversation goes because you don't want to hurt the other person's feelings. If you actually don't LIKE like them, then you just don't bring up the 'let's do this again' thing and then just don't text them."

What about if you do really LIKE like each other?

"Yeah, you probably would try to set something up again in the future. Maybe even right away that night, because you're overcome with the feeling that you *need this* and you need to do something quick."

As the above conversation shows, children have been known to contemplate the idea of romance, even before they experience it first-hand. When asked, children as young as eight can set the scene of a romantic date and describe it in great detail: Often it is a man and woman, sitting in a restaurant, with soft music and candlelight, eating "special" or "fancy" food (Bachen & Illouz, 1996). That children and adolescents can so easily craft a picture of a romantic date indicates that romance is an important enough concept to be discovered and elaborated on, even from a young age. Such descriptions suggest that children hold *relational schema*—or cognitive structures that represent "regularities in patterns of interpersonal relatedness" (Baldwin, 1992)—basically children develop working models of what romantic relationships "should" look like by internalizing information from the mass media or observations of others in their environment (e.g., family, friends, etc.). These schema reflect how children (and adults alike) develop their "romantic imagination"—not their capacity for make-believe, but rather "the set of symbols and meanings we use when trying to communicate to ourselves or others a *possible*, yet non-existent, situation" (emphasis original; Bachen & Illouz, 1996; p. 280). Our romantic imagination functions as an important sensemaking tool—a way for us to contemplate and understand our social world. Of course, its formation is affected by several individual factors, including: *age*—as we mature and our cognitive capacities develop, we focus on different forms of information and learn to process them differently. Our *personalities*, our *lifestyles*, and *experiences* in dating also shape our romantic imagination, as does the *biology* of our bodies as hormones fluctuate; all of these individual factors shape how we understand romance.

In addition to these individual factors, external forces like sexual politics, the economy, and religious beliefs have also exerted their influence on the environment in which we conduct romance. One factor in particular that has impacted our contemporary understanding of romance is *technology*. Innovations such as the postal mail service, the telephone, and the automobile have all contributed to the ways we date, mate, and relate. In this book, we will focus on a comparatively small portion of technological innovation by examining how Internet and mobile communication technologies have influenced our courtship and dating practices, and how we develop, maintain, and dissolve romantic relationships. To do this, however, requires examining historically our collective understandings and definitions of romantic love.

This chapter briefly discusses the historical evolution of the romantic imagination beginning in the early 1900s, with unique turning points in the 1920s and 1930s. We then trace the history of modern-day online and mobile dating by examining early computerized dating systems created in the 1960s. With this brief review, our goal is to provide a better understanding of how mobile and

Internet technology has developed alongside the practices and patterns of romantic courtship, dating, and relating. This sets the foundation for the rest of the book in which we explore how popular online and mobile dating technologies have fundamentally altered—sometimes facilitating, sometimes degrading—various functions of romantic communication.

A Historical Look at Romance and Dating

Today, we think of a romantic relationship as a shared connection between two partners that is both emotionally fulfilling and passionate. A couple is supposed to be united by love, commitment, and hot sex, as well as shared values, attitudes, and beliefs. That is a lot to expect from one relationship. But these contemporary expectations were not always the norm: Romance as we think of it today became part of a cultural consciousness that arose from several societal changes in the early part of the 20th century.

But let's begin at the end of the 18th century, when romance and dating looked very different than they do today. In America, for example, the idea that a single woman could unilaterally select her own romantic partner was unheard of—at that time, middle- and upper-class women, in particular, were often introduced to potential suitors by their parents, family members, or prominent members of their community. Although emotional connections between partners were encouraged, the family would first make sure that both partners were matched in terms of social position, class, and background. Men and women didn't go out on the town on dates. Instead a man would "call" on a woman he was interested in and visit her at her home—but he didn't come over to watch Netflix and chill. During a call, a man and woman might listen to music, play games, or converse, but always under the watchful eye of her family members.

It was during the end of the Industrial Revolution (1840s) that many young women began finding work outside the home as saleswomen, seamstresses, waitresses, or secretaries. Although they often drew much lower salaries than men, their new financial earnings presented them a fresh sense of independence—for example, rather than contribute to the family's collective income, some women decided to rent their own apartments (though many had to live together with other female roommates to make ends meet). In the early 1900s, women also began to receive more formal education, with many finishing high school and entering universities. In fact, between 1900 and 1930, high school enrollment in America increased by an astounding 650 % (Fass, 1977)! This increase in employment and education meant that young men and women spent more time with their friends at work and school, and less time at home with their families. College and university campuses also played a role, as the primary place that men and women met, interacted, and socialized.

The combined advancements in the 1920s of education, sexual contraception, and outside employment delayed the age of marriage for many women. As a result, dating took on a new significance and paved the way for changes regarding the possibilities and practice of romance. Three notable transformations regarding courtship took place at this time:

First, young women (and men) secured more freedom to select their own romantic partners. They no longer had to rely on parents or relatives to introduce them to men; they were able to make connections more freely for themselves and conduct courtship more privately. This allowed them the autonomy to decide whom to date, hook up with, (and eventually marry):

> [Dating] developed as youths were increasingly freed from the direct supervision of family and community and allowed the freedom to develop private, intimate, and isolated associations. Dating opened the way for experimentation in mate compatibility. The lack of commitment permitted close and intimate associations and explorations of personality, and isolation and privacy laid the ground for sexual experimentation, both as a means for testing future compatibility and as an outlet for present sexual energies. (Fass, 1977, p. 263)

Along with this new autonomy in mate selection comes a re-conceptualization of romantic relationships as being *intrinsically motivated* as opposed to *extrinsically matched*. That is, a true romantic connection was now considered to develop out of the pure pleasure of experiencing another person's conversation or company and less motivated by external reasons such as social position, rank, or economic needs (Simmel, 1971). A "real" romantic relationship in the 1920s was one that was built on a foundation of interpersonal connection, compatibility, personality, and emotional fulfillment. Given that women were able to support themselves, they were liberated to focus on matters of the heart, as opposed to matters of the pocketbook. This is the second notable change in the romantic imagination at this time, and it is perfectly illustrated in a newspaper column called "Heart Problems" printed in the *Richmond Palladium and Sun-Telegram* in 1920. A young woman writes to advice columnist, Mrs. Thompson, with the following dilemma:

> Dear Mrs. Thompson: I am 18 years old and have been keeping company with a young man I do not love. He loves me, however, and has asked father's permission

to marry me. Father likes him and gave the permission. I simply won't do it. The unpleasant part of it is that it has been made clear that I am no longer wanted at home and that it is the family's desire to have me marry, even if I don't love the man. Please give me your advice. I am desperate because I don't know what to do. –T. H. J.

And, Mrs. Thompson's response to T. H. J.:

Do not marry the man since you do not love him. It would be better to find a position and to live elsewhere than to spoil your whole life in a loveless marriage. At the age of 18 you are very young to start out in life alone. Your success depends entirely upon the quality of your own industriousness and character. Always remember that you want to be worthy of a good husband some day and that you must not compromise yourself.

Mrs. Thompson's advice demonstrates that the possibilities regarding romance and marriage in the 1920s were beginning to evolve. Although today's readers might feel that last piece of advice Mrs. Thompson gives seems antiquated (T.H.J., you better keep your hook-ups on the DL so as not to "compromise" yourself when your "good husband" comes along), she also advises T.H.J. to marry the man she wants—not the one her parents want for her. Love becomes a luxury that girls like T.H.J. can afford in the 1920s and 1930s; even though the age of 18 is "very young to start out in life alone," at least she has the option to support herself financially.

This shift in the cultural expectations for romance are also evidenced in Phyllis Blanchard's and Carlyn Manasses's book entitled *New Girls for Old* (1930) that discusses how "modern girls" of the time viewed important topics such as sexuality, family, education, and work. In the book, they discuss a "new kind of marriage" that was being advocated in the 1930s: "The modern union of man and woman is visioned as a perfect consummation of both personalities that will involve every phase of mutual living." (Let us just pause for a moment to consider the grandeur of this statement—romance is supposed to culminate in a marriage of perfect compatibility between partners involving *every* phase of living?! Sure, Phyllis and Carlyn, no pressure at all).

The third big change came as courtship moved out of the house. Men no longer had to call on women in their family homes. Instead, young men and women (by themselves, or in groups with their peers) could often see each other unchaperoned. The terms "going out" and "dating" become new, popular ways to describe courtship. As Spurlock (2015) notes, "By the end of the 1920s adult authorities had begun to view dating, and even "petting," as normal rituals leading to courtship" (p. 40). By the way, "petting" could include all kinds of stuff: according to Fass (1977) it could consist of "kissing" (mostly above the neck, nicknamed "necking"), "intimate caresses" or "physical fondling". . .(nice euphemisms, but we get the idea—those kids in the 1920s had their hands full). Oddly enough, it seems that in order to get any privacy to pet one another, couples had to go out in public. Staying at home was a surefire way to slow things down. In 1961, Ann Landers would advise young female readers of *Life* magazine that "the living room of your own house is the safest place to neck. And there must always be a light on. It goes without saying that a respectable girl never invites a boy into her house unless one or both parents are at home" (p. 75).

As the practice of dating becomes more public, it also became connected to *consumption*. Eating in restaurants, going to concerts and movies, and outings to the public dance hall were now integral to the performance and expression of romance (Illouz, 1997). In fact, the fourth big change for romance was its transition into an activity that requires money, effort, and time. (Note: though men and women both engaged in this new dating culture, women's meager salaries meant that they were still dependent on men to pay for the privilege of a night on the town and often had little say in the actual recreation or scheduling of the date itself, though they did maintain an "ambiguously understood veto" power over sex; see Spurlock, 2015).

In sum, moving mate selection, courtship, and dating out of the family home and directly into the hands of young men and women offered them more autonomy, but also made romance a more laborious and costly, prospect. With great power comes great responsibility, and for young adults on the precipice of this new generational shift in the romantic imagination, the possibilities of the dating scene might have seemed both exhilarating and daunting at the same time. They were now in charge of managing their own romantic destiny. As young people's "choices for dates, clothes, or conversation were their own" now (p. 133, Fass, 1977), the amount of effort required to manage those choices—which may have felt fresh and innovative in the 1930s—became a burden by the 1960s.

The Role of the Internet in Romance and Courtship

What's wrong with the young unmarried? Free as larks, they should be able to manage for themselves the way they always have, but no. They complain it has become almost impossible to meet members of the opposite sex, especially in the cities. Life, says one secretary, is an endless subway ride, a day at the office, an evening at home in a double-lock apartment. Such dates as are available are leftovers from friends of friends with whom one went to college ("New Rules for the Singles Game," 1967, p. 66)

As this passage from *Life* magazine describes, dating in the 1960s was securely in the hands of young men and women—and they found it difficult and exhausting. In the 1960s, a prodigious solution to the ongoing problem of mate selection and dating presented itself: computing technology. To be clear, various forms of technology had been intertwined with, and facilitated, romantic communication up to this point, including the love letter, the telephone, and (especially) the automobile. All of these advancements enabled relational development between romantic partners. As Ann Landers quipped:

> Today, almost every teenager can get four wheels under him at a moment's notice. And a car means more than just transportation. It can be a status symbol, an energy outlet and—as you know—a portable bedroom. The majority of teenagers who write to me about their sexual intimacies confess that the trouble started in a parked car. (1961, p. 74)

But the use of the computer (and later, the Internet, and mobile phone) would revolutionize the practice and process of dating, because the computer "promised to take the responsibility of choice out of the process of dating and marriage, and to do so using means that would be scientific and therefore somehow inarguably correct" (Hicks, 2016).

Though online and mobile dating is, today, commonly used and accepted, its history is complex. The origins of what we have come to recognize as online dating started with a computerized matching system called Operation Match. As Slater (2014) recounts, Operation Match was developed in 1965 by Jeffrey Tarr, Vaughn Morril, and David Crump, a group of Harvard students (Insert obvious comment about the parallel between these Harvard boys in 1960s and another group led by Mark Zuckerberg in the 1990s—all of them just chillin' in their dorm rooms deploying computing technology for the purposes of socializing and dating). Although college campuses had helped to revolutionize the dating scene in the 1920s and 1930s, by the 1960s, the formal gender segregation present on most American college campuses (including Harvard's) seemed old-fashioned. Tarr[1] and Morrill were frustrated by the endless blind dates and

---

1 Fun fact: Jeff Tarr's daughter, Jennifer Tarr, grew up and married Chris Coyne, who co-founded the online dating site OkCupid. Jennifer and Chris met at a party, not online, but it is still a pretty cool coincidence.

rounds of college mixers; they felt trapped by the dating scene. They wanted a new way to meet women. So, the three students set out to solve their problem with Operation Match, which would connect men and women using computing technology.

The Operation Match process began with a 135-question survey—impressively titled the "Quantitative Personality Projection Test V." Daters would mail back their completed surveys with a $4 subscription fee. Their questionnaire responses would then be transferred on to Hollerith "punch cards" which were run through the IBM 1401 computer, which was "the size of a bus" according to Crump, but cutting-edge in the 1960s. Matching results—the names, phone numbers, colleges, graduation dates, and addresses of six eligible daters—would be printed and mailed out a few days later, along with a letter that read:

Dear Participant,

Below are the names of the people with whom your responses indicate you were most compatible. The names are not in any preferential order. We cannot guarantee these results, nor can we endorse the characters of the individuals participating. We encourage you to contact these people, but suggest that you observe the normal precautions that you would follow before going on any blind date.

All of this sounds a lot like modern-day online dating—and indeed, Operation Match is clearly the great-great grandparent of many contemporary sites and apps that use a questionnaire model and provide recommendations, like OkCupid and eHarmony. But, notably, no photographs were exchanged in Operation Match's results letter. To see what people looked like, participants still had to go out on a face-to-face date (in an interview, Crump notes, "Man if we'd had pictures, we'd be billionaires").

Between 1965 and 1968, Operation Match distributed over one million questionnaires and generated $300,000 in earnings (worth approximately $2.23 million dollars in 2020). In fact, the idea of computerized matching seemed so profitable that others joined in, including MIT-graduate David Dewan, who founded Contact Incorporated. Both Operation Match and Contact Inc. made frustrated college kids on gender-segregated campuses their target market and got subscribers from as far away as California.

Across the pond, other inroads into online dating were being forged. The computerized dating company, Com-Pat, was founded in 1965, by Joan Ball. She already ran a successful escort service where female clients paid her to find men who could accompany them to important social events (note that *escort* really means escort here—services didn't include sex). Recognizing the potential of computing technology early on, Ball focused on computerized matching, re-branded her escort company as Computer Dating Services Ltd. (nicknaming it "Com-Pat" for short), and took on Marjorie Smith as her new business partner (Hicks, 2016). Together, the two women focused on matching young women with eligible bachelors. The demand was high and they drew in about 2,500 paying clients. That Com-Pat was run by women for women was notable; the fact that heterosexual marriage remained the "ultimate goal" of their service was not (Hicks, 2016).

John Patterson founded Dateline in 1966, after seeing the success of Operation Match at Harvard. It would go on to be one of the largest and most successful computerized dating companies in Britain, serving thousands of customers until Patterson sold it in 1998. Dateline focused not on college kids, but on "a population that had fresh reasons for needing help" and those reasons included financial instability, divorce, or immobility (Strimpel, 2017, p. 324). In addition to playing up the soulmate angle, Dateline also played to the new romantic imagination that was emerging in the 1980s, one that included sexual liberation and experimentation. The idea that Dateline could help daters find whatever they were looking for—from spouse to swinger—was appealing to many. Dateline highlighted the "epidemic" of loneliness in London in many of its advertisements, and marketed itself as a pragmatic, technologic, and agentic way to find romantic company through data and science.

Conclusion

Tracing the early history of computerized matching systems is important in that we can see the roots of today's online dating industry taking shape—including the reliance on user-generated data through dating profiles and questionnaires, the design architectures of popular sites and apps that facilitate ongoing communication functions between partners, and dating company marketing strategies culturally tailored to fit Western ideals of romance. In this book, we will explore the various effects of Internet and mobile technology on our contemporary experience of romance. In some cases, we will find that computing technology has vastly expanded the romantic imagination by providing new opportunities and ways for us to interact; in others, we will conclude that it has created unforeseen problems that modern daters must now face; and, in still other moments, we will conclude that Internet technology has simply facilitated the basic communication functions that have always been present in romantic dating. In the following chapters, we will explore topics as diverse as online relationship initiation, conflict between romantic partners that is mediated through computing technology, and even the public image of the dating companies themselves.

References

Bachen, C. M., & Illouz, E. (1996). Imagining romance: Young people's cultural models of romance and love. *Critical Studies in Mass Communication, 13*(4), 279–308. https://doi.org/10.1080/15295039609366983

Baldwin, M. W. (1992). Relational schemas and the processing of social information. *Psychological Bulletin, 112*(3), 461–484. https://doi.org/10.1037/0033-2909.112.3.461

Blanchard, P., & Manasses, C. (1930). *New girls for old*. The Macaulay Company.

Fass, P. S. (1977). *The damned and the beautiful: American youth in the 1920's*. Oxford University Press.

"Heart Problems." (1920, April 22). *Richmond Palladium and Sun-Telegram*.

Hicks, M. (2016). Computer love: Replicating social order through early computer dating systems. *Ada: A Journal of Gender and New Media & Technology, 10*. adanewmedia.org/2016/10/issue10-hicks/.

Illouz, E. (1997). *Consuming the romantic utopia: Love and the cultural contradictions of capitalism*. University of California Press.

Landers, A. (1961, August 18). Straight talk on sex and growing up. *Life, 51*(7), 74–79.

"New rules for the singles game." (1967, August 18). *Life, 63*(7), 60–66.

Rumur Inc. (2015). *Operation Match* [video file]. USA: FiveThirtyEight and ESPN films. https://fivethirtyeight.com/features/what-online-dating-was-like-in-the-1960s/

Slater, D. (2014). *A million first dates: Solving the puzzle of online dating*. Current.

Spurlock, J. C. (2015). *Youth and sexuality in the twentieth-century United States*. Routledge. https://doi.org/10.4324/9781315745596

Strimpel, Z. (2017). Computer dating in the 1970s: Dateline and the making of the modern British single. *Contemporary British History, 31*(3), 319–342. https://doi.org/10.1080/13619462.2017.1280401

Weigel, M. (2016). *Labor of love: The invention of dating*. Farrar, Straus and Giroux.

3

Good, Old-Fashioned Love: The Stage Model Approach to Understanding Romantic Relationships

The classic 1940 film *The Shop Around the Corner*, recounts the story of two gift shop co-workers, Klara Novak (Margaret Sullavan) and Alfred Kralik (James Stewart), who share a somewhat contentious working relationship. However, unbeknownst to one another, the two are also pen pal correspondents and budding sweethearts. In the modern remake, Kathleen Kelly (Meg Ryan) makes the online acquaintance of Joe Fox (Tom Hanks) in Nora Ephron's 1998 film *You've Got Mail*. As the two strike up an online friendship, they begin to disclose things to one another. In an opening scene of the film, Joe makes several relatively trivial self-disclosures in a voice-over:

> Brinkley is my dog. He loves the streets of New York as much as I do. Although he likes to eat pizza and bagel off the sidewalk, and I prefer to buy them. Brinkley is a great catcher who was offered a tryout on the Mets farm team. But he chose to stay with me so he could spend 18 hours a day sleeping on a large green pillow the size of an inner tube. Don't you love New York in the fall? Makes me want to buy school supplies.

Eventually Kathleen responds with her own similarly surface-level disclosures:

> Confession: I've read *Pride and Prejudice* about 200 times. I get lost in the language. Words like: 'Thither.' 'Mischance.' 'Felicity.' I'm always in agony whether

Elizabeth and Mr. Darcy are really going to get together. Read it. I know you'll love it.

As the similar plots of *The Shop Around the Corner* and *You've Got Mail* suggest, the introduction of technology into modern romance does not *necessarily* prove that romantic interactions are fundamentally different now than they were 40 years ago. To remake the film, after all, required remarkably little alteration of a nearly 60-year-old plot line. Similarly, we are hesitant to suggest that the Internet has fundamentally changed romance. It's not that we believe that technology hasn't had *any* effects on romantic relationships—if we believed that we probably wouldn't be writing this book. Rather, as scholars of CMC and social media, we believe that there is wisdom in being cautious about making grandiose claims about the groundbreaking effects of technology, because it certainly hasn't changed the fundamentals of romance. It is hard to pinpoint specific effects because as technology has developed, so have cultural mores, generational cohorts, and historical settings. In short, it's not just that new technologies have developed: generally speaking, a different cohort of suitors are meeting, falling in love, and navigating relationships. Is it the availability of new technologies to facilitate relational tasks that make relationships what they are now? Or, is it the case that any apparent changes in relational formation, development, maintenance, and dissolution can be traced to larger economic, political, and historical differences that transcend technology?

Another reason to be cautious about the effects of "new" technologies on romantic relationships is that while the technologies in question might be new, they may not lead to new effects. For example, Stafford and Reske's (1990) work exploring the effects of telephone conversations and letters sent through the postal service on long-distance romantic relationships suggested that these modes of interaction can create an idealistic view of one's partner. Similarly, Walther's (1996) hyperpersonal model predicts that partner idealization is also facilitated by use of CMC and social media in modern-day interpersonal relationships. Whether the technology is "new" like a computer or as old as a handwritten letter, similar effects can be observed. So, is the idealization of one's partner that occurs in textually-mediated interaction a "new" technology effect? Probably not, but at the same time, there are other aspects of technology that bring these kinds of effects to the fore.

Over the past 50 years, technologies have developed rapidly and have made their way into our lives. Those developments have certainly had an impact in terms of the ways that relational tasks are completed; however, although people use technology to accomplish goals they would have completed differently prior to the Information Age, it does not necessarily follow that technology has changed the fundamental aims of romance. For this reason, it seems prudent to spend some time discussing how scholars have approached romantic relational development prior to the dawn of the Internet.

Social Intercourse: Disclosure and Relational Development

Although there are a number of ways that interpersonal communication scholars have studied relational development over the span of romantic relationships, one particularly fruitful line of research has been to study the *stages* through which romantic relationships typically progress over the course of a couple's interactions. A few very good stage models exist that have driven research on relational development; among the most well-known is Knapp's (1978) *social intercourse model* which we use as an organizing framework for this book.

The disclosures between Tom Hanks and Meg Ryan's characters from the opening scenes of *You've Got Mail* are, at face value, fairly routine, but self-disclosures like these often form the building blocks of a budding romantic relationship. Knapp's (1978) social intercourse model of relational development grew out of ideas popularized by Altman and Taylor's (1973) social penetration theory. *Social penetration theory* suggests that as people get to know one another, both the quantity and quality of their self-disclosures change. As relationships progress, Altman and Taylor suggest that the breadth of self-disclosive behavior becomes wider and the depth of self-disclosures becomes deeper. As the short exchanges between Kathleen and Joe illustrate above, in the early stages of a relationship, self-disclosures tend to be relatively shallow. However, over time, as the relationship becomes stronger, self-disclosures become broader (i.e., covering a wider range of topics) and deeper.

The metaphor commonly applied to Altman and Taylor's (1973) work is that getting to know another person is a lot like peeling back the layers of an onion. In social penetration theory, getting to know another person means getting to know that person's personality and identity. Rarely, if ever, does a person make self-disclosures that completely represent their full, unfiltered selves in the very early stages of initial acquaintanceship. Instead, as people get to know one another, they progressively share more revealing information about more parts of their personalities and identities.

Types of communication in romantic relationships. Knapp (1978) substantially expands on Altman and Taylor's foundational ideas by arguing that romantic relationships progress through stages in which different types of self-disclosures occur. These stages serve as rough guidelines to the sort of social interactions and self-disclosures that typically take place at different moments in a relational lifespan. Knapp identifies several conversational *dialectics* that occur in relational growth or decay stages. We review several of these conversational dialectics here.

Communication in romantic relationships can vary in terms of topics covered: these can be *narrow* or *broad* in nature (Knapp, 1978). When Brandon and his wife Jen began their romantic relationship, they had been student workers in the admissions office at their undergraduate institution for some time. At the beginning of their acquaintance, their conversations were centered on their jobs, the college campus, and their classes. As their relationship became more romantic in nature, the topics they discussed began to extend beyond the mundane things they had previously spoken about. They began to discuss their families, their professional aspirations, and their long-term hopes and dreams. In short, the topics they discussed became substantially broader as their relationship developed.

Communication can also vary in terms of its *stylization* or *idiosyncrasies* (Knapp, 1978). Miller and Steinberg's (1975) work suggests that we can form different levels of knowledge about people as we come to know them. Early on in a relationship, or even preceding its development, two people may make predictions about another person based on what Miller and Steinberg call *cultural-level* or *societal-level* information. For example, when they were acquaintances, Brandon made predictions about Jen knowing that she was a fellow Michigander, and Jen made assumptions about Brandon knowing that he was a Christian. Miller and Steinberg suggest that when two people gain *psychological-level* knowledge about each other, this facilitates predictions about another person's behavior based on that person's idiosyncrasies. Such unique knowledge then, comes only after partners exchange broader and deeper disclosures and share information about themselves that is not widely known.

Walther (2019) further differentiates this concept by distinguishing psychological-level knowledge from true interpersonal knowledge. Walther reasons that while we can form idiosyncratic impressions and develop unique knowledge about a person, this type of knowledge only really represents personal, but not truly *interpersonal,* knowledge. Specifically, while we might have a pretty good idea of an individual's idiosyncrasies and behavioral tendencies based on a personal impression, interpersonal knowledge is unique in that it represents not just the idiosyncratic behaviors of a person *in general*, but also the specific idiosyncratic behaviors that person displays *with you*. In other words, knowing about another person's idiosyncrasies represents a certain kind of intimate knowledge about that individual, but only knowing how *your partner* treats *you*, uniquely, represents true interpersonal knowledge. As people develop deeper romantic relationships, novel communication patterns develop; as partners become closer, they become more likely to desire truly idiosyncratic interaction—that is, you would expect your interaction with your romantic partner to be *different and unique*, compared to how your partner communicates with others.

A third type of conversational dialectic that Knapp (1978) discusses is the degree to which the information shared in a developing relationship is *publicly* versus *privately* known. At one point in *You've Got Mail*, Kathleen corresponds with Joe using an instant message feature. In this exchange, he offers her some advice to help her deal with a problem (which, unbeknownst to him, is a problem he created for her—it really is an amusing film. If you haven't watched it, you should):

JOE: Hi. I can give you advice. I'm great at advice.
KATHLEEN: If only you could help.
JOE: Is it about love?
KATHLEEN: My business is in trouble.
JOE: I'm a brilliant businessman! It's what I do best. What is your business?
KATHLEEN: No specifics. Remember?

In this short exchange, we see that Joe has violated Kathleen's expectations about the depth of information that the two of them should be sharing. In other words, Joe asks a question Kathleen considers too intimate—given the current state of their relationship—for her to answer. As romantic relationships grow, suitors expect that their communicative exchanges will become more intimate and that deeper knowledge about one's partner will become appropriate to share.

While Knapp (1978) and Altman and Taylor (1973) identify several more dimensions of conversational dialog that vary over the course of romantic relationships, these three dimensions—breadth, idiosyncrasy, public/private—are most important for our purposes here, exploring the ways that romantic relationships vary across relational growth and decay.

Stages of Relational Growth

While Knapp's (1978) social intercourse model of relational development certainly is not the only stage model of relational development (for example, see also

Duck, 1982), it does a good job of conceptualizing both the stages of growth and decay within romantic relationships. Knapp identifies two general phases of relational development: those phases through which people transition as they grow closer to one another, and those phases through which people transition when they begin to grow apart.

Initiation. Knapp (1978) suggests that growth phases begin with an *initiation* stage. During the initiation stage people are sizing one another up, evaluating whether engaging with the other person is desirable or not, and determining that person's levels of attractiveness. Scholars who study behavior in this phase have explored the ways in which initial encounters create impressions of others. To begin examining the research on this relational stage, we list some foundational studies; but the body of research on impression formation is downright enormous, and these represent only the tip of a gigantic iceberg of literature: Albright, Kenny, & Malloy, 1988, Ambady & Rosenthal, 1993, Fiske & Neuberg, 1990, and Neuberg & Fiske, 1987. This research illustrates that although the initiation stage of a potential romantic relationship is *very* short, it can have long-term ramifications.

Generally speaking, communication during the initiation stage tends to be relatively conventional. Any self-disclosure that occurs tends to be very narrow in scope; people tend to reveal only information that they are comfortable being publicly available. Most information gleaned from a communication partner in this stage is nonverbal in nature (i.e., information that can be inferred from dress, appearance, bodily movement, etc.). While the initiation stage is important for the future development of a romantic relationship, it is over remarkably quickly— Knapp (1978), Albright et al. (1988), and Ambady and Rosenthal (1993) suggest that the information exchanged in this stage can last as little as 15 seconds.

Experimenting. After initiating communication in this first stage, people tend to move on to the *experimenting* stage, where they fundamentally seek to reduce uncertainty about their partners. Interpersonal communication scholars have theorized about communication strategies in the experimenting stage in a number of ways, but probably the most well-known theoretical perspectives are related to *uncertainty reduction theory* (Berger & Calabrese, 1975). Uncertainty reduction theory describes the process by which people get to know each other through information seeking and communication. Knapp (1978) offers that much of the communication that occurs during this phase is facilitated through *small talk*. While Knapp acknowledges that many of us profess some level of distaste for small talk, it fulfills several important functions for the experimenting stage. Most notably, small talk allows us to figure out promising topics for future exploration with a partner; it provides a way to "audition" another person for the role of romantic partner, and it provides a mechanism to inform a potential romantic partner about what topics of conversation are safe to probe further and which are not.

At this stage of relational development, potential romantic partners are carefully feeling out the relationship's future probability. Communication will be fairly narrow in scope; it will not reveal overly private or sensitive information; and partners' behaviors will generally adhere to societal norms (because behaving in normative ways is not particularly risky).

Intensifying. The initiation stage and the experimenting stage are phases of interaction that most human relationships progress to—romantic or casual; friend, enemy, or acquaintance. However, fewer of our relationships make it to the *intensifying* stage (Knapp, 1978). During the intensifying stage, people who have developed a friendship cautiously seek to deepen the intimacy they share with a relational partner. Communication during this phase is marked by an increase in the scope of topics people will discuss with one another. Partners will often begin to disclose things they have been holding back previously and will begin to share information that may not be considered fit for public presentation.

During this intensifying phase, partners will often develop a number of communication shortcuts that build on the shared knowledge and experiences of the couple. These shortcuts can be either verbal or nonverbal. For instance, Brandon and his wife Jen are both introverts. When spending time with a large group of people they both find it fun, but tiring. In order to unobtrusively leave such gatherings together, while still allowing the fun to continue among the other, more social, partygoers, Jen and Brandon developed a code to let one another know they were ready to leave. Someone (usually Brandon, because he has less social grace and patience than Jen) will say, "What do you think?" If the other person is not yet ready to leave, they will respond with a "Not quite yet." or a "Give me a minute." However, if the other person is ready to go, they respond to the question with a hearty, "I think so." If an outside observer were to witness this conversation, they would, no doubt, be quite confused. The question is vague, and the response doesn't seem to directly answer the question; but to Brandon and Jen, the meaning of this interaction is crystal clear.

Integrating. As a relationship develops to the point that partners' individual selves begin to take a back seat to the "couple identity," we identify the couple as being in the *integrating* stage. During this phase the couple will almost always consider themselves to be in a romantic relationship. Pairs of people in the initiating and experimenting stages typically do not consider the relationship they share to be an official, committed one. These feelings usually emerge first in the intensifying stage. In the integrating stage, couples' feelings of "oneness" become clear to those around them. It becomes apparent to friends and family that the relationship experienced by these two people is unique.

Walther's (2019) definition of *interpersonal* knowledge which we discussed earlier is applicable here. Partners in this phase have clearly developed an understanding not just about what their partner's idiosyncrasies are, but also how their partner treats them, specifically, in ways that those idiosyncrasies alone cannot explain. Moreover, in the integrating phase this level of interpersonal interaction becomes apparent not only to the couple themselves, but also to others around them who realize that there's something unique and special going on.

Bonding. The final stage of relational growth Knapp (1978) discusses is the *bonding* stage. The bonding stage is marked by some form of formalization of the relationship. In Western cultures this is typically in the form of marriage, civil union, or some other form of legal, or at least local community-recognized acknowledgment of the relationship. This formal recognition serves several functions—most notably, they add another layer of challenge if one or both partners would ever seek to terminate the relationship.

Bonding is unique among the stages of Knapp's (1978) model in that it functions in some ways as a clearly demarcated point in a relationship: one is either engaged or not engaged, married or not married, in a civil union or not. On the other hand, the formalization of a romantic relationship and agreeing to a relationship contract in front of a deity, community, or the state is an act—not a stage. And, in many ways, those in romantic relationships who are in the bonding phase are walking a tightrope between the integrating stage and the differentiating stage (which is a stage of relational decay which we will cover next). At times bonded pairs will experience relational uncertainty or turbulence (see Solomon, Knobloch, Theiss, & McLaren, 2016; Theiss & Solomon, 2006), will need to navigate some major life turning points (Baxter & Bullis, 1986) and will, inevitably, navigate (successfully or not) a wide variety of competing relational dialectics (Baxter & Montgomery, 1996).

Stages of Relational Decay

Differentiating. As noted previously, the bonding phase can be viewed as an extension of the integrating phase. When it is, partners will continue to integrate and further imagine their futures as a singular unit rather than separately imagining what is to come. However, in any romantic relationship (not just those doomed to fail), partners will eventually experience periods in which they *differentiate* from one another (Knapp, 1978). In the differentiation stage, partners come to the realization that their previously felt "oneness" is no longer the primary feeling in the relationship. Communication in this phase is often fraught with conflict, and often topics that were once safe areas of discussion become difficult and lead to conflict. However, it is important to note that although partners find once-safe topics conflict-inducing during interaction, they still tend to discuss these matters.

Circumscribing. If the differentiating stage is where partners identify some substantial conflict-inducing differences between each other, the *circumscribing* stage is where partners start avoiding communication about those differences. As lovers drift apart, conflict breeds avoidance. After identifying topics that are likely to result in undesirable, conflict-riddled interactions with their partners, many will avoid discussion of those topics. Sometimes a person will instruct their partner that a certain topic ought not be discussed, or even that previously affirmed relational contracts that had been agreed upon ought to be reassessed—for instance, shifting from a committed, romantic relationship to a friendship with new rules for what ought to be fair conversational game. While there is often still some interaction between partners, they work to avoid topics that they know will create tension or conflict.

Stagnating. As you might expect, once a couple has circumscribed enough topics, only a few things remain "safe" topics of discussion, and there is little left to say to a partner. Once this occurs, partners are said to be in a *stagnation* stage. Little private or personal information is shared at this stage. One unique feature—one that makes this stage relatively difficult—is that romantic partners are often still physically proximate to each other at this point—perhaps living together in the same house. Knapp (1978) suggests that this leads to messages being sent through nonverbal behavior more readily than by verbal messages.

Imagine two quarreling partners, Marvin and Betsy, who have circumscribed and whose relationship is now stagnating. One of the many ways that Marvin drives Betsy crazy is that she believes he spends too much money on his hobbies. On his way home from work one day, Marvin is driving by the model train store and simply cannot help himself. He knows Betsy would not approve, but he has found a good deal on some very life-like miniature shrubbery that would really pull together the whole 19th-century small-town vibe he has been hoping to recreate (see Figure 3.1). Upon his return home, Marvin tries to sneak in the door,

Figure 3.1: Marvin's trains. His passion for toy trains unfortunately doesn't translate to Betsy. Source: Kevin Phillips/Public Domain. https://www.publicdomainpictures.net/en/view-image.php?image=145770&picture=model-train

hoping Betsy won't see him. Unfortunately for Marvin, Betsy arrives home from work at exactly the same time as he does, and they walk into the house together. Betsy knows that *another* conversation with Martin will simply end in anger; so instead, she takes one look at his hobby store bag, rolls her eyes, and without saying anything pours herself a particularly generous glass of red wine. Marvin, who reads Betsy's exasperation clearly, storms off to his model train room and slams the door—just loud enough for Betsy to accurately interpret his anger.

Avoiding. Eventually, partners' relationship can decay to the point that neither wishes to inhabit the same physical environment as the other. When this occurs, Knapp (1978) suggests that the *avoiding* stage has begun. This stage is a clear harbinger of formal relational termination. Knapp suggests it can take several forms. Partners in this stage may achieve avoidance by arriving to appointments or scheduled events late, by very directly asking their partner not to make contact with them any longer, or by making excuses which preclude them from having to interact with their partner at all. Sometimes, partners cannot avoid being in the same physical environment (e.g., seeking to avoid a romantic partner who is also a current co-worker). In these situations, Knapp suggests that often couples will enact a forced avoidance by ignoring a partner. Research suggests that this *ostracism* has the effect of causing significant emotional harm to a partner (Eisenberger, Lieberman, & Williams, 2003; Williams, 2002, 2007).

Terminating. The most diverse stage of coming apart is *termination.* Interestingly, the fact that termination stage can come at any time (i.e., follow any other stage in the social intercourse model) makes it difficult to pin down the sequence of stages into a one-size-fits-all-couples pattern. For example, the relational termination that occurs directly after initiation is almost certain to be very different than the breakup of a marriage of 20 years. So it is difficult to pin down what the termination stage looks like because termination processes are often affected by how long the relationship has existed before it ended, and by the exact stage both partners were in before termination occurred. Generally, communication at the termination stage is vague and practical, and very little new personal or idiosyncratic information is shared. Many times, people will, during termination, come to an understanding of some of the ground rules of reduced access to their partners—especially if in their prior relationship partners had a great deal of regular interaction, shared property or major possessions, and/or had begun raising a child. On the other hand, if the relationship is terminating only after a few awkward text messages exchanged during the initiation stage, it will probably be much less formal, much more rapid, and will not cause nearly as much emotional strife.

How Relational Stages Function

You have probably guessed (and perhaps even personally experienced) that not every relationship progresses smoothly through these developmental stages and ends up at the bonding stage. In fact, it is likely that most of our interpersonal relationships never move much beyond the integrating phase. Even among our closest platonic friends, entering into the integrating phase may be unlikely. While we may intensify relationships with a platonic friend, humans usually reserve integration for their most serious of romantic relationships. But this leaves us with several important questions: How does movement occur among stages? Is there variance within stages of interaction? Can movement occur in multiple directions without having achieved the bonding phase?

Knapp (1978) suggests that, generally, people move through the stages in sequential order, *but* he suggests that movement may be either forward or backward. Take, for example, the fictional couple Ron and Jerri. Ron met Jerri at The Billy Goat Tavern one night while both were attending a conference in Chicago. The two immediately had an intense physical attraction to one another. The pair made plans to spend the next several evenings together, and as they did, they progressed quickly through small talk and their relationship began to intensify. As their disclosures deepened, though, Jerri noticed that Ron was somewhat brash and not as kind and gentle as he had hoped. Eventually, Jerri began to engage in more small talk. Eventually, by the end of their third evening together, their conversation was almost completely superficial. Although they had made plans to spend another night together, Jerri never showed up.

In the above example, we see one way that Knapp's (1978) model can function. In this scenario, Ron and Jerri moved quickly through the initiation and experimenting phase and on into the intensifying stage as their friendship developed. However, after some intensifying, Jerri developed a distaste for some aspects of Ron's personality. Eventually, their relationship returned to the experimenting phase and then terminated.

It is also important to note that these descriptive stages are simply attempts to capture what many people experience in developing relationships. Because of this, there will invariably be some movement within stages—and some couples may skip stages altogether or move across them in different orders. In even the strongest of marriages, for instance, some turbulence is expected, and even a well-integrated, bonded couple may experience communication characteristic of what one might expect in the circumscribing stage.

Conclusion

The purpose of this chapter has been to introduce the ways scholars have conceptualized and examined romantic relationships. We confess we have not provided you with an all-inclusive theoretical extravaganza that reviews all of the romantic relationship research in existence in encyclopedic fashion. Instead, we hoped to summarize some of the important research perspectives that have shaped interpersonal and relational communication research in the past several decades, paying specific attention to the scholarship that has been most important to analysts of romantic relationships in CMC and social media. We introduced the stage model framework because we use it to organize the book: Beginning with relational initiation stages, then progressing to maintenance, and finally termination, in each section we will explore how CMC, social media, and online and mobile dating technologies have changed, challenged, or facilitated the communication behaviors involved in the formation and dissolution of romantic relationships.

References

Albright, L., Kenny, D. A., & Malloy, T. E. (1988). Consensus in personality judgments at zero acquaintance. *Journal of Personality and Social Psychology*, *55*(3), 387–395. https://doi.org/10.1037/0022-3514.55.3.387

Altman, I., & Taylor, D. A. (1973). *Social penetration: The development of interpersonal relationships.* Holt, Rinehart, & Wilson.

Ambady, N., & Rosenthal, R. (1993). Half a minute: Predicting teacher evaluations from thin slices of behavior and physical attractiveness. *Journal of Personality and Social Psychology*, *64*(3), 431–441. https://doi.org/10.1037/0022-3514.64.3.431

Baxter, L. A., & Bullis, C. (1986). Turning points in developing romantic relationships. *Human Communication Research*, *12*(4), 469–493. https://doi.org/10.1111/j.1468-2958.1986.tb00088.x

Baxter, L. A., & Montgomery, B. M. (1996). *Relating: Dialogues & dialectics.* Guilford Press.

Berger, C. R., & Calabrese, R. J. (1975). Some exploration in initial interaction and beyond: Toward a developmental theory of interpersonal communication. *Human Communication Research*, *3*(2), 29–46. https://doi.org/10.1111/j.1468-2958.1975.tb00258.x

Brody, N., & Peña, J. (2015). Equity, relationship maintenance, and linguistic features of text messaging. *Computers in Human Behavior*, *49*, 499–506. https://doi.org/10.1016/j.chb.2015.03.037

Duck, S. W. (1982). A topography of relationship disengagement and dissolution. In S. W. Duck (Ed.), *Personal relationships 4: Dissolving personal relationships* (pp. 1–30). Academic Press.

Eisenberger, N. I., Lieberman, M. D., & Williams, K. D. (2003). Does rejection hurt? An fMRI study of social exclusion. *Science*, *302*(5643), 290–292. https://doi.org/10.1126/science.1089134

Fiske, S. T., & Neuberg, S. L. (1990). A continuum of impression formation from category-based to individuating processes: Influences of information and motivation on attention and interpretation. *Advances in Experimental Social Psychology*, *23*, 1–74. https://doi.org/10.1016/S0065-2601(08)60317-2

Knapp, M. L. (1978). *Social intercourse: From greeting to goodbye.* Allyn and Bacon.

Miller, G. R., & Steinberg, M. (1975). *Between people: A new analysis of interpersonal communication.* Science Research Associates.

Neuberg, S. L., & Fiske, S. T. (1987). Motivational influences on impression formation: Outcome dependency, accuracy-driven attention, and individuating processes. *Journal of Personality and Social Psychology*, *53*(3), 431–444. https://doi.org/10.1037/0022-3514.53.3.431

Solomon, D. H., Knobloch, L. K., Theiss, J. A., & McLaren, R. M. (2016). Relational turbulence theory: Explaining variation in subjective experiences and communication within romantic relationships. *Human Communication Research*, *42*(4), 507–532. https://doi.org/10.1111/hcre.12091

Stafford, L., & Reske, J. R. (1990). Idealization and communication in long-distance premarital relationships. *Family Relations*, *39*(3), 274–279. https://doi.org/10.2307/584871

Theiss, J. A., & Solomon, D. H. (2006). A relational turbulence model of communication about irritations in romantic relationships. *Communication Research, 33*(5), 391–418. https://doi.org/10.1177/0093650206291482

Walther, J. B. (1996). Computer-mediated communication: Impersonal, interpersonal, and hyperpersonal interaction. *Communication Research, 23*(1), 3–43. https://doi.org/10.1177/009365096023001001

Walther, J. B. (2019). Interpersonal versus personal uncertainty and communication in traditional and mediated encounters: A theoretical reformulation. In S. R. Wilson & S. W. Smith (Eds.), *Reflections on interpersonal communication research* (pp. 375–393). Cognella.

Williams, K. D. (2002). *Ostracism: The power of silence.* Guilford Press.

Williams, K. D. (2007). Ostracism. *Annual Review of Psychology, 58*(4), 25–52. https://doi.org/10.1146/annurev.psych.58.110405.085641

4

What is an Online Dating Platform? Defining, Describing, and Understanding Popular Dating Technologies

JERRY:	I still can't believe you're going out on a blind date.
ELAINE:	I'm not worried. It sounds like he's really good looking.
JERRY:	You're going by sound? What are we? Whales?
ELAINE:	I think I can tell.
JERRY:	Elaine, what percentage of people would you say are good looking?
ELAINE:	Twenty-five percent.
JERRY:	Twenty-five percent, you say? No way! It's like four to six percent. It's a twenty-to-one shot.
ELAINE:	You're way off.
JERRY:	Way off? Have you been to the motor vehicle bureau? It's like a leper colony down there.
ELAINE:	So what you are saying is that 90 to 95 percent of the population is undateable?
JERRY:	UNDATEABLE!
ELAINE:	Then how are all these people getting together?
JERRY:	Alcohol.

In this exchange from the comedy series *Seinfeld* (Seinfeld & David, 1995), Jerry cannot believe that his friend Elaine would consider going out on a blind date with someone she doesn't know and has never seen. Instead, Elaine has had to rely on the only impression she was able to form of her date, made based on how her date's voice sounded on the phone. In the 1990s when this scene was written, while a blind date was potentially risky because the other person could turn out to be unattractive or otherwise incompatible, it was still something that many romantic singles could arrange and experience. But today, considering the intertwining of computing technology and romantic dating, the idea of a blind date is not only risky—it is a very uncommon experience. We seek out information about our prospective dates through websites, mobile applications, and social media profiles; we can exchange text messages with them; we can even spot their physical location through geolocation data provided from their smartphones. And all of this information gathering and uncertainty reduction occurs before ever meeting that person FtF. With over 30 million Americans using some form of online dating site or mobile app, the number of us going out on truly "blind" dates seems to be shrinking.

But before we launch into thinking about how popular dating sites and apps affect things like blind dates, we should pause to consider what exactly these different technologies consist of—that is, what is an online dating platform, exactly? What specific features do they offer to users? We answer these questions by first providing an overarching definition of a dating platform; we then explore the various features that today's popular dating platforms have in common and offer a framework to organize those features; and finally, we discuss how these dating platforms influence the different communicative processes involved in romantic relationships.

Defining Online Dating Platforms

A basic search in the Apple App Store using the terms "dating app" pulls up a large number of results. Included in the list are industry originals like Match. com, OkCupid, and PlentyofFish, mixed in with established mobile apps like Tinder, Grindr, CoffeeMeetsBagel, and Bumble. Also on the list are lesser-known, "niche" dating apps like those oriented towards casual sex and hookups (OneNightHookup, CasualX), daters' ethnic and racial backgrounds (Chispa, BLK), multiple partners (3Sum), sexualities (Zoe), and sexual behaviors (Kinkoo, KinkD).

Online and mobile dating is clearly very popular—but with so many variations on a theme, it is easy to get lost in the sea of websites and apps. The purpose of this chapter is to describe and organize this vast landscape of dating platforms. We begin by introducing our definition, to which we will refer throughout this book:

We define "dating platforms" as Internet-based systems (i.e., mobile or web-based) designed to introduce or connect previously unacquainted adult individuals for the purpose(s) of (a) physical and/or (b) emotional intimacy.

This definition helps us understand what can be classified as a dating platform, and it also provides clear boundaries for what to exclude. The first definitional criterion we offer is the *acquaintanceship* between users. Note that there are many social computing platforms that use Internet technology to facilitate interpersonal connection and communication between people—the largest class of these involves social network sites (SNSs). Some SNSs like Facebook work by connecting people who typically already know each other offline (e.g., former classmates, friends, acquaintances, family members, neighbors), and so we will exclude from our definition of a dating platform.

You might also be wondering about other SNSs like LinkedIn, WeChat, Twitter, or Instagram that often introduce unacquainted strangers—would these count as dating platforms? It is true that some SNSs work to introduce unknown others, and they also sometimes facilitate romantic connections. But since they were not specifically designed for the purpose of developing physical or emotional (i.e., romantic) intimacy, we do not include them as dating platforms (although, they do play an important role in romantic relationships).

The second definitional criterion we highlight is the *shared purpose* of dating platforms, which bring together previously unacquainted users for romance/sex/dating. And although research has shown that people do report using dating platforms for multiple purposes including friendship, information gathering, self-validation/ego-boosting, and entertainment (Sumter, Vandenbosch, & Ligtenberg, 2017; Timmermans & De Caluwé, 2017; Van De Wiele & Tong, 2014), the primary intended purpose of these platforms is romance, emotional intimacy, and/or sex ("hookups"). And importantly, this primary purpose is not typically disputed or misunderstood by either developers or users (see also, LeFebvre, 2018).

Dating platforms are also unique in that they use Internet networks to facilitate connection and information exchange between people. Much like other forms of commercial media, the online and mobile dating industry has leveraged the global system of Internet connectivity. Although different platforms may offer different ways to access it (WiFi, cellular, etc.), almost all of these popular dating sites and apps rely on the Internet at their core.

Finally, we are careful to include the term *platform* in our definition, which reflects the larger space or environment where the dating app or website system is run. The term *platform* encompasses the relationship between the user, the software program or operating system, and the architecture or design of the hardware that is used to run that system. In this book, because we are examining the relationships between human behavior, technological systems, actual devices, and social and cultural practices of romance and relationships, we need a definitional term that captures it all (see, Apperley & Parikka, 2018; Burgess et al., 2016).

All of this is not to say that we won't be discussing the effects of non-dating social computing platforms on romantic relationships. In later chapters we will certainly do that—especially because most dating platforms have much to do with how a relationship begins, but play a much less important role (even to the point of disappearing completely) as the relationship develops between partners. SNSs like Facebook, Instagram, and Snapchat are important for communication in extant relationships, when romantic partners use social media to maintain their connections with each other. However, in this chapter, we explore the unique properties—or dimensions—of dating platforms that are worth defining, cataloging, and analyzing.

Shared Stages and Variable Dimensions of Online Dating Platforms

So far, we have established that dating platforms use Internet technology to facilitate romantic connection or intimacy, and they promote relational initiation processes between previously unacquainted adults. Additionally, although there are literally hundreds of different dating platforms on the market, many provide a relatively consistent experience for their users. Using Markowitz, Hancock, and Tong's (2019) stage model of online dating dynamics as a foundation, we examine how different dating platforms cultivate daters' experiences when interacting with technology and with other daters.

According to Markowitz et al. (2019), the process of online and mobile dating unfolds in a series of three stages they call *profile-matching-discovery*. To these three stages, we add a preliminary *registration* stage, where people initially decide to become users of the dating platform by creating a user account and consenting to the terms of service (TOS). After the registration stage, the next step is to develop a *profile*, in which users curate their self-image for presentation to other daters on the platform. In the *matching* stage, they engage in mate selection, searching the platform's pool of available daters for potential dates, selecting those they find most attractive, and initiating and receiving contact. Finally, through *discovery*, daters learn about each other through various means—including online information search, mediated message exchange, and phone conversations or video calls. If the information gleaned in the discovery process is deemed acceptable, the relationship progresses to FtF meetups.

Though most dating platforms facilitate this common dating experience, the specific features they offer to users at each stage of the process can vary. Table 4.1 (a) succinctly summarizes each *stage* and (b) details several *dimensions* along which dating platforms vary. Each dimension is conceptualized as a continuum that represents the various features that platforms offer that facilitate progress within and across each stage of the dating experience.

The Registration Stage

The *registration stage* is the first stage that occurs after an individual has decided to use an online or mobile dating platform to initiate romantic connectivity with other people. To become an active user, all dating platforms require people to create an account and provide some basic personal information to establish their identity.

Dimension 1: Authentication. Dating platforms vary in the kinds of *authentication* information they require—at the lowest level, web-based platforms will ask users for an email address; mobile apps require a phone number. At the other end of the continuum are those platforms that require additional personal information for authentication. *Linked registrations* through users' existing SNS accounts like Facebook, Instagram, or Snapchat provide additional forms of authentication for users' identities. Specifically, registrations linked to users' personal SNSs provide *warrants*—or evidence—that corroborate the authenticity of the person's identity and provide a sense of credibility about the account (DeAndrea, 2014; Walther & Parks, 2002). Linking multiple SNSs to a single dating account increases the overall number of warranting cues that serve to legitimize or validate that user's offline identity (DeAndrea, 2014). As we will see in later chapters, communicating one's own impression and establishing the veracity of a potential partner's identity are incredibly important!

Some websites like PlentyofFish and OkCupid are at the lower end of the authentication dimension as they only require users to enter a valid email address, password, a single photo, and some basic demographic information (such as birthday, gender, country of residence, ethnicity/race) in order to register an account on the platform. The League is a dating platform at the opposite end of the authentication dimension—in fact, during a January 9, 2019 episode of the podcast *Why'd*

You Push That Button (Carman & Tiffany, 2019), The League's CEO, Amanda Bradford, explained: "We use both Facebook and LinkedIn. We actually are the only ones that have double authentication. We require Facebook, then LinkedIn, then we put everyone into a waiting list. It's similar to a college admissions pool." Another example is the new dating app called The Lox Club, founded by Austin Kevitch in 2020 as "a private, membership-based app for Jews with ridiculously high standards" (loxclubapp.com). The Lox Club app claims it is "very discerning" in screening its user pool; not only does it verify potential users' "perceived authenticity," it also examines their "ambition" and "Instagram persona" before allowing people to complete registration (Lieberman, 2020). This suggests that apps like The League and The Lox Club occupy the extreme high end of the authentication dimension—they require specific, multiple warrants, evaluate each applicant's personal information, and allow only some to finish the entire registration stage.

Toward the middle of the authentication dimension are platforms that mandate specific forms of authentication, but without onerous vetting. As late as June 2018, the dating app Hinge required users to register using their Facebook accounts. But in a recent update, Hinge gave new users the option to register with a phone number instead (Perez, 2018). Additionally, at registration, Hinge users are required to input an email address, but bans all addresses that end in ".edu" (see Figure 4.1). So, while apps like Hinge do require specific kinds of authentication information, once those requirements are met, users can register. Other platforms like Tinder or Hily require phone numbers for authentication.

Figure 4.1: Authentication on Hinge. Illustration of the registration phase. Source: Authors

And although they prompt users to link to their Facebook or Snapchat accounts, respectively, both platforms ultimately allow users to choose for themselves which SNS accounts to use for authentication.

Dimension 2: Explicitness of Purpose and Functionality. In our definition above, we noted that in order to be classified as a dating platform, the mobile application or website must denote that its primary purpose is the facilitation of physical and/or emotional intimacy among its users. Though all dating platforms have this shared purpose, they will differ in how *explicitly* or *implicitly* they communicate it to users. For example, Tinder is relatively implicit in its statement of purpose. In other words, Tinder never clearly discloses that its purpose is to help users make romantic connections; instead, after users register, it simply offers brief explanations of the swiping features (left, right, up) that are used to create romantic matches within the app.

More *explicit* examples include Hily, which offers users a choice of functions for greater specificity that includes friendship and romantic connections—both short-term and long-term. Bumble began as a dating platform (Bumble Date), and later expanded into other segmented functions, including friendship building (Bumble BFF) and career/job networking (Bumble Bizz). As a result, the platform is very clear that it can be used to facilitate multiple kinds of relational connections, and people must indicate which kind of relationship networks they intend to build and which segment of the app they will use to do so. Interestingly, Bumble also explicitly states that it is built upon "kindness, empowerment, and respect"—thus, this dating platform offers explicit explanations regarding both the purpose(s) and the ethos of the platform for its users.

Other mobile apps and websites that have explicit explanations regarding purpose are sometimes described as "niche" dating platforms. Examples include Clover, which describes its purpose as "on-demand dating," which specifically encourages FtF meetups and shared activities between users. Chispa is similar to Tinder in that its overall purpose in facilitating romantic connection is more implicit, but it also explicitly asks users to specify their ethnic/racial "roots" as part of its purpose is to connect daters with Latino/Latina/Latinx backgrounds. Thus, the variable dimension of *explicitness* describes how a platform explains or announces its purpose(s) and environment for users.

The Profile Stage

After registration, users must craft an online profile to identify themselves to the other daters on the platform. The purpose of the profile is "to attract others' attention in an effort to develop future interactions and conversation" (Markowitz et al., 2019, p. 51). Since daters use others' profiles to form impressions, the profile serves as "a crucial self-presentation tool because it is the first and primary means of expressing one's self during the early stages of a correspondence and can therefore foreclose or create relationship opportunities" (Ellison, Heino, & Gibbs, 2006, p. 423).

Across most dating platforms, the profile shares common elements such as a featured photograph, information about physical characteristics (height, weight, body type), demographics (gender, sexual orientation, race/ethnicity), and self-authored biographical information. Although daters must decide how to construct their profiles, their decisions are made within each platform's specific profile specifications, which will vary in the *breadth* and *depth* of the content they will allow their users to include.

Dimension 3: Breadth of Profile Content. Almost all dating platforms allow users to divulge a fairly diverse *breadth*, or amount, of descriptive content to be shared with potential suitors. However, the purpose and functionality of the dating platform also affects the breadth of information displayed about a user in his or her profile. For example, on OkCupid or Match, users are offered a reasonably comprehensive breadth of information about a potential partner, including information about their likes, dislikes, hobbies, alcohol or drug use; whether they have children or not; and sometimes a short anecdote about an interesting life event. The breadth of information offered by web-based dating platforms differs from mobile dating applications. Dating apps are limited by the nature of their hardware—screens on smartphones, as we know, are much smaller than computer monitors. Correspondingly, the information that mobile profiles feature is often more sparse; personal information in these applications plays second fiddle to the number of (usually) flattering or suggestive photographs. In this way, mobile dating apps prioritize visual over the verbal; and as we will explore in other chapters, this key difference in the breadth of profile content will have downstream effects on other important relationship initiation processes.

Dimension 4: Depth of Profile Content. A platform's functionality and purpose also can affect the *depth* of information shared between users. For example, both OkCupid and Match are similar in terms of the breadth of profile information daters share about themselves, but the two websites vary in terms of depth. While Match only asks its users to fill out the "about me" portions of their profile, OkCupid not only asks its users for a "self-summary" but also prompts them to describe "what I'm doing with my life," "things I'm good at," and "the first thing people notice about me." Although both platforms clearly require daters to describe themselves to other daters, OkCupid's additional profile fields may prompt deeper self-disclosures.

Interestingly, many online and mobile dating platforms will not allow daters to skip certain required portions of their profile development. That is, most apps and sites will not release daters' profiles into the dating pool for others to view unless they complete *all* of the mandatory profile fields. One might think that dating sites and apps do this in order to ensure that the breadth and depth of the self-authored profile is sufficient for people to form impressions and select potential partners during the matching stage. A more cynical reader might question whether these companies want their users' personal information for more nefarious reasons. We explore the ethics of profile information ownership later; but for now, we want to point out how at the profile stage, dating platforms often vary in terms of the breadth and depth of personal information they expect their users to disclose.

The Matching Stage

After creating a profile to present themselves to others, users must then select dates from the pool of potential partners made available by the dating platform. At this stage, users often have their own set of preferences for selecting romantic partners. Users' mate selection during the matching stage is dependent upon the type of *decision making assistance* and *mutuality* that is offered by the platform.

Dimension 5: Decision Making Assistance. Dating platforms vary in the amount of influence they offer their users during the matching stage. At one end of the continuum are platforms like eHarmony that offer a high degree of *algorithmic influence* during mate selection, asserting that they "take the guesswork out of the dating equation" (eHarmony, 2017) by providing pre-selected matches that are made using daters' self-delineated preferences and answers to specific questions. Hinge also offers something similar to the Gale-Shapley algorithm in its "Most Compatible" feature, that employs users' data to calculate "the top daily Hinge member we think you'll be interested in dating, who is also most likely to be interested in *you*" (emphasis original, as cited in Carman, 2018). Such features offer a high degree of algorithmic recommendation, putting these two platforms toward the higher end of the decision making assistance dimension.

On the other end of the decision making assistance dimension are those dating platforms that provide little to no algorithmic influence over users' mate selections. Platforms like Match.com offer a variety of *search filters* that allow users to customize their search for romance. Users can select various characteristics of potential partners—gender, location, age, etc.—in essence, the platform gives its users a chance to narrow down the dating pool by using specific criteria. Thus, users control the choices they make, and how and when they make them—search filters like these give daters the greatest level of control and a customizable level of assistance, putting such platforms at the lower end of the spectrum on decision assistance.

Platforms like Tinder are in the middle of this dimension—though users are allowed to make their own choices among the people in Tinder's pool, the pool itself is not limitless. Users are shown a finite number of potential partners from which to choose, and those potentials are pre-determined by Tinder's algorithm. In the past, people speculated about how Tinder curated the pool for its users. An article in *Fast Company* (Carr, 2016) detailed Tinder's use of the Elo score that ranked users based on the kinds of swipes they received from others; a dater rose in ranking based on the number of Likes he or she got, and those Likes were weighted by the desirability of the swiper—the more Likes the swiper had, the greater the original dater's Elo ranking (see also, Tiffany, 2019). Presumably, Tinder got the idea for the Elo scores from competitive chess (they use a similar ranking system), but Tinder recently clarified that their algorithm does not rely on Elo rankings anymore. Instead it "prioritizes potential matches who are active, and active at the same time" and relies only on users' recent app activity, preferences, and location data to procure the pool (Tinder, 2019). Regardless of the inner workings of the algorithm (which Tinder says they will never reveal), it is clear that Tinder does influence its users somewhat by limiting the number and type of potential partners it makes available at any given time. But because users do get to make their own choices, we place platforms like Tinder that apply some influence in the middle of the decision making assistance dimension.

Dimension 6: Mutuality. Another dimension along which dating platforms can differ at the matching stage is in *mutual selection* (also known as "reciprocal interest"—see Markowitz et al., 2019). Some platforms like OkCupid give users the ability to match and message each other freely. Any user can initiate a match individually and then communicate with another dater simply by typing a message and hitting send. OkCupid calls this a *one-sided* match—and it does not inhibit users from initiating them; in fact, it encourages its users to "make the first move" by sending a message in the Discovery phase (see below).

Other platforms like Tinder require *mutual matching* where both daters must indicate romantic interest before interaction can continue. Mutuality is indicated with the "It's a Match!" notification from the platform, which has become so ubiquitous it has been integrated into other dating apps. Some platforms like

Bumble go one step further—not only do they require mutual matching between daters, they also impose *time limits* and *initiation restrictions* on those matches. Once users have indicated mutual interest, only female daters can initiate messages, and only for 24 hours. After that time, the mutual match expires and the opportunity for further communication is closed (Bumble, n.d.).

The Discovery Stage

Daters who match with one another then enter into *discovery*, which begins when they exchange messages and start interacting. Exchanges often commence on the dating platform itself and can include a variety of different kinds of communications at the start. Daters will then often move their interactions into other mediated channels such as text messaging, phone calls, and video chat before meeting up FtF. The discovery phase can vary in length, with some daters gathering information about prospective partners via their linked SNS accounts, or engaging in lengthy mediated conversations, and others progressing quickly toward FtF dates. Below, we elaborate on various dimensions that are important during the discovery phase.

Dimension 7: Interaction Engagement. This dimension describes the nature of communication supported by the dating platform. Most encourage direct messaging between daters, but the kinds of cues they offer for communication vary. At one end of the continuum are "platform-generated" cues—or those that are completely outside the control of the individual user. For instance, Match.com indicates whether users are "online now" and available for direct messaging. It also displays how active a user is on the platform by revealing the time of their last login through displays of status information such as, "Active 4 hours ago." Such cues signal users' availability for interaction, but are completely outside of a dater's control.

Other "one-click" or "paralinguistic" kinds of communications (Hayes, Carr, & Wohn, 2016) are controllable by daters, and can be used to indicate their romantic interest in another person. Easily done with a single click or swipe, these paralinguistic cues require such little communicative effort to send that we characterize them as *lightweight* in nature (Tong & Walther, 2011). An example of a lightweight cue would be "swiping up" in Tinder, which sends a "Super Like." The Super Like indicates something different than the standard right-hand matching swipe (discussed above); by sending a Super Like, a user is communicating that he or she is *very* interested in initiating a romantic connection with another dater. But because a Super Like is sent through a single, haptic swipe, the actual communicative costs of sending it are quite low—no witty joke, comment, or opening line is needed to signal romantic interest. Thus costs associated with message construction (i.e., cognitive effort, anxiety, delivery, etc.) are mitigated (note, this does not include the actual monetary cost associated with Super Likes, as it is a feature that requires a paid subscription. See Chapter 13 for more on customer fees and business models of the online dating industry). This makes Tinder's Super Like—and other one-click cues like the Match.com "Wink"—useful as lightweight communications within the platform (see also, Carman, 2017).

At the other end of the interaction engagement dimension is *interactive message exchange.* Dating platforms that support this kind of interaction allow their users to send messages back and forth, directly to each other, but vary in how much access they give to users. As mentioned above, some platforms like Bumble impose restrictions on the amount of time users have to initiate message exchange. Others like the Delightful dating app require users to pay for access to their own message inbox, and to respond to others' messages. Because truly interactive message exchange is a paid, upgraded feature in many platforms, many users might find themselves migrating away from the original dating platform and into other mediated channels, such as text messaging, phone, SNSs, or video conferencing.

Dimension 8: Mixed-Mode Meetups. Most platforms encourage their users to stay on the platform as long as possible during the discovery phase. By paying for more lightweight messaging cues and greater access to interactive tools, users continue to spend their money on the platform, contributing revenue towards the company's bottom line. Other platforms, however, actually push daters to shorten the discovery phase by encouraging them to make quick transitions between online discovery and offline dates. The Clover app promotes "on-demand dating" and urges its users to schedule "real time" meetups with each other. And (although it was acquired by IAC group in 2015) the HowAboutWe dating app had a feature called "Tonight" where users could suggest a date activity for a specific time, and the HowAboutWe app would search for other potential matches who were also interested in a date at that same time near the user's location (Crook, 2015). Platforms that have these kinds of on-demand dating features accelerate FtF communication during the discovery stage, and push daters to make quick mixed-mode transitions (see Chapter 7 for more on modality switching).

Dating Stage	Variable Dimensions of Features in Dating Platforms
Registration	**Authentication**: Is specific information (i.e., other social media accounts, email addresses) required to provide authentication or "warrants" of user identity?
	Little/No Authentication Required — Specific/Multiple Authentication Forms Required
	Purpose/Functionality: Is the platform clear about the kind(s) of contact it is facilitating for users? Does the platform outline a specific purpose for conduct?
	Implicit explanations — Explicit explanations
Profile	**Breadth & Depth of Profile Information**: How much of the profile's content is prepared by the user? How much is prompted or required by the platform?
	Extremely Narrow (name, photo, age, location) — Extremely Broad (several different categories of personal information)
	Shallow Profile Self-Disclosures — Deeper Profile Self-Disclosures (with many "required" by the system)
Matching	**Decision Making Assistance**: Does the platform guide daters' mate selection choices?
	System assistance — Autonomous choice
	Mutuality: Is reciprocal interest between daters required for the platform to create a match?
	Individually initiated — Mutual match required
Discovery	**Interaction**: What kinds of cues are available to facilitate interaction between daters? To what degree are those cues controllable by individual users of the platform?
	System-generated cues — Lightweight communication cues — Interactive message exchange
	Mixed-Mode Meetups: Does the platform push daters to meet up in person? Or do they promote prolonged online/mobile interaction?
	Facilitates mediated interaction on the system — Encourages quick online-to-offline transitions

Table 4.1: Stages & dimensions of dating platforms.

Conclusion

The ubiquity of online dating platforms requires users, developers, and scholars alike to consider the ways in which these technologies are influencing the patterns of romantic relationship initiation. The goal of this chapter was to offer a descriptive framework that could help define and organize the landscape of dating platforms; the dimensions in Table 4.1 provide a way to conceptualize the larger field of dating technologies that cuts across different websites and apps.

Lastly, we note that existing research has not examined all of these dimensions to the same degree: As you will find out in other chapters, early online dating research focused on the daters' development of web-based profiles (in terms of the breadth, depth, and veracity of information disclosures) and the issues surrounding the authenticity of impressions formed on the basis of those profiles (Ellison et al., 2006). Researchers have only more recently begun to consider how daters' personal goals intersect with the platform's architecture and design, and how these aspects combine to affect various relational outcomes (Ranzini & Lutz, 2017; Van De Wiele & Tong, 2014), positive or negative emotional experiences with dating technology (Beck, 2016), or the ways in which different kinds of automated decision making assistance embedded in platforms can affect mate selection (Levy et al., 2019).

So, while extant research has focused on daters' behavior in the early profile and matching phases—such as their self-presentation, impression formation, and mate selection—we know comparatively less about daters' interactions at discovery and beyond: What kind of cues do they rely on and what kind of information is actually exchanged when sending and receiving messages? We also know less about mixed-mode communication: How do daters decide when to migrate off of the initial dating app or site and onto other mediated platforms? How do they negotiate mediated interaction and FtF meet-ups? Questions like these suggest that there is still much room for continued investigation.

References

Apperley, T., & Parikka, J. (2018). Platform studies' epistemic threshold. *Games and Culture*, *13*(4), 349–369. https://doi.org/10.1177/1555412015616509

Bumble. (n.d.). "Bumble Date." https://bumble.com/en-us/date

Burgess, J., Baym, N., Bucher, T., Helmond, A., John, N., Nissenbaum, A., Cunningham, S., & Craig, D. (2016, October 5–8). Platform studies: The rules of engagement. Panel presented at AoIR 2016: The 17th Annual Conference of the Association of Internet Researchers. http://spir.aoir.org

Carman, A. (2017, October 17). Why do you Super Like people on Tinder? [Audio podcast episode]. In *Why'd you push that button?* https://www.theverge.com/2017/10/17/16482452/ tinder-super-like-whyd-you-push-that-button-podcast

Carman, A. (2018, July 11). Hinge's newest feature claims to use machine learning to find your best match. *The Verge.* https://www.theverge.com/2018/7/11/17560352/ hinge-most-compatible-dating-machine-learning-match-recommendation

Carman, A. (2019, January 9). People want exclusive dating apps to filter people out so they can swipe less. *Why'd you push that button?* [audio podcast] https://www.theverge.com/ whyd-you-push-that-button

Carr, A. (2016, January 11). I found out my secret internal Tinder rating and now I wish I hadn't. *Fast Company.* https://www.fastcompany.com/3054871/whats-your-tinder-score-inside-the-apps-internal-ranking-system

Crook, J. (2015, April 16). The new HowAboutWe will let you order a date on demand. *TechCrunch.* https://techcrunch.com/2015/04/16/the-new-howaboutwe-will-let-your-order-a-date-on-demand/

DeAndrea, D. C. (2014). Advancing warranting theory. *Communication Theory, 24*(2), 186–204. https://doi.org/10.1111/comt.12033

eHarmony. (2017, August 9). "What eHarmony is all about." https://www.youtube.com/watch?v= RXkPQlqXnD4

Ellison, N., Heino, R., & Gibbs, J. (2006). Managing impressions online: Self-presentation processes in the online dating environment. *Journal of Computer-Mediated Communication, 11*(2), 415–441. https://doi.org/10.1111/j.1083-6101.2006.00020.x

Hayes, R. A., Carr, C. T., & Wohn, D. Y. (2016). One click, many meanings: Interpreting paralinguistic digital affordances in social media. *Journal of Broadcasting & Electronic Media, 60*(1), 171–187. https://doi.org/10.1080/08838151.2015.1127248

LeFebvre, L. E. (2018). Swiping me off my feet: Explicating relationship initiation on Tinder. *Journal of Social and Personal Relationships, 35*(9), 1205–1229. https://doi.org/10.1177/ 0265407517706419

Levy, J., Markell, D., & Cerf, M. (2019). Polar similars: Using massive mobile dating data to predict synchronization and similarity in dating preferences. *Frontiers in Psychology, 10.* https:// doi.org/10.3389/fpsyg.2019.02010

Lieberman, S. (2020, December 19). Looking for nice Jewish guys with "standards"? Click here. *New York Times.* https://www.nytimes.com/2020/12/19/style/looking-for-nice-jewish-guys-with-standards-click-here.html

Markowitz, D. M., Hancock, J. T., & Tong, S. T. (2019). Interpersonal dynamics in online dating: Profiles, matching, and discovery. In Z. Papacharissi (Ed.), *A networked self: Love* (pp. 50–61). Routledge.

Perez, S. (2018, June 1). Dating app Hinge is ditching the Facebook login requirement. *TechCrunch.* https://techcrunch.com/2018/06/01/dating-app-hinge-is-ditching-the-facebook-login-requirement/

Sumter, S., Vandenbosch, L., & Ligtenberg, L. (2017). Love me Tinder: Untangling emerging adults' motivations for using the dating application Tinder. *Telematics and Informatics, 34*(1), 67–78. https://doi.org/10.1016/j.tele.2016.04.009

The Lox Club. (n.d.). https://www.loxclubapp.com/

Tiffany, K. (2019, March 18). The Tinder algorithm, explained. *The Goods, by Vox.* https://www.vox.com/2019/2/7/18210998/tinder-algorithm-swiping-tips-dating-app-science

Timmermans, E., & De Caluwé, E. (2017). Development and validation of the Tinder Motives Scale (TMS). *Computers in Human Behavior, 70,* 341–350. https://doi.org/10.1016/j.chb.2017.01.028

Tinder. (2019, March 15). Powering Tinder–The method behind our matching. [blog post]. https://blog.gotinder.com/powering-tinder-r-the-method-behind-our-matching/

Van De Wiele, C., & Tong, S. T. (2014). Breaking boundaries: The uses and gratifications of Grindr. In A. J. Brush, A. Friday, J. A. Kientz, J. Scott, & J. Song (Eds.), *UbiComp'14: ACM International Joint Conference on Pervasive and Ubiquitous Computing.* Seattle, WA (pp. 619–630). ACM Press. https://doi.org/10.1145/2632048.2636070

Walther, J. B., & Parks, M. R. (2002). Cues filtered out, cues filtered in: Computer-mediated communication and relationships. In M. L. Knapp & J. A. Daly (Eds.), *The handbook of interpersonal communication* (3rd ed., pp. 529–563). Sage.

5

Self-Presentation & Impression Formation in Online and Mobile Dating

If you type the phrase "dating profile tips" into Google, it will produce approximately 1.67 million search results. Apparently, a lot of people want advice about what information to put on their online and mobile dating profiles. This might seem strange since the content of a dating profile is pretty sparse—we're talking a few paragraphs (or less!) of self-description and some photographs. That's not a lot of words, and it seems fairly straightforward, so why are people so stressed out?

As we will discover in this chapter, composing the online profile is stressful because it is the means by which two integral communication processes occur in online and mobile dating. The first process is *self-presentation*, which consists of the deliberate behaviors that we perform in an effort to control how other people evaluate us (Goffman, 1959; Schlenker, 1980). We might reveal aspects of personality through our interactions with others, express ourselves through our clothing or jewelry, or tell people about our hobbies and interests—how we present ourselves can drastically influence how others see us. Researchers in communication have studied individuals' self-presentation behaviors in mediated dating platforms for many years and have explored several related topics. Early work on self-presentation looked at the content people put in their profiles and what motivated them to do so (Ellison et al., 2006; Ranzini & Lutz, 2017). Researchers have also examined whether or not the information people present on their dating profiles is fully honest, as well as the circumstances under which daters deliberately misrepresent themselves in order to appear more attractive to others (DeAndrea, Tong, Liang, Levine, & Walther, 2012; Duguay, 2017; Guadagno, Okdie, & Kruse, 2012; Hancock & Toma, 2009; Ward, 2017).

The flip side of self-presentation is *impression formation*, or the judgments we make about other people we meet. To form impressions of others, we use the information that people deliberately communicate about themselves, but also the unintended information that people let slip. Goffman (1959) distinguished between intentional and unintentional information, calling them "cues given" and "cues given off," and both kinds of cues influence our interpersonal judgments, as well as our decisions to interact with people in the future. With regard to impression formation in online and mobile dating, researchers have examined which information categories and cues (both visual and text-based) on the profile are most "diagnostic" for daters forming impressions of potential partners (Ellison et al., 2006; Tong et al., 2019), and how people evaluate either the credibility or *warranting value* of others' self-authored profile information (Corriero & Tong, 2016; Gibbs, Ellison, & Lai, 2011).

In this way, self-presentation and interpersonal impressions are linked together as the fundamental first phase of the online romantic relationship initiation process (see also Markowitz, Hancock, & Tong, 2019). Below, we provide a review of the literature on self-presentation and impression formation in online and mobile dating, then propose a set of new questions that researchers might investigate in future studies.

Foundational Concepts of Self-Presentation and Impression Formation

Goffman (1959) was a prominent theorist who considered how the ways we dress, describe ourselves, talk about our preferences, and interact with others work together to create a certain public self—or "face"—that we present to the world. In reciprocal fashion, others evaluate our publicly presented self-image by forming impressions about us. You've probably heard how important it is to "make a great first impression" and this is because those first impressions often determine whether or how others will interact with us in future situations. Positive impressions are indicative of social approval and respect, whereas negative impressions often lead to avoidance or rejection. According to Goffman, our public self-presentation is reflected back to us through others' impressions and treatment of us during social interaction.

Though we still rely on Goffman's foundational ideas, the ways that researchers think about self-presentation and impression formation have evolved as Internet technology has developed. In considering how self-presentation behavior may be altered in online settings, Walther (1996) proposed that it could be much more *selective* and strategic compared to FtF settings. Consider how much effort it takes to self-present in a FtF conversation—we have to monitor all of our nonverbal communication behaviors (e.g., tone of voice, gestures, facial expressions, physical appearance) and verbal communication behaviors (e.g., word choice, fluency, and structure of sentences). But in an online environment, we do not have to be so careful about our nonverbal behaviors—as you recall from Chapter 1, when communication occurs online, nonverbal cues like vocalics (e.g., tone, volume, pitch), proxemics (physical distance), physical appearance (e.g., grooming, wardrobe, hygiene), and haptics (physical touch) are "filtered out." The cognitive effort that we would have spent worrying about whether we have bad breath, or if we said the "right thing" in a nice tone of voice, can be reallocated toward monitoring those self-presentational cues that do remain under our control in mediated environments.

In online settings, the self-presentational cues that remain tend to be text-based or visual in nature. So, you can focus more of your attention on composing eloquent paragraphs of self-description for your OkCupid profile, typing out witty text messages, or selecting just the right profile photograph (i.e., the one that was taken in excellent lighting, features your good side, and that you edited with that fancy filter) for your Tinder account. Furthermore, when online, daters are often communicating *asynchronously*, so they can spend as much time as they want crafting and polishing their self-image. Lastly, text-based tools such as editing, deletion, cut-and-paste, and photo-based tools, such as cropping, lighting, and filters provide much more *control* over the presentation of visual information. To use Goffman's terminology, more cues are "given" rather than "given off" in online environments (Ellison et al., 2006). In summary, online self-presentation is much more selective because we can spend more time and put greater effort into choosing flattering information and presenting the best version of ourselves.

Self-Presentation: Putting Your Best Profile Forward

Early Investigations into Self-Presented Profiles. Nicole Ellison, Rebecca Heino, and Jennifer Gibbs were some of the first scholars to apply the concept of selective self-presentation in online dating research. In a series of interview studies with Match.com daters, they found that daters' self-presentation behaviors were motivated by two overarching, but competing, goals: (1) the need to self-present positive attributes to appear attractive and (2) the need to present their genuine, authentic selves. They argue that in online and mobile dating it is the *profile* that becomes the "crucial self-presentation tool because it is the first and primary means of expressing one's self during the early stages of a correspondence and can therefore foreclose or create relationship opportunities" (Ellison et al., 2006, p. 423). Although most of their participants reported that they tried to be accurate and truthful in their profiles, many also disclosed that they presented themselves as more athletic, younger, or thinner—in short, they presented a more desirable, *ideal* version of themselves in their dating profiles (Ellison et al., 2006).

Presentation of one's ideal self in dating profiles often involves making small self-enhancements: Daters report making incremental adjustments—like any person who wants to appear more attractive, we might subtract five pounds from our weight or under-report our age by a few years. In one experiment, Hancock, Toma, and Ellison (2007) recruited 80 male and female users of Match.com, Yahoo Personals, and American Singles from around New York City to participate in a study examining misrepresentations of height, weight, and age in dating profiles. Participants were brought to a laboratory where the researchers obtained a printed copy of each person's online profile. The researchers then measured participants' height (in inches) and weight (in pounds) and recorded participants' age from their drivers' licenses. In comparing people's self-presented dating profile information to the measurement data obtained in the lab, Hancock et al. found that "average deviation from the height reported in the profile and measured in the lab was 0.33 inches, ranging from 3 inches taller and 1.75 inches shorter than participants reported in their profile" (p. 451). Daters' weight deviations averaged about 5.68 pounds, ranging between 35 pounds heavier and 20.4 pounds lighter than reported in profile content. Finally, deviations between profile and observed age was 0.44 years, ranging from four years younger to nine years older.

As these results indicate, online and mobile daters routinely make small, self-serving claims about their height, weight, and age on profiles to project a more attractive self; but why did they stop short of presenting bigger discrepancies? What might be discouraging larger inconsistencies between self-presentation on a profile and reality? One factor might be daters' perceptions regarding the *social acceptability* of lying in one's online dating profile. In a follow-up experiment, Toma, Hancock, and Ellison (2008) asked their participants to rate the social acceptability of certain kinds of self-presentational discrepancies, which they defined as "the degree to which you believe it is acceptable to lie about this topic" (p. 1027). On the whole, daters seemed to think that self-presentation discrepancies on profiles were generally unacceptable—in fact, the most socially *unacceptable* category to misrepresent was one's relationship information (i.e., single, divorced, widowed). However, ratings of social acceptability of misrepresentation across other profile categories differed along gender lines: In particular, female daters considered it less acceptable to misrepresent their occupation and their education, compared to male daters. But overall, self-presentational discrepancies were not judged favorably among this sample of online daters.

Certain features of the CMC environment might also prevent online and mobile daters from making bigger, self-aggrandizing claims: First is the notion of *accountability* (Leary, 1995) through *anticipated future interaction* (Walther, 1996)—as we know from Chapter 4, daters who hit it off online are likely to set up FtF dates, eventually. The expectation of meeting another dater in-person some time in the future and being held accountable for profile distortions can discourage bigger lies: A dater who self-presents in his Match.com profile as a 25-year-old with an "athletic" build but is really a 55-year-old couch potato will be immediately labeled as a fraud. When such a blatant lie is eventually exposed, it will be clear that this person's intention was to deceive others entirely, not just subtract a few years off of his age. As such "to be caught distorting one's self-presentation is more embarrassing than being seen as dishonest and trying to conceal one's actual undesirable characteristics. The social cost of embarrassment prompts individuals to self-present more accurately" (DeAndrea et al., 2012). And because Internet information is *recordable* and *documentable*, the more inaccuracies daters place in their profiles, the more likely they are to be held accountable for those inconsistencies later on.

Recent Studies: Self-Presentation in Mobile Dating Apps

In examining daters' self-presentation behavior for this chapter, we interviewed several Tinder users and asked them what they put on their profile. Joshua, 22, told us:

> Well, I mean, I kind of make sure I have, like, clean, clear pictures of my face. I guess because, like, if you have weird pictures that's not good; or, I mean, don't have any shirtless pictures or anything like that. But, um, yeah I'm not doing anything special. I think I have some pictures that show I'm a student, that I'm doing stuff with my life. I just would say kind of what you would have on any normal social media type thing. Not too much information, but enough for people to get an idea.

Joshua's response shows the kind of thought that daters put into their profile photos—they want to portray a certain image (a student who is doing stuff with life), avoid other images (no shirtless, or other "weird" pictures), and provide "just enough" information for people to "get an idea" (i.e., form an impression), while leaving something to the imagination. When you consider all the things that Joshua is trying to convey to others through just a few photos and a little bit of text, it is a lot to accomplish in a small profile!

More recent research has built on the foundations of online web-based profiles and examined daters' self-presentation in mobile applications like Tinder and Grindr. Ward (2017) recruited 21 Tinder daters and asked them about the ways they managed their impressions on their profile. Daters discussed the specific image they wanted to create, as well as those impressions they wanted to avoid. Two respondents mentioned that appearing "too sexy" was something to be avoided: One female participant expressed that she "would never put up sexy pictures," and a male respondent said he wanted to appear "serious" to other daters, rather than "the guy who is starting with questions about sex" (p. 1651). Several respondents in this study also discussed experimenting with their self-presentation—sometimes putting forth a "philosophical" self-image, or presenting a more flirtatious self than they would normally portray offline—to see what kinds of responses they would receive on the app. People also described how as they gained more experience on Tinder and learned how matching worked, they would alter their profiles accordingly, hoping to attract specific sorts of people.

In addition to creating the content itself, Tinder users also considered how to arrange and order the content. Because a Tinder profile appears on a mobile device, users can only view one profile photograph at a time. To move forward and view more content, a dater must "swipe" through, to access additional photographs and profile text. Participants in Ward's (2017) interviews reported putting a great deal of thought into their primary profile photo—that is, the one that other daters see first—to make sure it was attractive enough to warrant continued scrolling and swiping.

The Influence of Individual Goals

Another factor that influences how people present themselves and develop impressions of others on dating websites and mobile apps is their individual romantic goals. The popular media often reports that daters are using apps like Tinder and Grindr solely for the hookups; and while scholarly research certainly reflects that casual sex is a shared goal among many online and mobile daters, study findings also reveal more diverse motivations for dating app use. The *uses and gratifications* (U&G) framework (Katz, Blumler, & Gurevitch, 1973; Figure 5.1) has been applied to examine people's motives for using online and mobile dating sites and apps. The U&G framework has two main background assumptions: (1) people's goals, needs, and desires influence their use of media, and (2) the consequences of that goal-driven media use attract and hold people's attention to that media content. Sometimes, the consequences of our media use are just as we expect, or what U&G refers to as *sought gratifications*, such as the entertainment we get through popular media like television, mobile apps and games. Other *obtained gratifications* refer to the actual outcomes of media use—things we may not have intended but which emerge as byproducts of our goal-directed media use, such as blurred vision or sleeplessness caused by too much screen time.

Van De Wiele and Tong (2014) used the U&G framework in their study of 525 Grindr users and uncovered six gratifications of Grindr use: social inclusion (i.e., the "ego boost" users felt when others would right swipe and find them desirable), casual sex/hookups, friendship, entertainment (i.e., looking at others' profiles for fun), romantic relationships, and location-based search. More recently, Timmermans and De Calwé (2017) replicated the use of this framework and found 13 motivations of Tinder use—in addition to those motives identified by Van De Wiele and Tong (2014), they also included: ex-partner surveillance, peer pressure, belongingness, sexual orientation, distraction, and curiosity.

You might be wondering why uncovering daters' uses and gratifications is so important. Research has shown that daters' goal-driven media use directly influences their self-presentation behavior and the ways they form impressions of others. For example, Ranzini and Lutz (2017) examined how daters' motivations for using Tinder, as well as their personality, influenced their perceptions about the authenticity and deceptiveness of their self-presentation behavior. They recruited 497 Tinder users to fill out an online survey that measured their various motivations for using Tinder, together with levels of self-esteem, loneliness, and narcissism. After reporting on their motives and personality, participants then reflected on how *real* their Tinder self-presentation was—measured as the extent to which they believed their Tinder profiles were "similar" to who they are offline; and how *deceptive* they believed their self-presentation was—as assessed by the extent they presented information on their profiles that wasn't representative of their "true" self. Ranzini and Lutz's results indicated that those participants who reported using Tinder primarily for hooking up/casual sex or for social approval (i.e., self-validating ego boost) were more likely to judge their own self-presentation as

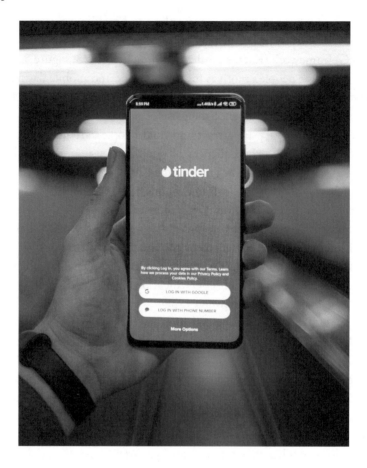

Figure 5.1: Uses and gratifications of Tinder. Source: Mika Baumeister/Public Domain

deceptive in nature. On the other hand, those who reported using Tinder to find friendship viewed their own self-presentation as more genuine. Regarding personality, people's narcissism and loneliness were not related to their self-presentation, but those who had greater self-esteem tended to feel as though they were more authentic and less deceptive in their self-presentation. This research suggests that our motives for media use and our individual personalities can influence the ways we present ourselves in mediated settings.

Finally, comparing the research examining daters' self-presentation in online websites to mobile apps shows predictable similarities, but also some key differences. Similar to Ellison et al.'s (2006) findings regarding online daters' self-presentation, Ward (2017) concluded that among Tinder users in her study: "All interviewees strove to make a positive impression, essentially aiming for a balance between an ideal and an authentic self-presentation" (p. 1652). Thus, the two competing self-presentation goals of putting forth a positive, attractive self-image to others, while also presenting one's genuine self, still exist in mobile apps. But some features of mobile dating apps, such as *locatability*, might alter or change certain self-presentation goals. For example, motivations to present an authentic self may be heightened in apps like Tinder and Grindr that use *geolocation* data to share an individuals' exact physical location.

Functioning as a "people nearby" app, Grindr advertises its ability to help daters find partners who are "0 feet away" (Grindr, n.d.) and to facilitate immediate in-person meetups among its users (Toch & Levi, 2013; Van De Wiele & Tong, 2014). The increased potential for, and speed with which, FtF dates follow matching in mobile dating apps may make authenticity an even greater concern when compared to online websites; since future interaction is anticipated to transpire more quickly, daters would be held accountable (and possibly called out) by others for any discrepancies or inconsistencies between their mobile dating profiles and physical appearance.

Forming Impressions in Online and Mobile Dating

Just as daters obsess over their own profiles, they spend just as much time analyzing and evaluating others' profiles. They scrutinize photos and bios, making judgments about attractiveness, personality, preferences, and abilities. The composite result of these judgments are the *impressions* they form, which subsequently inform their decisions about whether to initiate communication with a potential partner.

Regarding online impression formation, because so many (nonverbal) information cues on dating profiles are filtered out, those that remain often take on greater significance. Furthermore, because so many of the remaining cues are selective and self-authored (e.g., "given"), daters have to pay special attention to those that are "given off." Ellison et al. (2006) found that daters relied heavily on these "less intentional" cues to develop impressions—cues like grammar and spelling mistakes in profile bios became evidence for judgments of others' intelligence or (lack of) conscientiousness. Daters in these interviews also reported paying attention to seemingly innocuous information cues: *Chronemics*—or information about time—became a cue set that daters focused on. Some online dating websites will publish the date and time of a user's last login or site activity (see also Chapter 4), and from that information, people might make judgments about that user's habits, lifestyle, or (lack of) employment (Ellison et al., 2006). As this early research indicates, when the communication function of impression formation moves from offline to online, people still make judgments and inferences from others' personal information; however, in keeping with social information processing theory (Walther, 1992), their focus on available cues—even small ones—is sharpened in online settings.

Individual motivations for using dating sites and apps can influence self-presentation behavior, and they can also influence impression formation. Corriero and Tong (2016) surveyed 326 active users of Grindr to see if their reasons for using it influenced their desire to seek out interpersonal information about other daters who were also on the app. They hypothesized that those who were motivated to use Grindr to find casual sex would have a greater desire to remain *uncertain* about their potential hookup partners, which in turn would make them less motivated to search for information about those partners. Results indicated that when people reported using Grindr to hook up with others, their desire to remain uncertain about their sex partners corresponded to reduced effort spent on seeking out information about those partners. They concluded that those motivated to use dating apps for casual sex often enjoy the excitement of anonymous hookups, and this motive may have contributed to their overall disinterest in developing more detailed impressions of partners: "The risk associated with casual sex may also contribute to daters' excitement within Grindr" (p. 137).

The Importance of Being Honest: Warranting Theory in Online Impression Formation

The 2010 documentary film *Catfish*[2] explores the importance of being honest in the online realm. The film documents the friendship that Nev (the narrator) develops with a young artist, Abby, and later the romantic relationship Nev cultivates with Abby's half-sister, Megan. Throughout the course of his romantic relationship with Megan, Nev becomes suspicious about whether some of the things she is sharing with him are true or not. Eventually, motivated by curiosity

---

2   Since its release, the veracity the events that unfold in *Catfish* has been challenged. Some have suggested that some or even most of the elements of the plot were not discovered by filmmakers as presented in the film and that it represents a fake documentary—that is, a fictitious film presented in documentary style. The film's directors and main subject of the film dispute this claim (Longworth, 2010).

and suspicion, Nev makes a trip to rural Michigan and learns that he has never spoken with Meg, but instead has been interacting with Meg and Abby's mother, Angela.

Whether the events in this film are fact or fiction, the plot captures a real concern for those seeking to strike up a romantic relationship online: Is this other person *really* who they say they are? While instances of large-scale, identity-fabricating deception are probably rare in the online dating space—because, most of the time, romance seekers actually hope to meet the person they are communicating with—that does not stop people from being concerned that they could be duped. For this reason, it is probably not surprising that people who use the Internet to facilitate interactions with others whom they want to trust are constantly on the hunt for good, honest information.

While some daters may appreciate the uncertainty and anonymity that comes with Internet-initiated dating, for others developing a detailed, clear, and accurate impression of a potential partner is an important step toward launching a relationship. Given that so much profile information people rely on for online impression formation amounts to self-authored, selectively self-presented photos and text, daters often report concerns over its veracity (Gibbs, Ellison, & Lai, 2011).

Walther and Parks' (2002) warranting theory offers one theoretical explanation of how and why users trust some kinds of online information but are more skeptical of others. Warranting theory is among the easiest CMC theories to summarize: The more difficult it is to fake a piece of information, the more we trust that information. Walther and Parks are not the only scholars to ask about the role of trustworthy information in relationships. Warranting theory draws from Stone's (1996) thinking on how people verify their corporeal realities in virtual space. Similarly, Giddens (1991) and Dugay (2017) address online "authenticity."

Giddens' (1991), and later Dugay's (2017) authenticity, though, is different in some ways from what Walther and Parks (2002) discuss in warranting theory. For Giddens and later Dugay, authenticity represents a self-awareness which (as Dugay elaborates), can allow the self-aware user to capitalize on the affordances of computing technology in order to present an authentic version of the self. That is, one must have an understanding of who they are in order to represent an authentic version of oneself. Giddens and Dugay implicitly suggest that an authentic version of one's self is what an online dater would *want* to self-present. In many cases, this may well be true. However, there are challenges to conceptualizing authenticity in this way. First, knowing oneself isn't quite as simple as it may seem. A wide array of biases which cloud our ability to accurately judge ourselves—sometimes even when we seek to critically self-evaluate—are well documented (e.g., "The Dunning-Krueger Effect;" Krueger & Dunning, 1999; "The Barnum Effect;" Forer, 1949). Second, as enticing and chivalrous as it sounds to be motivated to represent oneself authentically, we suspect that the truth of a few more pounds, a few extra wrinkles, and a few more gray hairs, may be less important for a person to share than the promise of what they could be in the future (see Ellison, Hancock, & Toma, 2011).

Ultimately, we agree with Dugay that authenticity matters to those who use the Internet to find a romantic match. We also believe that authenticity, honesty, veracity (and it's been called all of those things by scholars seeking to address the same issue) most definitely matters a great deal to the *message receiver*. It may be normative for a message sender to moderately inflate self-presentation in an online dating environment (Ellison, Heino, & Gibbs, 2006), and a message recipient may be aware of this, but many online and mobile daters hope to form accurate impressions of potential romantic partners. It is because authenticity matters so much to message receivers that we find *warranting theory* so vital to providing a theoretical path to some of the questions that are most important regarding the online dating space.

Warranting theory (DeAndrea, 2014; Walther & Parks, 2002) is important because it offers explanatory guidance about the things people look for when they seek to make judgments about others' authenticity. As you might recall from Chapter 2, informational warrants are what we use to judge others' authenticity. In other words, this theory suggests that receivers' evaluation of informational warranting value can function to affect interpersonal impression formation outcomes. Some of the first research exploring how people make judgments of others according to warranting theory (Walther & Parks, 2002) analyzed the effects of self-generated versus other-generated information on impression formation. Walther, Van Der Heide, Hamel, and Shulman (2009), used the popular social networking website Facebook to demonstrate that other-generated information is preferred by observers over self-generated information, especially when that information is likely to have a favorable impact on a person's reputation. For instance, observers are more likely to believe that you are attractive if others in your Facebook network say you are attractive. This is much more believable than if you say it yourself. When considering someone's potentially positive characteristics, we understand that the person may have a vested interest in being judged favorably; because of this, we are more likely to judge as authentic what a friend (who has less to gain from lying about you) says about you, compared to what you say about yourself. We want to be careful with this finding. Although much of the early work on warranting theory focused on the ways that self-made claims did not carry the impression-bearing weight of others' statements, warranting theory is bigger than this particular finding alone. The self-versus-other dichotomy is simply one operationalization of warranting theory's central principle that information that is harder to manipulate is more believable.

Another type of information present on social media is communicated through *system-generated cues*. As noted in earlier parts of the book, system-generated cues are pieces of information about users that websites and mobile apps assemble and display on profiles. For example, Facebook still presents the number of "friends" one has, although not as prominently as it did in the past. If you add a friend, the system will add a number to your "Facebook friends" total. This information does not directly conform to the self-vs.-other dichotomy. This example of a system-generated cue is directly related to your behavior, but it is difficult to fake. The system simply calculates your number of friends and reports it. Warranting theory would predict that system-generated cues—because they are difficult to fake—ought to be perceived by an observer to be high in warranting value, and therefore to be trusted.

In online dating websites and mobile dating apps, there are system-generated cues that show up on profiles—daters do not have control over this information, but they often do use it to make impressions. As noted earlier, one important system-generated cue is the date and time of daters' activity on websites and apps. Most dating systems show a user's last login or activity by displaying cues such as "last active 4 hours ago" or "active now." These cues can trigger impressions about how "interested" or "available" a dater is (Ellison, Heino, & Gibbs, 2006, p. 431).

Daters also form impressions from the algorithmic matching scores that some dating platforms offer. For example, OkCupid has an algorithm that calculates "match" and "enemy" scores between daters. This algorithm takes into account the basic "looking for" profile information of both daters (i.e., desired partner's location, age, gender, sexual orientation), as well as "question compatibility" or how similarly they answered the questions posed by the system during the profile-generation phase (OkCupid, n.d.). Although these algorithmically-generated elements can guide daters' impressions of potential partners and even affect their decisions to pursue relationships, research shows that people lack awareness regarding the influence of system-generated cues over their impression-making behavior (Sharabi, 2021; Tong, Hancock, & Slatcher, 2016).

System-generated cues are important pieces of information that can have high warranting value, which means daters will often draw on them when forming impressions. Many other cues exist in mobile apps too—like geolocation data—but more research is needed about the influence of system-generated information, especially in terms of their effects on initial impression formation. We will return to this topic later in the chapter.

Are Daters' Self-Presentations and Observers' Impressions Consistent?

Having been introduced to self-presentation and impression formation as two processes involved in online relationship initiation, you may be wondering about the degree to which these two processes correspond. That is, do people's self-presentation and others' impressions of them match each other? Are others' views of your personality similar to how you see yourself? One technique that has been used to examine the consistency between people's self-presentation and observers' impressions of them is the *lens model analysis*. The lens model was introduced by Brunswik (1956), a psychologist who wanted to understand how a clinician might make inferences about a patient's personality. A lens model analysis examines how people *encode*—or self-present—information about their own personality through various kinds of information cues or behaviors. Brunswik termed this encoding process *cue validity* and it refers to those personality traits or elements of an individual's self-concept that are self-presented. Cues are also utilized by observers to *decode* profile-owners' personalities, in a process called *cue utilization*. The extent to which the observer's impressions of the profile-owner corresponds to the profile-owner's personal evaluation of self is known as *functional achievement*. Importantly, the cues that a profile-owner uses for encoding and the cues that an observer uses for decoding need not be the same—and sometimes this lack of overlap, or *cue sensitivity*, can lead to inconsistencies between self-presentation and others' interpersonal impressions.

The lens model approach has been used to examine encoding, decoding, and functional achievement in Twitter tweets (Qiu, Lin, Ramsay, & Yang, 2012), blog entries (Yarkoni, 2010), and Facebook profiles (Hall, Pennington, & Leuder, 2014). Within the online dating context, Tong, Corriero, Wibowo, Makki, and Slatcher (2019) conducted a lens model analysis of the self-authored "about me" portions of daters' profiles. The researchers analyzed the "about me" paragraphs of 190 online daters, separating them into seven categories of linguistic cues: humor, specific qualities/characteristics, spending time with others, leisure, personality, life aspirations, and interest in relationships.

The researchers also asked participants to fill out a survey assessing their personality along the dimensions of the "Big 5"—emotional stability (i.e., neuroticism), extraversion, openness to experience, conscientiousness, and agreeableness. To examine the self-presentation side of the lens model, the researchers explored whether any of the daters' personality characteristics were encoded through the language they used in their self-authored paragraphs. Results showed that this sample of online daters was able to encode their extraversion, conscientiousness, and emotional stability through their descriptions of their life aspirations and their desire to spend time with their family and friends.

To complete the other side of the lens model analysis, seven outside observers were asked to read the "about me" paragraphs and rate each profile-owner along the same Big 5 dimensions. By correlating observers' personality judgments to the use of language in the profiles, the researchers could determine the extent to which this content was used by observers when decoding daters' personalities during impression formation. As in the encoding side, life aspiration words were useful for observers' judgments of emotional stability and openness. But whereas messages about time spent with others provided a useful set of linguistic cues for self-presentation, they were not used by observers in the impression formation process. Instead, observers relied on specific personality or quality cues, like daters' self-described characteristics, such as "honesty," or being "fun" or "funny."

Although daters were able to encode aspects of their personality and observers did form impressions, this study indicates a lack of consistency between the two processes. As Tong et al. (2019) note, their results "show some misalignment between the cues used to encode one's self-concept versus those used to develop impressions on the observer's end. The mismatch between the cues used for encoding impression displays and the cues utilized for impression formation may provide partial explanation for the unmet expectations that can arise when online daters meet face-to-face" (p. 887). What might be causing this inconsistency between encoding and decoding? On the self-presentation side, it may be that the architecture of dating sites and apps encourage "stock" profiles: Daters are all producing the same formulaic content, which reduces the diagnostic value of language—if every single person claims to like long walks on the beach, hanging out with their friends, cute puppies, and pepperoni pizza, how does that make them unique and attractive? On the observers' side, impressions may be influenced by individual characteristics such as romantic goals, gender, age, and people's general belief that they possess more complex, multifaceted personalities than others do (Sande, Goethals, & Radloff, 1988). As none of these factors were measured in this study, we do not know the extent to which they may have influenced observers' impression formation. We might classify Tong et al.'s (2019) study as *descriptive* research—that is, their work uncovered the inconsistency between self-presentation and impression formation, but it did not examine specific reasons why that inconsistency occurred. Future explanatory studies that concentrate on *causality* will be better suited to determine the circumstances under which the discrepancy between self-presentation and impression formation among online and mobile daters exists.

Conclusion

As two halves of the initial stage of online dating, self-presentation, and impression formation—mainly through the dating profile—compose the gateway through which daters communicate about themselves and learn about potential partners. Regarding self-presentation: Many smart readers might be thinking, "People misrepresent themselves all the time—it's not like it only happens online." Very true. As an important aside, we note that people are often driven by self-presentation goals that transcend medium or channel—it is a communication process that occurs in many environments. For example, young women adhering to Westernized socio-cultural standards of beauty often strive to self-present as thinner or younger (Fitzsimmons-Craft et al., 2012). Thus, if prompted, they would be likely to under-report their weight or age in all kinds of situations, not just in their online dating profiles. Our point here is that selective self-presentation—while very likely to occur in online dating settings—clearly happens in many other (offline) settings, too. In fact, however, little research has systematically explored whether deceptive behavior is more or less prevalent online or offline. Certainly, scholars have demonstrated that online daters perceive that *others* are frequently dishonest on dating platforms (Ellison et al., 2006), but in terms of the base rates of dishonesty in self-presentation on the dating scene from online to offline, is there a difference? (For more reading on this issue, see DeAndrea et al., 2012).

Moreover, more research needs to be done to clarify what, precisely, dishonesty is. As Ellison et al. (2006, 2011) suggest, our own self-descriptions may be impeded by the fact that we often fail to see ourselves accurately—a problem Ellison et al. (2006) label the "foggy mirror" phenomenon (and a point that recent work by Levine [2019] expounds upon at some length). Also, humans have become rather comfortable with the forms of "deception" we use offline, so much so that in some cases, we don't even think of them as being deceptive. For example, prior to a date, most of us would take the opportunity to shower, put on deodorant, shave, put on make-up, and wear clothing that makes us look our best. We wouldn't bat a (false) eyelash at most of these behaviors. But the moment someone digitally removes a pimple, we scream, "deception!" The problem with this is that at their core, both types of behavior seek to dress up the impressions others form of us. As future work seeks to understand the prevalence of deceptive behavior in all types of romantic interaction (both online and offline) it is very important that scholars continue to develop and define precisely what we mean when we discuss "deceptive behavior" in self-presentation.

Additionally, some new dating platforms seem to capitalize on several of warranting theory's (Walther & Parks, 2002) core contentions with respect to impression formation. As noted in Chapter 2, many dating sites and apps urge (or sometimes require) users to link their social media accounts to their dating profile at the registration stage. For example, the Hinge app used the (established) Facebook network to match daters with other potential partners who are connected by one degree of separation (i.e., potential matches are friends of friends). One of the components of warranting that Walther and Parks discuss is that observers are more likely to trust and value information that arises from within a networked environment because that information has been "vetted" by members of the shared social network. In other words, although photographs from Facebook or Instagram may be just as carefully self-curated by an online dater as the photographs they upload to their dating profile, it may be that an online dater's willingness to share photos that they have *already* shared with their broader social network may be perceived as more believable and authentic by observers on dating platforms.

Recent technological developments in mobile dating platforms also bring to mind classic theories of interpersonal attraction. For instance, in the past decade, location-based dating applications have begun to spring up. Now, many platforms proudly display approximately how far in miles or kilometers you are from a prospective match. Newcomb's (1956) classic *proximity attraction principle* suggests that we are attracted to those in close proximity to us. We suspect that a great deal of interesting new research might be generated by this system-generated proximity variable. On one hand, *everyone* a person "meets" on an online dating platform is in a sense the same distance away—as far as the screen to an observer's eyes. On the other hand, when a person's geolocation data is offered through the dating app, the knowledge that someone is geographically proximate may close the psychological distance between a dater and a potential match. Could this sense of proximity have an effect on the perceived attractiveness of the other person? Might we like a person more if they we know that they are physically nearby? Might we *trust* a person more if they are in within walking or driving distance? Is there a proximity-based halo effect (see Nisbet & DeCamp Wilson, 1977; Thorndike, 1920) which makes the geographically close seem more similar, more authentic, and more beautiful than it would otherwise seem? These questions, like others raised in this chapter, are complicated by the fact that as online and mobile dating platforms change, so do the contexts for self-presentation and impression formation. CMC researchers should be very busy in the years ahead.

References

Beck, J. (2016, October). The rise of dating-app fatigue. *The Atlantic Online.* https://www.theatlantic.com/health/archive/2016/10/the-unbearable-exhaustion-of-dating-apps/505184/

Brunswik, E. (1956). *Perception and the representative design of psychological experiments.* University of California Press.

Carman, A. (host), & Tiffany, K. (host). (2019, January 9). *People want exclusive dating apps to filter people out so they can swipe less* [audio podcast]. *The Verge.* https://www.theverge.com/2019/1/9/18170256/the-league-raya-exclusive-dating-apps-membership-whyd-you-push-that-button-podcast

Corriero, E. F., & Tong, S. T. (2016). Managing uncertainty in mobile dating applications: Goals, concerns of use, and information seeking in Grindr. *Mobile Media & Communication, 4*(1), 121–141. https://doi.org/10.1177/2050157915614872

DeAndrea, D. C. (2014). Advancing warranting theory. *Communication Theory, 24,* 186–204. https://doi.org/10.1111/comt.12033

DeAndrea, D. C., Tong, S. T., Liang, Y. J., Levine, T. R., & Walther, J. B. (2012). When do people misrepresent themselves to others? The effects of social desirability, ground truth, and accountability on deceptive self-presentations. *Journal of Communication, 62*(3), 400–417. https://doi.org/10.1111/j.1460-2466.2012.01646.x

Duguay, S. (2017). Dressing up Tinderella: Interrogating authenticity claims on the mobile dating app Tinder. *Information, Communication & Society, 20*(3), 351–367. https://doi.org/10.1080/1369118X.2016.1168471

Ellison, N. B., Hancock, J. T., & Toma, C. L. (2011). Profile as promise: A framework for conceptualizing veracity in online dating self-presentations. *New Media & Society, 14*(1), 45–62. https://doi.org/10.1177/1461444811410395

Ellison, N., Heino, R., & Gibbs, J. (2006). Managing impressions online: Self-presentation processes in the online dating environment. *Journal of Computer-Mediated Communication, 11*(2), 415–441. https://doi.org/10.1111/j.1083-6101.2006.00020.x

Fitzsimmons-Craft, E. E., Harney, M. B., Koehler, L. G., Danzi, L. E., Riddell, M. K., & Bardone-Cone, A. M. (2012). Explaining the relation between thin ideal internalization and body dissatisfaction among college women: The roles of social comparison and body surveil-lance. *Body image, 9*(1), 43–49. https://doi.org/10.1016/j.bodyim.2011.09.00

Forer, B. R. (1949) The fallacy of personal validation: A classroom demonstration of gullibility. *Journal of Abnormal Psychology, 44*(1), 118–121. https://doi.org/10.1037/h0059240

Gibbs, J. L., Ellison, N. B., & Lai, C. H. (2011). First comes love, then comes Google: An investiga-tion of uncertainty reduction strategies and self-disclosure in online dating. *Communication Research, 38*(1), 70–100. https://doi.org/10.1177/0093650210377091

Giddens, A. (1991). *Modernity and self-identity: Self and society in the late modern age.* Polity Press.

Goffman, E. (1959). *The presentation of self in everyday life.* Doubleday.

Guadagno, R. E., Okdie, B. M., & Kruse, S. A. (2012). Dating deception: Gender, online dating, and exaggerated self-presentation. *Computers in Human Behavior, 28*(2), 642–647. https://doi.org/10.1016/j.chb.2011.11.010

Hall, J. A., Pennington, N., & Lueders, A. (2014). Impression management and formation on Facebook: A lens model approach. *New Media & Society, 16*(6), 958–982. https://doi.org/10.1177/146144481349516

Hancock, J. T., & Toma, C. L. (2009). Putting your best face forward: The accuracy of online dating photographs. *Journal of Communication, 59*(2), 367–386. https://doi.org/10.1111/j.1460-2466.2009.01420.x

Hancock, J. T., Toma, C., & Ellison, N. (2007, April). The truth about lying in online dating profiles. In *Proceedings of the SIGCHI Conference on Human Factors in Computing Systems* (pp. 449–452). ACM Press. https://doi.org/10.1145/1240624.1240697

Katz, E., Blumler, J. G., & Gurevitch, M. (1973). Uses and gratifications research. *The Public Opinion Quarterly, 37*(4), 509–523.

Kruger, J., & Dunning, D. (1999). Unskilled and unaware of it: How difficulties in recognizing one's own incompetence lead to inflated self-assessments. *Journal of Personality and Social Psychology, 77*(6), 1121–1134. https://doi.org/10.1037/0022-3514.77.6.1121

Leary, M. R. (1995). *Self-presentation: Impression management and interpersonal behavior.* Westview Press.

Levine, T. R. (2019). *Duped: Truth-default theory and the social science of lying and deception.* The University of Alabama Press.

Levy, J., Markell, D., & Cerf, M. (2019). Polar similars: Using massive mobile dating data to pre-dict synchronization and similarity in dating preferences. *Frontiers in Psychology, 10.* https://doi.org/10.3389/fpsyg.2019.02010

Longworth, K. (2010, September). Doc or not, Catfish is stranger than fiction. *Village Voice.* https://www.villagevoice.com/2010/09/15/doc-or-not-catfish-is-stranger-than-fiction/

Markowitz, D. M., Hancock, J. T., & Tong, S. T. (2019). Interpersonal dynamics in online dating: Profiles, matching, and discovery. In Z. Papacharissi (Ed.), *A networked self: Love* (pp. 50–61). Routledge.

Newcomb, T. M. (1956). The prediction of interpersonal attraction. *American Psychologist, 11*(11), 575–586. https://doi.org/10.1037/h0046141

Nisbett, R. E., & DeCamp Wilson, T. (1977). The Halo effect: Evidence for unconscious alter-ation of judgments. *Journal of Personality and Social Psychology, 35*(4), 250–256. https://doi.org/10.1037/0022-3514.35.4.250

OkCupid. (n.d.). How is the Match score calculated? https://help.okcupid.com/article/128-how-is-match-calculated

Qiu, L., Lin, H., Ramsay, J., & Yang, F. (2012). You are what you tweet: Personality expression and perception on Twitter. *Journal of Research in Personality, 46*(6), 710–718. https://doi.org/10.1016/j.jrp.2012.08.008

Ranzini, G., & Lutz, C. (2017). Love at first swipe? Explaining Tinder self-presentation and motives. *Mobile Media & Communication, 5*(1), 80–101. https://doi.org/10.1177/2050157916664559

Sande, G. N., Goethals, G. R., & Radloff, C. E. (1988). Perceiving one's own traits and others': The multifaceted self. *Journal of Personality and Social Psychology, 54*, 13–20. https://doi.org/10.1037/0022-3514.54.1.13

Schlenker, B. R. (1980). *Impression management.* Brooks/Cole Publishing Company. https://doi.org/10.1037/0022-3514.54.1.13

Seinfeld, J. (writer), & David, L. (writer), Ackerman, A. (director). (1995). The Wink (Season 7, Episode 4) [TV series episode]. In L. David, G. Shapiro, & H. West, *Seinfeld.* NBC.

Sharabi, L. L. (2021). Exploring how beliefs about algorithms shape (offline) success in online dating: A two-wave longitudinal investigation. *Communication Research, 48*, 931-952. https://doi.org/10.1177/0093650219896936

Stone, A. R. (1996). *War of desire and technology at the close of the mechanical age.* MIT Press.

Thorndike, E. L. (1920). A constant error in psychological ratings. *Journal of Applied Psychology, 4*, 25–29. https://doi.org/10.1037/h0071663

Timmermans, E., & De Caluwé, E. (2017). Development and validation of the Tinder Motives Scale (TMS). *Computers in Human Behavior, 70*, 341–350. https://doi.org/10.1016/j.chb.2017.01.028

Toch, E., & Levi, I. (2013). Locality and privacy in people-nearby applications. *In Proceedings of the 2013 ACM International Joint Conference on Pervasive and Ubiquitous Computing, Zurich, Switzerland* (pp. 539–548). ACM Press. https://doi.org/10.1145/2493432.2493485

Toma, C. L., Hancock, J. T., & Ellison, N. B. (2008). Separating fact from fiction: An examination of deceptive self-presentation in online dating profiles. *Personality and Social Psychology Bulletin, 34*(8), 1023–1036. http://doi.org/10.1177/0146167208318067

Tong, S. T., Corriero, E. F., Wibowo, K., Makki, T., & Slatcher, R. B. (2019). Self-presentation and impressions of personality through text-based online dating profiles: A lens model analysis. *New Media & Society*, 1–21. https://doi.org/10.1177/1461444819872678

Tong, S. T., Hancock, J. T., & Slatcher, R. B. (2016). Online dating system design and relational decision making: Choice, algorithms, and control. *Personal Relationships, 23*(4), 645–662. https://doi.org/10.1111/pere.12158

Tong, S. T., & Walther, J. B. (2011). Relational maintenance and computer-mediated communication. In K. Wright & L. Webb (Eds.), *Computer-mediated communication and personal relationships* (pp. 98–118). Peter Lang Publishing.

Van De Wiele, C., & Tong, S. T. (2014). Breaking boundaries: The uses and gratifications of Grindr. In A. J. Brush, A. Friday, J. A. Kientz, J. Scott, & J. Song (Eds.), *UbiComp'14: ACM International Joint Conference on Pervasive and Ubiquitous Computing.* Seattle, WA (pp. 619–630). ACM Press. https://doi.org/10.1145/2632048.2636070

Walther, J. B. (1992). Interpersonal effects in computer-mediated interaction: A relational perspective. *Communication Research, 19*(1), 52–90. https://doi.org/10.1177/009365092019001003

Walther, J. B. (1996). Computer-mediated communication: Impersonal, interpersonal, and hyperpersonal interaction. *Communication research, 23*(1), 3–43. https://doi.org/10.1177/009365096023001001

Walther, J. B., & Parks, M. R. (2002). Cues filtered out, cues filtered in: Computer-mediated communication and relationships. In M. L. Knapp & J. A. Daly (Eds.), *The handbook of interpersonal communication* (3rd ed., pp. 529–563). Sage.

Walther, J. B., Van Der Heide, B., Hamel, L., & Shulman, H. C. (2009). Self-generated versus other-generated statements and impressions in computer-mediated communication: A test of warranting theory using facebook. *Communication Research, 36*(2), 229–253. https://doi.org/10.1177/0093650208330251

Ward, J. (2017). What are you doing on Tinder? Impression management on a matchmaking mobile app. *Information, Communication & Society, 20*(11), 1644–1659. https://doi.org/10.1080/1369118X.2016.1252412

Yarkoni, T. (2010). Personality in 100,000 words: A large-scale analysis of personality and word use among bloggers. *Journal of Research in Personality, 44*(3), 363–373. https://doi.org/10.1016/j.jrp.2010.04.001

6

"To the Left, To the Left": Mate Selection in Online and Mobile Dating

Although searching for a romantic partner is not a new phenomenon, moving that search into online and mobile environments may fundamentally change some parts of that process that used to take place FtF. Notably, some researchers have argued that mobile apps like Tinder, Bumble, and Grindr have "cheapened" the mate selection process by placing too much emphasis on quick judgments of physical appearance. Indeed, research studies and anecdotal accounts from daters underscore the importance of the *profile picture* as the key factor in initial judgments of attraction. This is, of course, reinforced by the fact that the basic architecture of most dating apps prioritizes visual information by prominently displaying a dater's profile photo on the smartphone screen.

As noted in the introduction, we conducted several informal interviews with daters about how they approach online and mobile platforms, what their experience is like, and how they think communication might be changed, stifled, or amplified by the technologies they use. The people we talked to confirmed that the profile picture is the first cue that they see, and, therefore, the first thing they interpret and use in their decision making.

Valerie was new to Tinder, having only used it for two months. But she noted two "poses" that men posted in profile pictures that would earn an immediate left swipe, or rejection:

"If they do the 'neck pose,' I'm out. I don't swipe right, unless they have some other nice pictures in there. Or, like, a picture in the mirror with their abs. That, I also usually swipe left on it."

What, exactly is the neck pose?

"It's like the duck lips thing—but more annoying."

Maria told us that a guy was "in contention" if he "looked like a nice person." After this vague response, she elaborated on specific cues she looked for in men's profile pictures that influenced her decisions:

Usually, I'll look at the photo and if it's, like, a nice photo, that's a good thing. If it's a weird angle or if their shirt is off, and you know, um, that's not really my thing. So if I think the photo looks kind of nice, I'll look at their location and stuff, and see if they have anything in their description. Usually if there's not a lot there [in the profile]—like, if there's only one photo—I get a little nervous, and I pass on those. I like when they put things in their descriptions, because it just makes me feel like they're a real person.

Such responses reflect concepts we discussed in Chapter 5, which detailed how daters form impressions of others based on the profile. Many people spend a lot of time thinking about their profiles—they agonize about which photos to post and what information to share. But exactly how apps like Bumble and Tinder are affecting the processes of mate selection and subsequent interaction is a hotly-contested topic. Take for instance, two opinions offered in the *New York Times*. On the one hand are company representatives like Tinder's "in-house dating and relationship expert" Jessica Carbino, who suggested the following in her interview with the newspaper: "Research shows when people are evaluating photos of others, they are trying to access compatibility on not just a physical level, but a social level. They are trying to understand, 'Do I have things in common with this person?'" (Bilton, 2014).

On the other hand, in his *New York Times* opinion piece published just one year later, the psychologist Eli Finkel (2015) argued that date selections made on Tinder on the basis of others' physical attractiveness are "superficial" ones that can never lead to true judgments of romantic compatibility: "Curated text and a handful of pictures will never be able to tell you whether the first-date conversation will crackle or whether you'll feel a desire to discover what makes this person tick."

Although they take different positions, there are some things that company reps like Jessica Carbino and researchers like Eli Finkel can agree on: Dating apps like Tinder, Hinge, and Bumble prioritize visual information like photographs, and (in doing so) they put physical appearance front-and-center for daters reviewing multiple profiles. But how does putting pectoralis or bicep muscles on center stage affect our decisions to swipe left or right? Do those collogen-filled duck lips really influence us to contact or message a dater? This chapter examines the processes that kick in after initial impressions are formed. After daters view a potential partner's profile, how do they decide whether to swipe left or swipe right? How do they initiate connections on mobile? What kinds of messages do they exchange? And because many of these connections will fail to develop into lasting relationships, how do they deal with rejection?

"I choose you!" Mate Selection in Online Dating Profiles

Nature: Evolutionary perspectives on mate selection. Obviously, people were selecting romantic partners long before Tinder, Match, or OkCupid came on the scene. For generations, men and women have been evaluating each other, trying to decide whether or not this person would make a good romantic date or long-term partner. One well-researched theoretical perspective from *evolutionary psychology* contends that men's and women's romantic partner preferences and selection behaviors are driven by an innate biological need to reproduce. Parental investment theory (Trivers, 1972) suggests that mate preferences are driven, at least in part, by the different degree of resources and effort that each sex commits to the care and survival of their offspring. According to this view, the sex that invests more in its offspring's development seeks to protect that investment and so looks for evidence that their potential mate is strong, fit, and willing to provide for offspring. For most mammals (including humans), it is the female who expends greater effort and investment (labor, breast feeding, etc.), which makes them the choosier sex.

Other scholars built upon parental investment theory, suggesting that both women and men have evolved to form preferences for distinct traits in opposite-sex mates that serve the goal of reproduction. For example, *sexual selection* theories (Buss, 1989; Buss & Schmitt, 1993) have noted women's evolved preference for men who display *dominance*, because it reflects the ability to protect offspring and maximize resource-provisioning; women also prefer male *altruism*, which signals a stronger inclination to share those resources with others (Barclay, 2010; Buss, Shackelford, Kirkpatrick, & Larsen, 2001; Jensen-Campbell et al., 1995). Men have evolved to prefer altruism too, as well as mates who are healthy, fit, and show evidence of reproductive potential (i.e., ability to gestate, birth, and care for offspring).

Accordingly, women and men have developed a keen sense of attraction to certain physical and behavioral characteristics that reflect these preferred traits. For example, because male dominance is signaled through height and muscu-lature, women often prefer taller men who are physically fit (see, Cunningham et al., 1990; DeBruine et al., 2006). Evolutionary-based theories also contend that women place importance on men's gift-giving behavior as a signal of altru-ism (for more on this topic, see Hughes & Aung, 2017). Contrastingly, men pay close attention to women's waist-to-hip ratios, bust lines, and age—as charac-teristics that offer specific physical evidence of fertility and reproductive fitness. Importantly, theorists note that these evolved sexual strategies of mate selection are almost exclusively non-conscious; an individual's attraction to a potential mate (e.g., a preference for certain physical features or temperaments) is not merely a reflection of one's desire to reproduce, but a behavioral tendency that services that ultimate goal (Tong & Matheny, 2017).

With so many daters trying to get through the revolving door of swipes, the *intra-sex competition* in dating sites and apps can be fierce—men are competing against other men for women's attention (note that women are also vying against one another for male daters' attention, too). Given this competition, and as if on cue, out come the shirtless pec pics, neck poses, and duck lips: Commonly known as "thirst traps," these represent daters' attempts to visually stand out in the sea of online dating profile pictures scrolling by on a phone screen. Through the lens of evolutionary theory, profile pictures featuring physical stature, muscu-lature, facial symmetry, and a desirable hip-to-waist ratios emerge as modern-day courtship signals (Figure 6.1).

Nurture: The importance of social roles. As you know from Chapter 5, photo-graphic profile content is important, but there are other parts of the dating profile that may motivate daters' mate selection decisions. Similarly, there may be other forces besides evolutionary ones that may influence mate selection. According to *social role theory*, evolved mate preferences (such as those described above) may be intensified or dampened depending on the extent to which a person holds certain beliefs about men's and women's roles in society (Eagly & Wood, 2016). For example, in the United States "traditional" (some might say *stereotypical*) attitudes toward gender roles and the division of labor place men in the "strong

Figure 6.1: *Thirst trap* [thurst trap] (noun). Any statement or picture used to intentionally create attention or "thirst" (urbandictionary.com, 2020). Source: Public Domain/ https://www.publicdomainpictures.net/pictures/30000/velka/along-came-a-spider.jpg

provider" role and women in the "softer, domestic" role. These attitudes and beliefs about gender roles can manifest as attitudes known as *hostile sexism* (or the degree of prejudice people display toward strong women who challenge beliefs in male dominance), and *benevolent sexism* (or approval of "traditional" gender roles, with women as caretakers and men as providers) (Eastwick et al., 2006; Glick & Fiske, 1996).

A set of studies (Tong & Matheny, 2017) examined the intersection of evolutionary and social role theories in online mate selection. Since women are the "choosier" sex, researchers wanted to see how their attitudes toward gender roles affect their preferences for dominant or altruistic male dating partners on the popular online dating site, OkCupid. Female participants viewed one of four hypothetical (i.e., experimentally-developed) OkCupid profiles (see Figure 6.2 for an example). Each profile depicted the same man, but the "About Me" descriptions reflected different amounts of dominance/aggression (high and low) and altruism (high and low). Four different self-descriptions were created to instill these different personality traits in a 2 × 2 experimental design.

28 • Detroit, MI • Man

About   Photos   Questions   Personality

My self-summary

People describe me as dynamic, dominant, and in your face, and competitive too. I am loud when I need to be (and I find I usually need to be!). I know what I want and I'm not afraid to go for it. I'm an optimist and I don't believe in excuses. I'm hardworking and demanding of myself and others, so I don't take crap from people. My friends know that I can be snarky and impatient, but they know that all my teasing is in good fun. Life is a game and I play to win.

What I'm doing with my life

I currently work as a freelance media consultant. I like my job because it allows me to be creative, bold, and innovative. And I get to be my own boss! I love it because I have to be aggressive and scrap for my clients and accounts, but I don't mind because I'm pretty damn successful! If you want to know the truth, I'd like to someday run my own company and make my way to the top. I'll be honest, I do work a lot, but because no one is going to look out for number one but me, myself, and I!

I'm really good at

You want me on your trivia team! I'm competitive and enjoy a challenge. I'm also a good team captain (ask my softball squad). This is going to sound weird, but I'm a good driver. I am the party planner among my group of friends. Nothing makes me happier than being the life of the party surrounded by people I love.

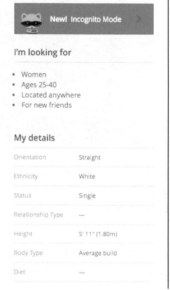

New! Incognito Mode

I'm looking for

- Women
- Ages 25-40
- Located anywhere
- For new friends

My details

Orientation	Straight
Ethnicity	White
Status	Single
Relationship Type	—
Height	5' 11" (1.80m)
Body Type	Average build
Diet	—

Figure 6.2: Sample experimental profile (identity hidden, for confidentiality). Based on his profile, can you tell whether this guy would have an altruistic or dominant personality? Source: Authors

In the first study, the goal was to ensure that the self-authored profile language could actually instill impressions of the man's altruistic or aggressive personality. After confirming that each of the four profiles was being perceived as intended, a second experiment was conducted that began by measuring female daters' hostile and benevolent sexism attitudes, before asking them to view one of the four profiles. After looking at a profile, each woman was asked to indicate how attractive she thought the man in the profile was and his suitability as a potential romantic date.

Following evolutionary theories, it was predicted that female daters would factor these two particular traits of dominance and altruism into their dating decisions. First, it was expected that women would prefer altruistic men overall—a phenomenon known as the "altruism hypothesis." Women's desire for male dominance was expected to be a little more complex; hypotheses predicted that these preferences would follow a pattern known as the "dominance dilemma" in which a man's dominance is attractive to women, but only if he simultaneously seems altruistic (Jensen-Campbell et al., 1995). Lastly, it was also expected that women's basic desires for male dominance and altruism described above might be moderated (i.e., affected) by their personal attitudes toward gender roles.

Results revealed some interesting patterns:

(1) support for the *altruism hypothesis* (Barclay, 2010)—overall, women preferred more altruistic men as dates;

(2) evidence of *the dominance dilemma*—that a man's dominance was most attractive to women when he also demonstrated altruistic tendencies;

(3) finally, evidence of a *moderation* effect, in which women who had lower benevolent sexism attitudes found male dominance displays to be less attractive compared to women with higher benevolent sexism attitudes. In other words, the more that the women in our study disavowed traditional gender roles, the less attractive they found the dominant men among OkCupid daters.

What can we conclude from these results? First, that while individuals can make quick judgments based on profile photos, they can also glean important personality information from written biographic information, if they are sufficiently motivated to do so. Secondly, daters' preferences seem to be guided by both nature *and* nurture. These results suggest that women's preferences for dominance or altruism followed patterns predicted by evolutionary theory, but (consistent with social role theory) these preferences were also moderated by their beliefs regarding gender roles.

Of course, this study has some limitations: Studying only heterosexual female daters' selection of male profiles does not allow us to say much about how men engage in female mate selection, or men or women in same-sex mate selection (for more on same-sex mate selection from an evolutionary perspective, see Gobrogge et al., 2007). Furthermore, these daters did not have to question the authenticity of profile information—all profiles were shown within a hypothetical experimental setting, so women's concerns about warrants and the credibility of the man's self-presented content were less of an issue. An astute reader might also point out that study participants were unusually motivated to drill down into the detailed portions of the OkCupid profile in these experiments, since they were asked to view and evaluate only a single profile, with as much time as they liked. When daters are faced with multiple profiles to look through, such detailed, careful review may not actually occur. Finally, while this procedure may reflect how web-based mate selection works in online dating sites, this experiment is not exactly characteristic of the mobile dating environment. In apps like Tinder or Hinge where biographic information is limited to 300–500 characters and the profile picture is prioritized over written self-description, do the mechanisms operate the same way? How might the mobile interface influence daters' mate selection?

Moving Mate Selection to Mobile: More Swiping at Faster Speeds

When faced with multiple profiles, daters' decision-making behavior may not be as detail-oriented as that exhibited by the participants in these prior experiments. Indeed, recent estimates report that for a typical mobile dater, a single login to an app like Tinder, Hinge, or Badoo can last anywhere between seven to 17 minutes, with most daters logging an average of six to eight logins per day; furthermore, in each session, a dater can expect to review, judge, scroll, and swipe on between 10 and 20 profiles (Bilton, 2014; Kolhoff et al., 2020, Peat, 2018). This also suggests that daters might easily reach the daily limit on profiles set by different apps—for example, the upward limit set for Tinder users is 100 profiles a day. In the move to mobile, mate selection becomes short, fast, and often.

What dating apps *have* done is put our decision-making muscles into over-drive. Mobile platforms are changing the *speed* and *quantity* of mate selection judgments. Levy et al. (2019) examined a massive data set of over 421 million matches made on the Hinge app. They found that men spent an average of 6.7 seconds reviewing a profile before deciding to swipe left or right, while women spent an average of 11.1 seconds. This is between eight and four seconds fewer than we spend in offline impression formation (Ambady & Rosenthal, 1993); as we saw in Chapter 3, "thin slices" of initial information exchange in FtF settings can occur in as little as 15 seconds—to put all of this into perspective, 15 seconds is the current minimum length of a TikTok video.

Mobile apps are also changing the *kinds of information* we rely on to make mating decisions. As we noted above, dating apps prioritize visual information.

As Levy et al. (2019) noted in their study of Hinge daters, "given that faces are likely to draw the users' attention first, followed by the text...we suspect that visual information was processed for a long time during the decision" (p. 6). So the time and effort that daters spend on their profile pictures might not be such a bad investment. And the self-authored biographical information? Its effects seem to differ across sex: One study of Tinder daters found that 42% of women in their sample had blank bios in their profiles, compared to only 30% of men (Tyson, Perta, Haddadi, & Seto, 2016). The effect of biographical information (or its lack) on subsequent matching differed across sex, too. Women did not seem to suffer from the absence of a Tinder bio—with or without it, the average female Tinder dater received a similar number of matches. For men, however, having some sort of Tinder bio increased his matching potential—a profile with a blank bio received an average of 16 matches, while men with Tinder bios saw a four-fold increase, upwards of 69 matches! This led Tyson et al. (2016) to conclude that "in all cases, the profiles with bios do far better" (p. 466). Tyson et al.'s results are consistent with what Tong and Matheny (2017) saw in their study of online profile review and mate selection in OkCupid: Women are more likely to pay attention to other parts of the profile in addition to the photos. This more extensive profile review may account for the longer time they spend viewing mobile profiles on average, compared to men.

Other Trends in Online and Mobile Mate Selection: Similarity and Choosiness

When examining their massive Hinge dataset that contained 421 million matches, Levy et al. (2019) also relied on evolutionary theories. In particular, they looked to the theory of positive *assortative mating*, which suggests that, biologically speaking, mate selection decisions are based on the similarity of partners' characteristics. Similarity between people is a powerful factor that influences interpersonal attraction among both humans and non-humans (Burley, 1983). In fact, similarity has been shown to extend into many areas like partners' personality traits, physical attractiveness, education levels, socio-economic status, and personal preferences. Assortative pairing also extends across different kinds of relationship, including marriage and dating partners, and also friends. Oddly, just the *perception* that we are similar to another person can be enough to drive interpersonal attraction, even if we are not *actually* similar to them at all (Montoya, Horton, & Kirchner, 2008).

In their analysis of online daters, Levy et al. (2019) concluded that "assortative mating holds across almost every characteristic that can be assessed in our data" (p. 16). That claim was based on their analysis of all kinds of characteristics from their 421 million Hinge matches, including: height, education, race, religion, relationship preferences, hometown, occupation, number of friends on social media, and even type of phone (Android vs. iPhone). They note that their results parallel previous results regarding the power of similarity and assortative mating in mate selection by daters in online sites (Hitsch, Hortacsu, & Ariely, 2010) and in-person speed dating (Tidwell, Eastwick, & Finkel, 2012). While this suggests that online dating can produce endogamous couplings, a related question is: in comparison to those who meet each other offline, are couples who meet online more similar to one another or more diverse? We return to this question in Chapter 8; for now we note that similarity is a powerful force that drives interpersonal attraction to romantic partners.

Other mobile dating experiments have produced evidence that women are the "choosier" sex: In their study of Tinder, Tyson et al. (2016) created hypothetical "dummy" profiles featuring "average" male and female daters to conduct field experiments. They began by "injecting" their hypothetical profiles "into a locale to collect data" (p. 462). They wrote a software script that automatically reviewed the Tinder profiles of other daters within a 100-mile radius of their location, then systematically "liked" each one with a (automated) right-hand swipe (Tyson et al., 2016). For the right swipes that generated mutual Tinder matches, the researchers recorded the profile data of the matched dater. This automated procedure yielded a dataset of approximately 230,000 male profiles and 250,000 female profiles. Tyson et al. found that the male daters in their selected sample were much more likely to reciprocate a female-initiated right swipe, whereas women were more selective. In fact, male-reciprocated right swipe matches numbered 8,248 compared to female-reciprocated 532 matches. Interestingly, the patterns changed with regard to messaging: Men in the study followed up with messages to their matches only 7% of the time, but women were three times more likely to engage, sending messages 21% of the time. The average length of that initial message also differed by sex. Women daters' initial messages average approximately 122 characters, whereas men's average opening message was only 12 characters long (and 25% of those messages average six characters or less). Male daters' opening lines are probably simple greetings ("hi," "hello," etc.), suggesting, shall we say, that they are not necessarily sending thoughtful opening messages. From this information, Tyson et al. (2016) concluded that women were "more careful with whom they like and therefore consider it more worthwhile to send a message"

(p. 464), an interpretation that seems consistent with evolutionary ideas of female selectivity.

Levy et al. (2019) also found evidence of female choosiness in their analysis of men's and women's decision making "streaks"—which they defined as consistently swiping right to indicate their interest or left to indicate they were uninterested on several profiles in quick succession. By looking at daters' choice sequence behavior, they found that among women who exhibited decision making streaks, right-swipe streaks were fairly rare (only 1.3% of the sample). Instead "the majority of women (43.1%) are likely to have their longest streak of saying 'no'" rejecting on average around 37 male profiles (Levy et al., 2019, p. 14). Male daters, on the other hand, were equally divided, with 26% of the sample going on swipe right "binges" and 24% exhibiting swipe left streaks, saying "no" on average to approximately 30 women at a time. Women, then, appeared to be more selective, exhibiting evolutionary principles of female choosiness with more leftwards swiping, whereas men were equally inclined to both leftwards and rightwards swipe streaks.

From these studies of mobile mate selection behaviors, we can draw some conclusions. First, attractiveness, as assessed through visual information, is still paramount in the mobile mate decision making process—but so is similarity. Daters are more likely to match and exchange contact information if they are similar to each other. According to Levy et al. (2019): "given the selection strategies we observed, it is likely that users start the choice process by focusing on salient attributes such as visual features and basic observable characteristics (i.e., characteristics that suggest similarity in taste)" (p. 15). Although photos seem to motivate most swipes, daters still rely on other parts of the profile to form impressions and make decisions. Biographical profile information, even in limited amounts, still factors into mobile matching. It is particularly important for female daters, who still exhibit greater control over mate selection in modern online and mobile dating domains.

Friendly Advice: Social Contextual Approach to Romantic Relationships

The basic phenomenon of mate selection is oftentimes imagined to hinge on personal choice. That is, we are accustomed to thinking about mate selection as an *individualistic* proposition: Each person forms preferences and makes up his or her own mind when choosing a romantic partner. This is the dominant perspective on mate selection—at least in individualistic cultures like the United States. Nonetheless, people often feel the need to consult others at some point in the relationship initiation process. The *social contextual approach* (Sprecher, 2011) to relationships suggests that a true understanding of people's romantic relationships requires considering the larger network of existing relationships into which these new romantic connections will enter. Most romantic relationships that move past the initiation and experimenting stages and into further development are supported through the actions of the friends, family members, and acquaintances that constitute the daters' social networks (Sprecher & Felmlee, 1992). Without that network support, most romantic relationships are very difficult to maintain.

In fact, the role of the network is abundantly clear in popular representations of romance. It figures everywhere in the plotlines of movies, television shows, and plays. Consider these well-known themes:

(1) *Wicked stepmothers breaking apart new lovers.* What happens when your mom doesn't approve of your match (or needs to feed her own ego)? She will try to break up your relationship. This is a popular plotline of many Disney princess movies (*Sleeping Beauty, Cinderella, Snow White*). A more modern interpretation is the 2005 romantic comedy *Monster-in-Law*, pitting Viola (played by Jane Fonda) against her daughter-in-law, Charlie (played by Jennifer Lopez.).

(2) *Overprotective fathers forbidding daughters to marry inappropriate male suitors.* Protection by the patriarch of the family is reflected in movies like *Meet the Parents* (2000). There, Robert De Niro's character, Jack, tries everything to prevent Gaylord Focker (played by actor Ben Stiller), from marrying his daughter, Pam (played by actress Terri Polo).

(3) *Friends don't let friends hook up with losers* or *true friends will help their friends find true love.* In other words, friends can make or break a budding romance. These themes play integral roles in romantic comedies like *Failure to Launch* (2006) and musicals like *Grease* (1978) and *West Side Story* (1957).

Thus, we see the importance of the social network reflected back to us in modern media: popular books, movies, and love songs remind us of the important role that friends and family play within the larger romantic imagination. Star-crossed lovers like Romeo and Juliet would probably have failed to move into the integrating stage in real life. Communication research clearly suggests that romantic relationships can develop only with the support of partners' networks; without such support, romantic relationships often break apart (see Parks & Adelman, 1983).

I Swipe Right…with a Little Help from My Friends. Until very recently, being introduced to new romantic partners through shared network connection was the most common way for singles to form romantic connections. But today, we know that such mutual introductions have been supplanted to some degree by online and mobile dating (Rosenfeld, Thomas, & Hausen, 2019). If our friends are no longer introducing us to new partners, this is not to say they have entirely vanished from the scene. Might our friends still influence the mate selection decisions we make online? And to what extent are they involved when mate selection moves to mobile?

There are several good reasons to suspect that friends still play an integral part in the modern mate selection process. First, in some mobile apps, friends' feedback is actually built into the system. For example, Tinder's *profile sharing feature* allows daters to share profiles of prospective partners that they think a friend might like. In 2017, Bumble also released a similar feature called "Share to a Friend" that allows users to recommend profiles to one another (Jalili, 2017). Other niche dating apps are trying to take advantage of group-assisted dating. The platform Wingman was developed with the goal of having friends take control over an individual's dating profile and mate selection decisions. Here, a trusted friend, or "wingman," is invited on to the application to look for potential matches and buffer the impacts of potential rejection (Farokhmanesh, 2017). The person being matched can review information added or changed about them in their profile, but they are completely left out of the initial decision making process. Similarly, an app called Chorus formally reinstates the role of friends as matchmakers: "Friends have always helped friends navigate relationships; there's no reason that should stop just because everything is moving online" (Chorus, 2020). In Chorus's "matchmaking" function, the primary "dater" creates a profile, but lets their "matchmaker" do the swiping. Chorus states that the advantage of its friend-based app is that it allows "matchmakers to stay in the know" while "daters get a break." A Chorus dater can invite as many matchmakers as they want—and a person can function as both a primary dater and a matchmaker for a friend, simultaneously.

Aside from engaging with specific features and affordances of dating apps, friends might still engage in *social mobile dating*, defined as "sharing access of a personal mobile dating account with at least one other person during a session in which they engaged in any kind of dating app behavior" (Kolhoff, Rochadiat,

Tong, & Matheny, 2020, p. 9). In this study, researchers surveyed and inter-viewed 34 Tinder users, ages 18–22, to investigate two overarching research questions: How prevalent is social mobile dating? And—if people are using dat-ing apps with friends—why are they doing it?

In the opening questions of this study, participants reflected on a "typical week" of their Tinder use. They estimated the percentage of their time they spent using Tinder alone versus how much time they spent using Tinder with friends. This sample reported that approximately 73.1% of weekly Tinder use was solo and 26.8% was social. Thus, while social mobile dating sessions do not make up the bulk of a dater's week, results indicated that using Tinder with friends is not necessarily unusual (see Table 6.1 for other usage statistics that describe the sample).

The interview findings indicated that participants' social Tinder use was motivated by a variety of different goals and functions; we highlight four in par-ticular—*entertainment, affiliation, perspective taking,* and *social approval.*

(1) Those who reported basic *entertainment* functions simply noted that social mobile dating was a way to "break up the monotony of individual Tinder use" (p. 19). One participant mentioned that he would give his phone to his friend and allow him to write whatever he wanted on his profile or even exchange messages with other daters on his behalf.

(2) Another theme that came up was an *affiliation* function. Participants suggested that the popularity of dating apps within their friendship net-works made it a shared activity that they could do together and talk about. Using Tinder socially increased *common ground* (Clark & Brennan,

Table 6.1: Tinder usage statistics

Participants' Estimates of Personal Tinder Use	*M (SD)*
Time Spent per Single Tinder Session (in minutes)	16.69 (12.14)
Individual Sessions (i.e., logins) per Day	2.36 (4.09)
Total Right Swipes per Single Tinder Session	11.61(9.03)
Total Matches made in one Tinder Session	4.78 (3.55)
Estimated Amount of Weekly Tinder Use Spent with Friends	26.8% (27.7%)
Estimated Amount of Weekly Tinder Use Done Alone	73.1% (27.77%)

Source: Authors

1991)—or mutual beliefs, knowledge, and assumptions—which are crucial to create meaningful interaction and strengthen friends' bonds.

(3) *Perspective taking* was noted by almost all participants but was especially evident among participants who engaged in social mobile dating with opposite-sex platonic friends. These friends often provided important opposite-sex perspectives that daters found integral at several phases: profile development, matching, and discovery. For example, one participant noted how at the discovery phase of mobile dating, he would hand his phone to his best female friend so she could read through the message exchange: "I may not even realize something or notice, and they're there to point it out....ladies would know this better than guys" (p. 23). Interpersonal communication literature has pointed out the "insider information" that opposite-sex friends can give each other, about how members of the opposite sex think, feel, and behave (see, Monsour, 1997, p. 376).

(4) Participant responses also represented *social approval* motives. Participants reported that their friends provided a sounding board as they formed impressions of other daters—they provided affirmation for participants' positive judgments and right swipes, confirmed suspicions about deceptive profiles, and sometimes reinforced daters' own misgivings about interacting with other, potentially problematic, daters.

Interestingly, these social mobile dating motives parallel previous research that uncovered social motives for other kinds of media use, such as watching television with others (see Lull, 1980). Shared mobile dating activity also reflects ideas from the social contextual approach to relationships: Daters seek out their friends' advice about their personal romantic partner choices—not only because doing so is fun, but to ensure that their friends approve of their relational decisions, and also as a way to build their friendships. Clearly, friends still play an important role in mate selection. They may not be going on mutual double dates or be the primary bridge between a friend and their potential romantic match, but they are still very much involved in the early stages of romantic relationship initiation (for more on this topic, see also Sobieraj & Humphreys, 2021).

Conclusion

With respect to well-articulated theories of mate selection, there is still a lot to learn about how dating platforms moderate or otherwise influence the process.

We know that these platforms motivate us to make more selections at faster speeds, but the ways in which we make these choices—evaluating physical attributes and personality characteristics, estimating similarities, and relying on our social networks—are still critical features of the selection process. In the future, researchers might further investigate the psychological effects of this increase in choice-making behavior (see also, Chapter 12), and delve more deeply into how the role of friends and family is being altered by mobile dating platforms. Although our initial interviews have established the basic prevalence of and motivations for social mobile dating, we have yet to uncover whether friends actually influence our swipes, and if so to what extent. And how might our friendships be strengthened by this shared swiping? Because friends bring into play different aspects of our identity, we might also investigate whether and how shared perspective taking in social mobile dating affects our sense of self—that is, if we allow our friends to write our profiles, does their perspective of us change how we feel about ourselves, romantically or otherwise? Or potentially, how our friends view us?

Finally, taking a broader perspective, might the practice of shared mobile dating differ across cultures? Those of us who grew up in more individualistic cultures might find the idea of shared swiping to be a little strange; it might be unsettling to think of ceding control over mate selection, even to a trusted buddy. But those readers with a more collectivist perspective might find the influence of family and friends over mate selection to be very normal—even welcome. These are just a few of the questions still lingering for future research to examine.

References

Barclay, P. (2010). Altruism as a courtship display: Some effects of third-party generosity on audience perceptions. *British Journal of Psychology, 101*, 123–135. https://doi.org/10.1348/000712609X435733

Bilton, N. (2014, Oct). Tinder, the fast-growing dating app, taps an age-old truth. *New York Times.* https://www.nytimes.com/2014/10/30/fashion/tinder-the-fast-growing-dating-app-taps-an-age-old-truth.html

Burley, N. (1983). The meaning of assortative mating. *Ethology and Sociobiology, 4*(4), 191–203. https://doi.org/10.1016/0162-3095(83)90009-2

Buss, D. M. (1989). Sex-differences in human mate preferences: Evolutionary hypothesis tested in 37 cultures. *Behavioral and Brain Sciences, 12*, 1–14. https://doi.org/10.1017/S0140525X00023992

Buss, D. M., & Schmitt, D. P. (1993). Sexual strategies theory: An evolutionary perspective on human mating. *Psychological Review, 100*, 204–232. https://doi.org/10.1037/0033-295X.100.2.204

Buss, D. M., Shackelford, T. K., Kirkpatrick, L. A., & Larsen, R. J. (2001). A half-century of mate preferences: The cultural evolution of values. *Journal of Marriage and Family, 63*(2), 491–503. https://doi.org/10.1111/j.1741-3737.2001.00491.x

Cameron, C., Oskamp, S., & Sparks, W. (1977). Courtship American style: Newspaper ads. *Family Coordinator, 26*, 27–30.

Chorus (n.d.). How Chorus works. https://getchorus.co/

Clark, H. H., & Brennan, S. E. (1991). Grounding in communication. In L. B. Resnick, J. M. Levine, & S. D. Teasley (Eds.), *Perspectives on socially shared cognition* (pp. 222–233). American Psychological Association. https://doi.org/10.1037/10096-000

Cunningham, M. R., Barbee, A. P., & Pike, C. L. (1990). What do women want? Facialmetric assessment of multiple motives in the perception of male facial physical attractiveness. *Journal of Personality and Social Psychology, 59*(1), 61–72.

DeBruine, L. M., Jones, B. C., Little, A. C., Boothroyd, L. G., Perrett, D. I., Penton-Voak, I. S., et al. (2006). Correlated preferences for facial masculinity and ideal or actual partner's masculinity. *Proceedings of the Royal Society B—Biological Sciences, 273*, 1355–1360.

Eagly, A. H., & Wood, W. (2016). Social role theory of sex differences. *The Wiley Blackwell Encyclopedia of Gender and Sexuality Studies*, 1–3. https://doi.org/10.1002/9781118663219.wbegss183

Eastwick, P. W., Eagly, A. H., Glick, P., Johannesen-Schmidt, M. C., Fiske, S. T., Blum, A. M., ... & Manganelli, A. M. (2006). Is traditional gender ideology associated with sex-typed mate preferences? A test in nine nations. *Sex Roles, 54*, 603–614. https://doi.org/10.1007/s11199-006-9027-x

Ellis, B. J. (1992). The evolution of sexual attraction: Evaluative mechanisms in women. In J. H. Barkow, L. Cosmides, & J. Tooby (Eds.), *The adapted mind: Evolutionary psychology and the generation of culture* (pp. 267–288). Oxford University Press.

Farokhmanesh, M. (2017, April 19). If you trust your friends to pick dates for you, there's an app for that. *The Verge*. https://www.theverge.com/2017/4/19/15355990/wingman-dating-app-ios-friends-select-dates-facebook

Finkel, E. (2015, Feb). In defense of Tinder. *New York Times*. https://www.nytimes.com/2015/02/08/opinion/sunday/in-defense-of-tinder.html

Glick, P., & Fiske, S. T. (1996). The ambivalent sexism Inventory: Differentiating hostile and benevolent sexism. *Journal of Personality and Social Psychology, 70*(3), 491–512. https://doi.org/10.1037/0022-3514.70.3.491

Gobrogge, K. L., Perkins, P. S., Baker, J. H., Balcer, K. D., Breedlove, S. M., & Klump, K. L. (2007). Homosexual mating preferences from an evolutionary perspective: Sexual selection theory revisited. *Archives of Sexual Behavior, 36*(5), 717–723. https://doi.org/10.1007/s10508-007-9216-x

Hitsch, G. J., Hortaçsu, A., & Ariely, D. (2010). Matching and sorting in online dating. *American Economic Review, 100*(1), 130–63. http://www.aeaweb.org/articles.php?doi=JO. 1257/aer.100.1.130

Hughes, S. M., & Aung, T. (2017). Modern-day female preferences for resources and provisioning by long-term mates. *Evolutionary Behavioral Sciences, 11*(3), 242–261. https://doi.org/10.1037/ebs0000084

Jalili, C. (2017, June 23). Bumble lets you send guys' profiles, so now you can send your friends your leftovers. *Elite Daily.* https://www.elitedaily.com/dating/bumble-guys-profiles-update/2001272

Jensen-Campbell, L. A., Graziano, W. G., & West, S. G. (1995). Dominance, prosocial orientation, and female preferences: Do nice guys really finish last? *Journal of Personality and Social Psychology, 68,* 427–440. https://doi.org/10.1037/0022-3514.68.3.427

Kolhoff, S., Rochadiat, A. M. P., Tong, S. T., & Matheny, R. (2020). "I know their type better than they do": Understanding the social use of mobile dating applications. [Paper presentation.]. Annual Conference of the International Communication Association. Online.

Levy, J., Markell, D., & Cerf, M. (2019). Polar similars: Using massive mobile dating data to predict synchronization and similarity in dating preferences. *Frontiers in Psychology.* https://doi.org/10.3389/fpsyg.2019.02010

Lull, J. (1980). The social uses of television. *Human Communication Research, 6*(3), 197–209. https://doi.org/10.1111/j.1468-2958.1980.tb00140.x

Monsour, M. (1997). Communication and cross-sex friendships across the life cycle: A review of the literature. *Annals of the International Communication Association, 20*(1), 375–414. https://doi.org/10.1080/23808985.1997.11678946

Montoya, R. M., Horton, R. S., & Kirchner, J. (2008). Is actual similarity necessary for attraction? A meta-analysis of actual and perceived similarity. *Journal of Social and Personal Relationships, 25*(6), 889–922. https://doi.org/10.1177/0265407508096700

Parks, M. R., & Adelman, M. B. (1983). Communication networks and the development of romantic relationships: An expansion of uncertainty reduction theory. *Human Communication Research, 10*(1), 55–79 https://doi.org/10.1111/j.1468-2958.1983.tb00004.x

Peat, J. (2018, January 23). Millennials 'spend 10 hours a week on dating apps'. *The Independent.* https://www.independent.co.uk/life-style/dating-apps-millenials-10-hours-per-week-tinder-bumble-romance-love-a8174006.html

Rosenfeld, M. J., Thomas, R. J., & Hausen, S. (2019). Disintermediating your friends: How online dating in the United States displaces other ways of meeting. *Proceedings of the National Academy of Science, USA, 116*(36), 17753–17758. https://doi.org/10.1073/pnas.1908630116

Sobieraj, S., & Humphreys, L. (2021). The Tinder Games: Collective mobile dating app use and gender conforming behavior. *Mobile Media & Communication.* https://doi.org/10.1177/20501579211005001

Sprecher, S. (2011). The influence of social networks on romantic relationships: Through the lens of the social network. *Personal Relationships, 18*(4), 630–644. https://doi.org/10.1111/j.1475-6811.2010.01330.x

Sprecher, S., & Felmlee, D. (1992). The influence of parents and friends on the quality and stability of romantic relationships: A three-wave longitudinal investigation. *Journal of Marriage and the Family,* 888–900. https://doi.org/10.2307/353170

Tidwell, N. D., Eastwick, P. W., & Finkel, E. J. (2013). Perceived, not actual, similarity predicts initial attraction in a live romantic context: Evidence from the speed-dating paradigm. *Personal Relationships, 20*(2), 199–215. https://doi.org/10.1111/j.1475-6811.2012.01405.x

Tong, S. T., & Matheny, R. (2017, January). Mate selection preferences: Dominance & agreeableness in online dating. [Paper presentation.]. Annual Conference of the Society for Personality & Social Psychology. San Antonio, TX.

Trivers, R. L. (1972). Parental investment and sexual selection. In B. Campbell (Ed.), *Sexual selection and the descent of man*. Aldine.

Tyson, G., Perta, V., Haddadi, H., & Seto, M. (2016). A first look at user activity on Tinder. In The proceedings of *IEEE/ACM International Conference on Advances in Social Networks Analysis and Mining (ASONAM)* (pp. 461–466). San Francisco, CA, USA. https://doi.org/10.1109/ASONAM.2016.7752275

7

Navigating the Great Modality Shift: From Tinder to Text to Snapchat to Starbucks

Tricia, Ashir, and Jenna are all college students who used Tinder or Bumble to meet new people. Tricia was the newest user, with only two months' experience; Ashir had been using Tinder for 13 months. All three of them had matched with other daters on Tinder, messaged some of those matches online, and also arranged in-person dates. All three of them recounted their experiences to Stephanie, during interviews excerpted below.

Case Studies in Modality Shifting

As a new college freshman, Tricia used Tinder to meet new friends and find dates near her new university. She described the first FtF date that she arranged using Tinder: "I remember it was kind of awkward."

How so?

". . .I don't know, talking to people and, like, seeing them online. And, like, never seeing them in person. I don't know, it was just kind of weird. Like things don't always match."

Can you explain that more? Like, did you feel like that person was true to how you thought they were going to be? Or not?

"Yeah...well, for the most part? But I think also—it was an age thing, too. Because he was trying to be too serious. . .. He was like, 22, and it was just kind of like, I don't know. I felt kind of pressured to, like, be someone I wasn't. Kind of like, I don't know, too 'adult' or something."

Gotcha. So, you were more into having fun, he was too serious?

"Yeah."

Ashir described what he experienced when he talked to women on Tinder, then subsequently met them on FtF dates:

"[Meetups] are fine. But it's like, if you're in person, not online, it's kind of formal."

Okay. How so?

"Um, I don't know. . ..It's because within 30 seconds, you know, you can tell if you like someone. But with Tinder, you can't know that really. . .you won't get that until you meet them. And they have this weird information about them online. So, kind of—you get high expectations [you feel] like you should like them, but then you meet up and really don't. And you're like, 'Wow, that was a waste of time.'"

Interesting. What is it about that change from online to in person? Why do you think that happens? That you feel like you should like them when you meet them?

"I think because like, [online] I can't see past filters, and I can't see past like their faces, I guess? So they can look gorgeous on there. They can look one way, or like they could become a better person if you see them in the flesh. But then they look better online than they do in person. . .and it's such a letdown. So, I get that a lot."

Finally, Jenna described her first date arranged off of Bumble:

"I get really, really—I get really nervous to, like, meet new people. I like, feel uncomfortable. So I was scared to do it. But, I guess that's kinda what drew me to Bumble. Um, I think it [the date] was kind of awkward, a little bit. Like, I don't know. Meeting with him was a little bit scary. Because you don't know the person and you're getting to know them. But then when we laughed, it was just kind of awkward. Like, he walked me to my car and he gave me a hug. It was just like, 'Bye.' I don't know. I guess I would say I wasn't totally satisfied, but it was also not as bad as I thought. . .Like afterwards."

Tricia, Ashir, and Jenna's accounts all reflect the inevitable messiness inherent in *mixed-mode communication*—specifically in the move from online messaging to offline dates. Almost all the daters we talked to recounted similar progressions that went something like: Tinder → Text messaging → Snapchat → Starbucks. Filled with "mismatches" and "awkwardness," the online-offline transition can be "uncomfortable" for so many reasons, such as: the formation of impressions and (unmet) expectations, and the differences between "formal" and "informal" communication modes. How do daters navigate this great modality shift?

Notably, scholars have been researching the online-offline blend of communication between relational partners for many years. Walther and Parks (2002) defined a *mixed-mode relationship* as one that begins in an online space and then migrates offline.[3] In fact, a significant portion of CMC research has concerned itself with this overarching question: How are the impressions and connections we form of others through online interaction different than those we form when we interact with them FtF? Different theoretical perspectives about this question have informed research over the years.

One theoretical camp has suggested that when people communicate in CMC using text-only modes of interaction, our nonverbal cues are stripped from our communication; as a result, it is more difficult (if not impossible) to exchange relational information online (e.g., Kiesler, Siegel, & McGuire, 1984). Theories sharing this perspective have been collectively referred to as the *Cues-Filtered-Out* (CFO) perspective (Culnan & Markus, 1987, see also, Chapter 1). Those in the CFO camp would predict that initial online interactions would feel impersonal and partners would find each other cold. But after a modality shift, when partners meet up FtF, their use of nonverbal communication would once again allow for the development of stronger impressions and connections than could form online.

Another camp of theorists (e.g., Reicher, Spears, & Postmes, 1995) approach these questions differently. Informed by the *social identity model of deindividuation effects* (SIDE), these theorists might argue that when people communicate online, not only do they have reduced nonverbal cues, they are often *visually anonymous* and can only see what another person says via text. As a result, people tend to rely on group-level information to "fill in the blanks," and make guesses about others' characteristics and personalities when chatting online. For

---

3 A smart reader might also ask, "What about relationships that begin offline and move online?" That, too, could be counted as a mixed-mode relationship, but here we focus specifically on the transition from online introduction to offline meeting.

example, if you are chatting with another person online whom you can't see or hear and you only know that they are British, you may start filling in some of the things that you do not know about them with stereotypes that you may hold of British people (stiff upper lip, not very emotional, likes tea, etc.). SIDE theorists might expect that those who meet in CMC through text-only, visually anonymous interactions form impressions about their partners based on group-level stereotypes. But when the modality shifts and they meet up FtF, they will come to see each other as individuals, and stop relying on stereotypical group-level attributions to develop more detailed impressions. In other words, a SIDE theorist might expect that greater *individuation* occurs when online acquaintances turn into offline friends.

A third camp, informed by Walther's (1992) *social information processing theory* (SIPT) might predict something else. SIPT theorists would argue that when people communicate online using text, they will find creative ways to use that text in order to compensate for the lack of nonverbal cues. Even though SIPT argues that people are smart and can adapt to a reduced-nonverbal-cue environment, it also notes that information exchange between partners will take longer online than it would FtF. That is because the information that would have been communicated via nonverbal cues in FtF settings has to be translated into verbal text—and as we all know, reading, typing, and exchanging text messages takes longer than looking and listening and talking in a FtF conversation! Regarding modality shift, a SIPT theorist (in contrast to CFO theorists), might expect that when partners who meet initially online are given adequate time to interact, they will be able to develop a strong interpersonal connection. Moreover, the *hyperpersonal model* (Walther, 1996) suggests that in some cases, a significantly more intimate relationship may develop between partners online, than might have happened offline. It is this set of disparate predictions about what might happen in these mixed-mode relationships that has captivated researchers for decades.

A Review of Modality Shift Research

At some point almost all romances that start online eventually cease to be solely online ventures. While colorful examples of relationships that start and continue using only online communication methods—even through marriage—certainly exist, this is not how the "typical" romance progresses. Moreover, as many couples who have met online and gone on to develop established relationships will attest, the first FtF meeting is among the most anxiety-ridden moments in their budding relationship. Will she sound the way I think she'll sound? Have I been picturing her accurately? Will she be disappointed by *my* appearance? In short, couples who meet online and move on to a FtF meeting have many questions about whether or not their partner is what they are expecting them to be, and vice-versa.

To understand how communication scholars approach these questions, we need to understand the roots of modality shift research. Ramirez and Zhang (2007) define *modality shifts* as the process that occurs when people change communication channels that they use to interact with one another. Ramirez and Zhang note that research findings surrounding the shift from online to offline display some inconsistencies. For example, McKenna, Green, and Gleason (2002) find that people who meet one another online then shift FtF tend to experience *more* liking for one another. However, Ramirez and Zhang also note other research indicating that the opposite may be true. For instance, some scholars theorize that impressions developed online are often inconsistent with those developed during FtF meetings (Jacobson, 1999), and that when people communicate online, people's potential to portray themselves inaccurately increases (Conwell & Lundgren, 2001). Moreover, this research argues that when people portray themselves inaccurately online, FtF meetings will be less pleasant, because any obvious physical deceptions perpetrated online will likely be exposed. So, what is the truth about modality shifts in online dating? To answer that question requires reviewing the research.

Evidence from Experiments

Ramirez and Zhang set out to understand, and hopefully draw together under a single unifying theoretical apparatus, these seemingly conflicting findings. They first identified an existing theoretical discrepancy, then pitted one of the most popular CFO theories, *social presence theory* (Short, Williams, & Christie, 1976) against the *hyperpersonal model* (Walther, 1996) to determine which theory could best predict what would happen in different modality-switching scenarios. Ramirez and Zhang recruited a number of previously unacquainted people, assigned them to dyads (pairs), and followed each dyad as they interacted over a nine-week period. Participants were randomly assigned to interact with their partner in one of four different ways that mirrored variations in single-modality or mixed-modality conversations: (a) only CMC, (b) first CMC, then FtF, (c) only FtF, or (d) first FtF, and then CMC[4]. They found that those partners relying only on CMC reported greater levels of *intimacy* and *social attraction* than did partners assigned to other conditions, consistent with the hyperpersonal model (Walther, 1996). Additionally, those participants who communicated first via CMC and then switched to FtF interactions at the end of the experiment reported greater *uncertainty* than all other conditions, also consistent with the hyperpersonal model.[5] In sum, their research demonstrated that the effects of modality switching were most consistent with SIPT and the hyperpersonal model (Walther, 1992, 1996).

Ramirez and Wang (2008) continued this line of research into modality switching, this time examining the phenomenon through the lens of Burgoon's (1993; Burgoon & Hale, 1988; Burgoon & Jones, 1976) *expectancy violation theory* (EVT). To summarize briefly: EVT suggests that people often hold basic expectations about others' behavior during interaction. When those expectations are violated, it causes *arousal*, which focuses their attention on the source of that arousal, namely the behavior that caused the expectancy violation and the person who enacted it.

As an example, imagine that your supervisor—whom you admire and like a great deal—comes by your cubicle at work and places her hand on your shoulder while delivering a message. She usually doesn't make physical contact when she speaks to you, so this causes arousal and catches your attention. This is an example of a nonverbal expectancy violation cueing an *orienting* response to that particular violation—that is, you start to search for a reason or way to make sense of your supervisor's behavior.

EVT proposes that the next step in this process occurs as a person makes an *assessment* of the violation—how do you judge your supervisor's behavior? When expectancy violations are judged as ambiguous, EVT suggests that a

---

4   The inductions of modality in Ramirez and Zhang (2007) were actually more complex than are depicted here, but we have excluded some of the specifics for ease of reading. If you're interested in modality-shift work, we recommend that you read the article itself to gain a full understanding of the experimental inductions.

5   It should be noted that Ramirez and Zhang (2007) also provide some of the strongest evidence that exists in support of the often cited, but rarely directly empirically tested, social information processing theory (Walther, 1992).

communicator's reward valence—your overall judgment about the costs and bene-fits of interacting with a message sender (in this case, your supervisor)—will help you interpret the nonverbal expectancy violation. So, if you trust your supervisor and you consider her a friend, EVT suggests that you will interpret this particular expectancy violation positively, perhaps as a sign of camaraderie or solidarity. If you already had misgivings about your supervisor, however, you may arrive at a very different—probably negative—conclusion.

Ramirez and Wang (2008) further examined modality switching through the lens of EVT, reasoning that when dyad partners made the switch from CMC to FtF, they would encounter a lot of unexpected nonverbal social information from their partner. They suspected that this would be especially true among partners who interacted for a longer period of time through CMC, because making the switch from CMC to FtF communication would create greater opportunities for nonverbal expectancy violations. Moreover, people who associated with another person for quite some time using CMC, but then switched to FtF communication, were expected to evaluate their partners' unexpected behaviors more negatively. Ramirez and Wang conclude that the types of unexpected social information one gathers after a modality switch often do create expectancy violations. This is an interesting finding as it suggests that switching modalities from CMC to FtF is more likely to cue EVT processes than a modality switch from FtF to CMC.

Ramirez and Wang (2008) also conclude that the *length of time* people inter-acted prior to modality switching affected the ways that expectancy violations were interpreted. They found that when people interacted for only a short time using CMC (approximately three weeks) and then switched modalities, they rated their partners more favorably in subsequent FtF interactions; however, peo-ple who had longer-term (approximately nine weeks) CMC interactions before switching to FtF had more negative interactions when they finally met FtF, com-pared to those who continued to communicate via CMC and who never made the switch. In short, people who thoroughly get to know one another using CMC and then connect FtF do not find meeting their partner nearly as pleasant as those who only use CMC for a short time before quickly switching to in-per-son interactions. Ramirez and Wang reasoned that this was because people who interact for a longer period in CMC may develop *idealized* perceptions of one another. Once a FtF interaction occurs, the partner is simply unable to live up to the unrealistic, idealized version that the other has developed. Consequently, FtF interactions tend to negatively violate a partner's expectations and lead to increases in uncertainty.

Mixed Modalities Outside of the Lab

The studies we reviewed above introduce a lot of important evidence suggesting how impressions develop and change once we move from online to offline interaction settings. And while these carefully planned studies featured great experimental control, they do not tell us much about what goes on after the nine-week interaction period. Additional research has examined modality switching in the context of a *longitudinal field study*. McEwan and Zanolla (2013) studied an existing online community that had occasional planned in-person "meet-ups" where people who knew each other only from their online interactions met in-person. Participants were first asked a series of questions about a specific member of the community that they had previously known only online, but whom they intended to meet in-person in the near future. Then, after the two people had met, researchers contacted these participants and asked another series of questions. Ultimately, this work reveals several mixed findings. Some of the data were consistent with the CFO approach; participants who met up offline became significantly more satisfied with their interpersonal relationship than those who maintained a solely online relationship. However, researchers also concluded that those individuals who had extremely positive online interactions at the outset were disappointed with their FtF interactions when they met their partners in-person. This is consistent with what we might expect according to the hyperpersonal model.

In part, McEwan and Zanolla's (2013) study may have arrived at mixed findings because it could not carefully control as many variables as did earlier experimental studies, reviewed above. Given the selected method and sample, this is to be expected. In part, what McEwan and Zannolla set out to examine was what happens when relational partners leave the laboratory and make their way out into the world. So, their finding—consistent with the CFO perspective—that individuals who eventually met offline were significantly more relationally satisfied and closer than those who only knew one another online may have been due (either completely or in part) to the fact that those who met another person offline *chose* to meet that person offline. It would be reasonable to expect that CMC friends who choose to meet FtF may simply like each other more than those who choose not to meetup FtF. While this issue and others like it are a challenge to field studies, such research helps to push the study of modality switching beyond the confines of the experimental laboratory. In doing so, it highlights the complexities and vast number of uncontrolled but potentially meaningful variables that may affect the modality switching process when it occurs in the wild.

Mixed Modalities in Relational Reconnection

While previous work has looked at modality switching between relatively unacquainted partners, Ramirez and Bryant (2014) sought to tackle *relational reconnection*, in which people use social media to revive dormant relationships. They note that once partners re-establish connection online, they will frequently maintain more FtF interactions (Ramirez, Hu, Spinda, Feaster, Hoplamazian, Zhang, & Horton, 2009). With this in mind, Ramirez and Bryant (2014) conducted a survey which queried college students' experiences with relational reconnection and modality switching. Additionally, this work sought to better understand the ways that those who reconnect online engaged in *multimodal channel expansion*, which occurs when people begin to increase the numbers of channels they use to communicate with others. Until this point in the history of modality switching research, most studies had focused on the behavioral and relational impacts of switching from a single, usually text-based form of communication, to a FtF meeting. This was one of the first studies to consider multiple modes of communication.

This study found that people who reconnected with distant partners were likely to have had a more solid relationship in the past, before they lost contact. Additionally, Ramirez and Bryant found that participants with persistent relational reconnections also used a greater number of modalities, consistent with multimodal channel expansion expectations. However, several limitations that challenged McEwan and Zanolla's (2013) longitudinal study also affected Ramirez and Bryant's (2014) relational reconnection and modality switching study. Namely, because of the non-experimental nature of the data, it becomes difficult to determine if those who successfully reconnected with past associates offline did so successfully because meeting FtF is a superior modality to CMC, or if they simply had a stronger relationship before they ever lost touch and reconnected.

As we know, both kinds of research—experiments and field studies—provide an important foundation for more modality shift work. Experiments are particularly well-suited to explain the specific causes and effects of moving online to offline, while field studies are exceptionally effective in shedding light on how people who experience modality switches in their everyday lives *actually* communicate with their partners. Now that we have reviewed the background research and defined some key theoretical ideas, we can explore how these findings about modality switching might apply to dating relationships which exist in a multimodal communication media environment.

Modality Shifts as a Part of the Online Dating Process

After reading that review, the astute reader will, no doubt, have predicted where the research on modality shifts was headed: What we know from prior work is that modality switching matters in terms of the way people form online connections, and then move offline. Furthermore, the pattern of results seems to be "cleanest" among those people who are unacquainted before they meet online, and then transition offline. It follows, then, that the next place to explore the effects of modality switching would be in online dating. Among the first scholars to suggest that understanding modality switching might provide insight into the online dating process were Gibbs, Ellison, and Heino (2006). However, it wasn't until almost a decade later that Ramirez, (Bryant) Sumner, Fleuriet, and Cole (2015) directed substantial attention to the phenomenon of modality switching in terms of the ways that it specifically affects online dating.

As we mentioned at the beginning of this chapter, among the daters we talked to, modality switching occurred relatively quickly. As we discussed above, Tricia, Ashir, and Jenna were all able to match with others on dating apps like Tinder or Bumble and exchange phone numbers with their matches for text messaging, before moving on to other platforms, such as Snapchat. Most daters we talked to reported moving off the dating app relatively quickly—after about a day or two—but the period of texting prior to meeting up FtF varied considerably. Some arranged FtF dates with partners in as little as one week, others chatted with their partners online for a month before meeting in-person. One dater we talked to, Rosa, mentioned she messaged a man for five months before they had their first FtF date:

> "I met up with this guy I had talked to for, like, five months and he was actually really cool. Which was surprising because I didn't expect that from Tinder. And we went on two dates and now we're just friends. So that was actually a good experience."

So you guys talked for five months? Was that all on Tinder? Or did you switch to a different app?

> "We switched to a different app like after the first conversation."

After the very first conversation?

> "Yep."

What did you switch to?

"Um, I think it was Snapchat."

Right. Did you exchange phone numbers or anything else, up to that point?

"Oh yeah, we did that, too. Texts every day."

Ramirez et al. (2015) examined how variations in the amount of mediated messaging online daters engaged in might influence their satisfaction with their first offline date: In their study, they predicted that those who communicated very little or a great deal online prior to meeting FtF would perceive their relational communication more negatively, but that there would be a "sweet spot"—that is, that those who communicated online only a *moderate* amount would report higher levels of satisfaction with relational communication after meeting FtF.

To test these predictions Ramirez et al. conducted a survey of adults who had used some online dating platform in the past. Generally speaking, the data supported their predictions: Participants who reported communicating *very little* (in terms of both the amount of *time* participants had communicated and in terms of the *number of mediated messages* they had previously exchanged) online prior to a FtF meeting reported lower satisfaction with their relational communication; those who reported a *moderate* level of online exchange prior to meeting reported more favorable relational communication during their FtF meeting. Participants who reported communicating online a *great deal* prior to a FtF meeting, however, did not achieve more favorable relational communication outcomes. In short, they found a "Goldilocks" effect—too little or too much online interaction resulted in less satisfying FtF meetings between partners, but just the right amount of texting and messaging led to better FtF dates. Those online daters who engaged in a modality switch after a moderate amount of online communication confirmed Ramirez et al.'s predictions.

But other investigations of modality switching between romantic daters offer less robust support for these theoretical perspectives. One longitudinal study of online communication and first date (FtF) success, for instance, has demonstrated mixed support for SIPT and the hyperpersonal model (Sharabi & Caughlin, 2017). This study employed a longitudinal design which first collected data from online daters about a person they intended to meet, then collected data again shortly after participants met FtF. After participants met a potential romantic partner FtF, their message history was also collected, which allowed for analysis of the actual online message behavior between the potential romantic partners that preceded their in-person meeting. In spite of mixed results, Sharabi and Caughlin report an overall *decrease* in reported attraction following daters' first FtF date. This finding is what one would expect if participants had been engaged in hyperpersonal communication that led to inflated (and unsustainable) impressions of one another that came crashing down in their in-person meeting (Walther, 1996).

Other recent research has begun to develop Ramirez and Bryant's (2014) work on modality switching and relational reconnection. While these researchers' early work focuses on the general communicative function of relational reconnection (with no presumption that these reconnections are romantic in nature) they do acknowledge that romantic reconnections are a particularly interesting, if not common, type of reconnection. Moreover, recent work has begun to explore the ways that these reconnections occur not only among younger adults but also among more mature adults (Sumner, Ramirez, & Fletcher, 2019). These lines of research should prove theoretically rich and practically meaningful, and ultimately may lead to new questions that push beyond the rigid technological boundaries they have previously observed.

The Future of Modality Shift Research in Online Relationships

As we consider the future of modality shift research, one of the key considerations will be the degree to which some of the most prevalent theoretical frameworks adequately help push future research forward. Most of the modality switching research is primarily motivated by the hyperpersonal model (Walther, 1996) and predicted outcome value theory (Sunnafrank, 1986). Future research in this area, however, will need to consider the efficacy of these models to understand modality switching effects beyond initial relationship formation stages. While the hyperpersonal model and predicted outcome value theory work well to explain initial contact and modality switching between daters in early developmental stages, neither model has been applied to longer-term relational development across stages. Predicted outcome value theory seeks to describe how people make predictions about the future advantages of reducing uncertainty about a potential partner. This theoretical frame has been exceptionally useful thus far because key questions in online romance often consist of how people's expectations of future relationships may form differently or deviate from the expectations they form in FtF settings. SIPT is often used to predict what may happen when relationships initiated online, move offline. The hyperpersonal frame, too, has been useful because it has (relatively accurately) anticipated some of the elation and disappointment some people feel when initial interactions conducted in online settings traverse through a modality shift. But other unanswered questions still remain.

Multi-Way Modality Shifts in Relationships

Early experimental CMC research primarily compared modality differences in between-subjects experimental designs, in which some pairs of partners were randomly assigned to interact via CMC while others were randomly assigned to FtF conditions. More contemporary mixed-mode and modality switching literature developed as researchers observed what occurs when people switch from CMC to FtF communication in a controlled, linear manner (as in Ramirez & Zhang, 2007; Ramirez & Wang, 2008). Up to this point, however, modality switching research has largely been explored in this one-way manner, whereby partners traverse the boundary between online and offline.

Increasingly, the transition between online and offline modes of communication within a relationship has become substantially more fluid. As relationships progress, modality switching between online forms of communication and FtF are quite common. When writing this book, for instance, Stephanie and Brandon communicated with each other using lots of text messages, email, some phone calls, and occasional FtF meetings. Each of these modes may provide unique relational benefits, and each may have relational drawbacks.

One potential benefit to the layering of modality switching for more established relationships is that this practice may assist partners in accomplishing tasks that would require considerable investment or effort in one communication mode, but prove relatively easy to complete in another. Nonverbal communication in romantic relationships has the potential to both add to and detract from relational satisfaction—that is, *how* something is said can be just as important as *what* is being said. An emotionally warm facial expression or tone of voice can helpfully convey to a romantic partner that they are cared about, even when the verbal content of a message is not particularly romantic or emotionally charged in nature. For example, a warm smile while asking if the dishes have been washed this morning has the potential to allow the verbal content of the message to be received by one's partner without evoking their ire—or at least evoking *less* of their ire. However, nonverbal emotional exchange is often challenging to manage in vocal-verbal conversation (i.e., conversations that happen FtF or on the telephone). At the end of a long work day when fatigue has set in, after the children have been driven to ballet and drama and soccer and baseball practice, after the dogs have been walked, etc., the task of carefully managing the nonverbal cues that accompany verbal chat with one's romantic partner may be a little too much to manage. Under these stressful circumstances, it's more likely that the same inquiry about the dishes being washed will be asked with a sigh of frustration rather than a warm smile. Here, using communication modes that relieve us of the obligations of nonverbal cue management may offer substantial relational benefits. A text message that can be carefully crafted to convey one's "<3" (i.e., "love") for their partner may be substantially less challenging than accomplishing the same emotional work in a FtF conversation.

As future scholars consider this possibility, they may ask other novel research questions about how established relational partners manage even the most mundane conversations using multiple modes to communicate. Perhaps, throughout the work day romantic partners are more likely to text than they are to call. There may be many practical reasons for such a choice, but it would be an interesting choice, nonetheless. Even more interesting, however, are the effects this choice may have on relational satisfaction and liking for one's partner. Is it the case that staying in touch via text throughout the day is superior in terms of a couple's relational satisfaction to placing phone calls?

It is worth noting that the practice of modality shifting to accomplish relational maintenance tasks is not a new one. The practice of writing letters to a distant lover (or love interest) can be traced *at least* as far as back the celebrated exchange of Heliose and Abelard, the doomed 12th-century couple. A more recent (and less tragic) example is the collection of letters that Ronald Reagan, former President of the United States, wrote to Nancy Reagan, his wife (Reagan, 2000; Figure 7.1). President Reagan (regardless of your stance on his politics) was by most accounts both deeply in love with and devoted to his wife, and also a dedicated public servant.

These (sometimes oppositional) callings—one to public service and one to his role as husband—made it challenging to maintain his marriage. Reagan accomplished routine relational maintenance tasks by writing love letters and telegrams to his wife. While these messages were not delivered by way of the Internet, they did represent an attempt to stay connected to a significant other by changing the modalities of interaction. When a FtF conversation or phone call may not have been possible or practical due to international travel or national emergency, President Regan wrote a love letter.

Figure 7.1: The Reagans. President Ronald Reagan and his wife, Nancy Reagan routinely exchanged love letters throughout their relationship. Source: Public Domain/ WikiMedia: https://commons.wikimedia.org/wiki/File:Ronald_Reagan_and_Nancy_Reagan_aboard_a_boat_in_California_1964.jpg

This and other research questions arise when we start to consider modality switching as a complex process that occurs not just during the early stages of dating but serves as an ongoing process underlying the communication practices of established, long-term partnerships. Elsewhere in this book (see, Chapter 9) we discuss the process and effects of mediated maintenance, since this is one especially promising vein of mixed-mode research.

Conclusion

As we alluded at the end of the previous section, a satisfying, life-long romantic relationship demands a wide variety of communication functions. In the early stages of a romantic relationship, forming an accurate impression of one's partner is very important. As a relationship progresses, however, impression formation takes a back seat to maintenance functions or social influence functions, to name a few. Because the body of modality switching research is, first, relatively young and second, largely conducted with voluntary samples of undergraduate college students, the focus of this work has, thus far, been on the initiation stages of relationships, and on the ways in which impression formation is affected by switching modalities from online to offline. However, as this research area matures, it will be important to understand how multiple modalities affect the romantic relational functions that occur among older adults and those in longer-term romantic relationships.

There is still much that scholars do not understand about the ways people switch modalities to accomplish basic relational functions. Some theorists have suggested that different media (or modes of communication) are better than others at supporting complex messages (see *media richness theory*; Daft & Lengel, 1986), and that therefore people tend to select a communication modality which best suits the purpose of their message. Other theorists (Kock, 2004) have argued, from an evolutionary perspective, that all communication which is not accomplished FtF is in some way unnatural. This is to say, because humans evolved over millions of years to communicate using a full complement of facial expressions, gestures, words, etc., any mode of communication which curtails this system of interaction hampers interaction. Importantly, *media naturalness theory* suggests that FtF communication represents a *communicative ideal*—a "gold standard" which humans will strive to satisfy if at all possible. While these perspectives are certainly intuitively appealing, they struggle to explain why romantic partners often choose to use a cell phone to send a text message rather than place a phone call or use a video connection to chat with their significant other.

These perspectives often make several implicit assumptions about FtF communication. First, they tend to assume that people have a remarkable level of control over their nonverbal behavior in FtF communication episodes. Both media richness theory (Daft & Lengel, 1986) and media naturalness theory (Kock, 2004) seem to presume that in general, when people use FtF communication their nonverbal behavior is firmly under their control and primarily positively valenced. Ekman (1978) discusses three main types of nonverbal behavioral control: *simulation*, when a communicator attempts to nonverbally show emotion when they have none; *inhibition*, wherein a communicator seeks to show no emotion when they actually are experiencing an emotion; and *masking*, where a communicator seeks to show one emotion when they are, in fact, experiencing another. We believe that when humans communicate FtF they occasionally fail at managing these nonverbal behavioral controls. However, when people use mediated forms of communication, they may realize a greater ability to manage their emotional expression.

Another implicit assumption that these theories make about FtF communication is that humans have a great capacity to accurately identify and utilize the nonverbal meaning in FtF communicative episodes. We would argue it is not necessarily clear that people are always better at accurately interpreting a communication partner's emotion in person than online. Ekman's (1978) behavioral control typology seems to explicitly assume that people interacting FtF at very least occasionally seek to alter others' perceptions of the emotions they are experiencing. In other words, Ekman assumes that at times, communicators are explicitly *trying* to withhold their true emotional state from her or his partner. The idea that people are more able to accurately identify others' emotions in FtF than in CMC is admittedly an intuitively appealing one. After all, for a mode of communication which removes nonverbal behavior—humans' primary mechanism of emotional expression (Burgoon & Hale, 1987)—it seems quite possible that, comparatively, CMC ought to be less good at transmitting emotion. But part of the challenge in validating this belief empirically is that we rarely have a good comparison point. We can all recall times when an email conversation or text message that we sent with an intended tone was totally lost on the recipient—sometimes with disastrous effects. Unfortunately, however, we don't usually have a FtF comparison point for such exchanges. Would the results of that disastrous online email exchange have been quite so bad if it had been conducted FtF? Would it have been helpful to see the nonverbal response of a communication partner so that one could have adjusted their message in real time? Do such things help or hinder communicators? The answer to most of those questions is that we just do not know. It seems to be true that people *perceive* that FtF communication is better at conveying emotion than CMC; however, whether the reality matches that perception is not quite settled, in our view.

As modality shift research moves forward, we believe that Ekman's (1978) forms of nonverbal behavioral control might serve as interesting jumping-off points to spur future research into modality shifting in longer-term relationships. As people in longer-term, and often more developed, relationships seek to navigate different relational functions, it is possible that different modalities provide various ways to regulate the emotions one's partner perceives. These modality choices will likely not be driven by necessity like those at the outset of a romantic relationship that begins through an online or mobile dating platform. Instead, these modality shifts may be shifts of convenience that address the following not-even-close-to-exhaustive list of research questions: If I am tired and down at the end of a long day, am I more likely to shift to a text-based modality, one that allows me to better conceal my exhaustion from my spouse or partner? Are people better at responding with (or even simulating) excitement or happiness when they receive others' good news via text, or rather in person? When people seek to appear measured and logical about a touchy or conflict-inducing topic, is CMC or FtF better at allowing a person to inhibit their emotion and convey their message? Such questions about modality shifts and choices relational partners make will be important for future study.

References

Burgoon, J. K. (1993). Interpersonal expectations, expectancy violations, and emotional communication. *Journal of Language and Social Psychology*, *12*(2), 13–21. https://doi.org/10.1177/0261927X93121003

Burgoon, J. K., & Hale, J. L. (1987). Validation and measurement of the fundamental themes of relational communication. *Communication Monographs*, *54*(1), 19–41. https://doi.org/10.1080/03637758709390214

Burgoon, J. K., & Hale, J. L. (1988). Nonverbal expectancy violations: Model elaboration and application to immediacy behaviors. *Communication Monographs*, *55*(1), 19–41. https://doi.org/10.1080/03637758809376158

Burgoon, J. K., & Jones, S. B. (1976). Toward a theory of personal space expectations and their violations. *Human Communication Research*, *2*(2), 131–146. https://doi.org/10.1111/j.1468-2958.1976.tb00706.x

Conwell, B., & Lundgren, D. C. (2001). Love on the Internet: Involvement and misrepresentation in romantic relationships in cyberspace vs. realspace. *Computers in Human Behavior*, *17*(2), 197–211. https://doi.org/10.1016/S0747-5632(00)00040-6

Culnan, M. J., & Markus, M. L. (1987). Information technologies. In F. M. Jablin, L. L. Putnam, K. H. Roberts, & L. W. Porter (Eds.), *Handbook of organizational computing: An interdisciplinary perspective* (pp. 420–443). Sage.

Daft, R. L., & Lengel, R. H. (1986). Organizational information requirements, media richness and structural design. *Management Science*, *32*(5), 554–571. https://doi.org/10.1287/mnsc.32.5.554

Ekman, P. (1978). Facial signs: Facts, fantasies, and possibilities. In T. Sebeok (Ed.), *Sight, sound, and sense* (pp. 124–156). Indiana University Press.

Gibbs, J. L., Ellison, N. B., & Heino, R. D. (2006). Self-presentation in online personals: The role of anticipated future interaction, self-disclosure, and perceived success in internet dating. *Communication Research*, *33*(2), 152–177. https://doi.org/10.1177/0093650205285368

Jacobson, D. (1999). Impression formation in cyberspace: Online expectations and offline experiences in text-based virtual communities. *Journal of Computer-Mediated Communication*, *5*. Retrieved 13 May, 2019 from https://onlinelibrary.wiley.com/doi/full/10.1111/j.1083-6101.1999.tb00333.x

Kiesler, S., Siegel, J., & McGuire, T. W. (1984). Social psychological aspects of computer- mediated communication. *American Psychologist*, *39*(10), 1123–1134. https://doi.org/10.1037/0003-066X.39.10.1123

Kock, N. (2004). The psychobiological model: Towards a new theory of computer-mediated communication based on Darwinian evolution. *Organization Science, 15*(3), 327–348. https://doi.org/10.1287/orsc.1040.0071

McEwan, B., & Zanolla, D. (2013). When online meets offline: A field investigation of modality switching. *Computers in Human Behavior, 29*(4), 1565–1571. https://doi.org/10.1016/j.chb.2013.01.020

McKenna, K. Y. A., Green, A. S., & Gleason, M. E. J. (2002). Relationship formation on the internet: What's the big attraction? *Journal of Social Issues, 58*(1), 9–31. https://doi.org/10.1111/1540-4560.00246

Ramirez, A., Jr., & Bryant, E. M. (2014). Relational reconnection on social network sites: An examination of relationship persistence and modality switching. *Communication Reports, 27*(1), 1–12. https://doi.org/10.1080/08934215.2013.851725

Ramirez, A., Jr., Hu, M., Spinda, J., Feaster, J., Hoplamazian, G., Zhang, S., & Horton, B. (2009, November). *Social networking technology and re-engaging friendships from the past: Two studies comparing cross-sex and same-sex friendships.* [Paper presentation in the Interpersonal Communication Division.] Annual meeting of the National Communication Association, Chicago, IL.

Ramirez, A., Jr., Sumner (Bryant), E. M., Fleuriet, C., & Cole, M. (2015). When online dating partners meet offline: The effect of modality switching on relational communication between online daters. *Journal of Computer-Mediated Communication, 20*(1), 99–114. https://doi.org/10.1111/jcc4.12101

Ramirez, A., Jr., Sumner, E. M., & Hayes, J. (2016). Reconnect on Facebook: The role of information seeking behavior and individual-and relationship-level factors. *Cyberpsychology, Behavior, and Social Networking, 19*(8), 494–501. https://doi.org/10.1089/cyber.2015.0630

Ramirez, A., Jr., & Wang, Z. (2008). When online meets offline: An expectancy violations theory perspective on modality switching. *Journal of Communication, 58*(1), 20–39. https://doi.org/10.1111/j.1460-2466.2007.00372.x

Ramirez, A., Jr., & Zhang, S. (2007). When online meets offline: The effect of modality switching on relational communication. *Communication Monographs, 74*(3), 287–310. https://doi.org/10.1080/03637750701543493

Reagan, N. (2000). *I love you, Ronnie: The letters of Ronald Reagan to Nancy Reagan.* Random House.

Reicher, S. D., Spears, R., & Postmes, T. (1995). A social identity model of deindividuation phenomena. *European Review of Social Psychology, 6*(1), 161–198. https://doi.org/10.1080/14792779443000049

Sharabi, L. L., & Caughlin, J. P. (2017). What predicts first date success? A longitudinal study of modality switching in online dating. *Personal Relationships, 24*(2), 370–391. https://doi.org/10.1111/pere.12188

Short, J., Williams, E., & Christie, B. (1976). *The social psychology of telecommunications.* Wiley.

Sumner, E. M., Ramirez, A., Jr., & Fletcher, J. (2019, May). *An examination of older adults' relational reconnection on social network sites.* [Paper Presentation]. Annual Meeting of the International Communication Association, Washington, DC.

Sunnafrank, M. (1986). Predicted outcome value during initial interactions: A reformulation of uncertainty reduction theory. *Human Communication Research, 13*(1), 3–33. https://doi.org/ 10.1111/j.1468-2958.1986.tb00092.x

Walther, J. B. (1992). Interpersonal effects in computer-mediated interaction: A relational perspective. *Communication Research, 19*(1), 52–89. https://doi.org/10.1177/009365092019001003

Walther, J. B. (1996). Computer-mediated communication: Impersonal, interpersonal, and hyperpersonal interaction. *Communication Research, 23*(1), 3–43. https://doi.org/10.1177/ 009365096023001001

Walther, J. B., & Parks, M. R. (2002). Cues filtered out, cues filtered in: Computer-mediated communication and relationships. In M. L. Knapp & J. A. Daly (Eds.), *Handbook of interpersonal communication* (3rd ed., pp. 529–563). Sage.

8

Intragroup and Intergroup Interaction Patterns: Online Dating across Age, Race, and Gender

When asked to describe the "typical" online dater, many will conjure images of straight, twenty-something college graduates, new to cubicle life in a big city, who turn to Tinder because they have no time to date "in real life." While it is true that online and mobile dating is most common among men and women ages 18–29, other usage statistics might surprise you. For example, use of dating platforms is much more common among lesbian, gay, and bisexual (LGB) adults compared to heterosexuals—55% of LGB adults report having used these dating platforms versus 28% of straight adults. And, although mobile apps are often thought of as technology for younger users, roughly 33% of Americans over age 50 have tried some kind of dating app or website (Anderson, Vogels, & Turner, 2020), suggesting that dating online is not just the domain of the under-30 crowd.

In accordance with these usage trends, developers are looking toward creating niche platforms tailored for specific audiences. As we discussed in Chapter 2, popular dating platforms clearly announce their focus on users' age, race, culture, religion, or sexuality as part of their explicit purpose and use. Some dating platforms, including OurTime.com and SilverSingles, are designed specifically with older adults in mind. Other platforms focus on daters' cultural, religious, or racial background, such as The Lox Club, Jdate, Muslima.com, or Chispa, aimed at Jewish, Muslim, and Latina/Latino daters, respectively. These *niche* dating platforms' characteristics and design features can help users from specific populations define and achieve their romantic and sexual goals more readily than a platform that caters to a broader base of users.

In this chapter, we examine intra- and intergroup characteristics to introduce the ways in which dating technologies cut across various demographic categories. We know we cannot capture the full extent of daters' diversity of experiences in a single chapter; however, we hope to introduce you to the ways in which our personal backgrounds can affect our views on intimacy, and the ways we use technology to fulfill our romantic goals and needs.

Social Categorization in Online and Mobile Dating

As you saw in Chapter 6 on partner selection, in the complex social world of online and mobile dating, daters are tasked with wading through a large and diverse pool of potential partners. When faced with an endless parade of options, daters must make a series of evaluations based on others' profiles. Interestingly, this first step of the profile review phase often involves *social categorization*, which is "the process of understanding what something is by knowing what other things it is equivalent to and what other things it is different from" (McGarty, 1999, p. 1).

Broadly, social categorization involves forming impressions by sorting people into known categories of gender, race, sexuality, culture, religion, political affiliations, and more. As humans, we are motivated to interpret the world around us in quick and efficient ways, and this process of categorization facilitates speedy sensemaking (Allport, 1954; Fiske & Neuberg, 1990). As such, social categorization "plays a fundamental role in virtually all downstream forms of social cognition" including our impressions of other people, our memory of them later on, and our evaluation and response to their behaviors (Maner, Miller, Moss, Leo, & Plant, 2012). Social categorization also facilitates *self-reference*—through the process of classifying others, we come to know our own place within our surroundings, or what Henri Tajfel called "self-definition in a social context" (1978, p.61). Overall, social categorization is a useful process that helps us organize our social environment and influences how we communicate with others. As outlined in the previous chapters, many dating apps push their users to make judgments very quickly, with the swipe of a finger or click of a keyboard. Within online dating, social categorization provides a rapid way for daters to separate a "potential partner" from "this person is not my type."

Clearly, relating to people on the basis of social cues and group-level categories can be both advantageous and problematic. For example, if you are a Muslim man who wants to continue practicing your religion with your new partner or spouse, you may seek out someone who is also Muslim. A site like Muslima.com would save you the trouble of having to apply search filters and wade through others' profiles on a larger site like Match.com or Tinder, looking for someone who shares your religious values. Because everyone on Muslima would likely be a Muslim as well, you can safely present your religious background and your preferences for someone who shares your beliefs. As discussed in Chapter 6, we often desire mates who are similar to ourselves in terms of values, beliefs, personality, education, and even physical characteristics. Thus, dating sites that cater to specific audiences can facilitate positive *assortative mating* by providing quicker access to similar others. So, one group-level outcome of niche dating apps and sites might be greater *endogamy*, wherein a group tends to enforce, fairly strictly, coupling within a single social group according to certain characteristics (e.g., religion, race/culture, age, lifestyle).

But just as dating platforms can help connect us with others like us, they can also break us out of our comfortable "social bubbles." Our offline social networks tend to be filled with friends who are similar to ourselves. The saying "birds of a feather flock together" describes a relational mechanism known as *clustering* (Simmel, 1950), in which we tend to become friends with the friends of our friends. Within such homogamous relational networks, it may be unusual to randomly meet a potential partner who differs from us in terms of age, race, ethnicity, or religion—in part because the content of our friendship network just does not allow for these types of connections to be made. And it is also unlikely that our friends will introduce us to anyone drastically different (because our friends' friends, too, are just like us). However, sites and apps can facilitate connections among complete strangers, and because of this they are sometimes responsible for more diverse, *exogamous* couples, matching people with partners who are outside of the social groups that they routinely associate with. By structurally widening the dating arena, online and mobile platforms can push us toward new matches that we would have never met or considered in our offline environments, increasing "the baseline probability of a diverse match for most social characteristics, in such a profound way that it might drown out any and all endogamy-encouraging mechanisms online" (Thomas, 2020, p. 1260). In other words, simply having access to unknown others increases our chances of dating someone who comes from a completely different social network, or a different neighborhood from our own, or who has a very different background than ours (Granovetter, 1995).

In this way, some scholars have suggested that another important social-level outcome of modern online and mobile dating is greater *social integration and diversity* (Thomas, 2020).

Just as the time-saving heuristics offered through social categorization can facilitate effects of within-group similarity and intergroup contact like those described above, they can sometimes foster deleterious *outgroup differentiation* effects like group stereotyping and judgment bias. In this chapter, we will also examine the ways that group-level categorization can lead to patterns of exclusion and rejection among people of different ages, races, ethnicities, and genders. Additionally, we offer a brief review of the literature regarding the goals, motivations, and behaviors of online and mobile daters through a group communication lens, specifically focusing on the *age*, *race*, and *gender*. For each demographic group, we review intragroup and intergroup outcomes suggested by the literature, and conclude each section with ideas for future research.

Adult Swim: Older Adults in the (Online) Dating Pool

According to the US Census, in 1900 there were 3.1 million people living in the United States aged 65 or older; by 2000, that number had grown to 35 million (Roberts, Ogunwole, Blakeslee & Rabe, 2018). In 2016, the American Community Survey (ACS) estimated that the number of people in the United States over age 65 was 49.2 million. Clearly, the American population is aging; and as it does, so does the mismatch between the numbers of men and women over 65. Given their longer life expectancy, senior women (27.5 million) outnumber senior men (21.8 million), and this discrepancy is also reflected in older adults' *marital status*. A closer look at the 2016 US Census shows that overall, there are a lot of women—and comparatively fewer men—who find themselves romantically single in later stages of life. As such, the dating pool for men over age 65 can look different from the dating pool for women of the same age (see also, Sassler, 2010).

The remarkable aspects of romantic (re)partnership later in life. Quite a bit of interesting research suggests that there are several things that affect the ways that people (re)find love later in life. For example, Carr and Borener (2013) found in their study's sample of older widows that while 42% of respondents reported an interest in pursuing a potentially romantic relationship, only 10% of the sample reported any actual dating activity. The gap between older adults' interest in dating and actual dating behavior may be the result of several issues that arise when older adults pursue new romantic partnerships at later points in their lives. First, because relational goals often become more diverse and varied with age, it can be harder for older adults to find someone else who shares their outlook, goals, expectations, and the circumstances that come with more life experience. For example, older men tend to be interested in (re)marriage and cohabitation, whereas older women prefer autonomy to remarriage (Moorman, Booth, Fingerman, 2006). In fact, many women—particularly widows—note that as their caretaking obligations for husbands decline later in life, they obtain a "freedom" or "selfish ability" to do what they want (Mahay & Lewis, 2007; Sassler, 2010). Single women report worrying that romantically (re)partnering later in life could jeopardize this new-found autonomy. For them, taking on new caretaking responsibilities is not a worthwhile tradeoff for the romantic intimacy or companionship they would gain by moving their relationships into the bonding stage, with a public declaration like marriage (Davidson, 2002; McWilliams & Barrett, 2014).

Secondly, older adults face barriers that may prevent them from actually pursuing new romantic partnerships. For example, those who are divorced, separated, or widowed may already have raised children with a previous partner. Older adults may feel they have fulfilled their parenting duties and might have less desire to be inducted as the new family member of a partner's existing family. Similarly, older adults also entertain concerns about how to introduce a new romantic partner into an existing family unit with grown adult children (Carr & Borener, 2013). A final barrier to relational initiation for some older adults is that they may be reticent to upset the balance of their well-established households, finances, and advanced careers, and may be anxious about merging and sharing these hard-won assets with new partners. Their more developed and established circumstances might make it difficult to fully integrate a new partner into their lives. For all these reasons, some older adults adopt "living apart together" arrangements that allow partners to live separately in one-person households, but share the intimacy, emotional support, and connection that is characteristic of a romantic relationship (Davidson, 2002; De Jong Gierveld, 2004).

Third, just like 20- and 30-year-olds, older adults also report frustration with dating in "traditional" spaces such as churches, bars, social clubs, or neighborhood events. Older adults have noted the lack of eligible partners in these spaces and how the awkwardness of trying to date within their own social network can lead to unique issues like "dating a dead friend's husband—too much history and too much talk" (McWilliams & Barret, 2014, p. 422). Others noted that having to compete against younger women and men left them feeling embarrassed and awkward as they attempted to navigate singledom after many years away from the contemporary dating scene.

Advantages and Challenges for Older Adults Dating Online

Given the unique issues that older adults face, the development of online avenues to romance presents them with both advantages and challenges. Some research emphasizes the advantages. Online and mobile dating, for example, can provide older adults access to new networks of potential partners and the ability to search for partners in non-traditional online spaces. With greater control over interaction offered by dating platforms, older adults report being better equipped to decide how and when to pursue new partners and relationships, and how to tailor a search to their personal romantic goals. McWilliams and Barret (2014) suggested that older men used dating platforms to look for potential partners interested in marriage or longer-term relationships, whereas older women asserted their desire for slower-paced relationship development by using computing technology to get acquainted with men before forging a relationship.

But for all these advantages, there are also challenges and risks for older daters. Just like any online daters struggling to create a profile, older adults have several decisions to make about photos, bios, and content. However, they also report grappling with impression management problems unique to their stage in the life cycle—specifically, balancing the authentic self-disclosure of their age, while presenting a vibrant, youthful attitude (Adams et al., 2003). From an evolutionary psychology perspective, we have already reviewed literature that indicates men often prefer female mates whose youth suggests their reproductive health (see Chapter 6). But older women also report preferring younger men: Women's longer life expectancies also suggest that they want a partner who can keep up and maintain an active lifestyle. Women often note that an older man's youthful attitude reflects both his physical and psychological health. Indeed, signaling one's personal health and vitality is a significant self-presentation feature found in older adults' dating profiles: In Alterovitz and Mendelson's (2009) study of "young-old" (60–74 years old) and "old-old" (75 and older) adult daters' online personal advertisements, the older group of daters mentioned their personal health more often in their personal ads (39.3%) compared to younger group (19.3%). Also, as older adults often report feeling younger than their actual chronological age, the pressure to accurately present their age, combined with both perceived and actual competition from younger suitors who seek to land the same romantic partner as older folks, can create an overall "tension between authenticity and social approval" that has to do specifically with their age (McWilliams & Barret, 2014, p. 416).

Another challenge is the differential (discriminatory) treatment that older daters face from online and mobile dating companies compared to their younger counterparts. In 2018, Tinder was found guilty of age discrimination when it was revealed that it charged older daters higher subscription fees for its "Tinder Plus" premium service. Younger users aged 18–29 were charged only $9.99 compared to $19.99 monthly fees for those 30 and over. Though Tinder noted that dynamic pricing such as student discounts were offered by other tech-service companies like Amazon, a California court ruled that Tinder owed an $11.5 million payout to an estimated 230,000 older subscribers of the Tinder Plus service who were discriminated against due to their age. In this way, Tinder and other dating apps and sites may be hindering intergroup contact between older and younger daters. It can be pretty daunting to dive into the online dating pool when the company running it is quite literally charging a premium on age (Lee, 2019).[6]

Some older daters also lack familiarity and dexterity with computing and mobile communication technology. Sometimes called "The Greatest Generation" those individuals born before 1946 did not grow through adolescence with much access to computing technology. Although adults of this generation may have used computers or smartphones at work or home, not all of them would have been exposed to or become proficient with technology. As such, some may find the adoption of these technologies for romantic purposes to be intimidating. Lack of computing efficacy can also translate into less awareness of how to protect their identities online, less likelihood of spotting risks or predators, and (once targeted) less ability to deal with the fallout of scams or harassment (Wion & Loeb, 2015). This lack of efficacy makes older adults in online dating spaces an attractive target for cyber criminals—the FBI's Internet Crime Complaint Center's (IC3) annual report in 2015 confirmed that individual citizens lost an astounding

---

6 Judge William F. Highberger presided over the class action lawsuit, Lisa Kim v. Tinder Inc., et al. (Case No. 2:18-cv-03093 in US District Court for the Central District of California). The 70-year-old district court judge has a pretty good sense of humor: "Because nothing in the complaint suggests there is a strong public policy that justifies the alleged discriminatory pricing, the trial court erred in sustaining the demurrer. Accordingly, we swipe left and reverse" (Dunaway, 2018). Well played, Judge Highberger . . . Super Like on this ruling.

$203,390,531 to online romantic confidence frauds and scams. The IC3's report also noted that as a group, it was those aged 60 and over who had the greatest number of victims who were scammed out of $100,000 or more.

However, as the American population ages, older adults' experience and efficacy with computing technology will improve, perhaps making cybercrime victimhood less of an issue. Baby Boomers (born between 1946 and 1964) may be much more amenable to using online and mobile technology for romance. As older adults adopt online and mobile dating platforms, more detailed investigation into patterns of use, behaviors, and outcomes will become crucial. At present, the overall number of older online daters is somewhat small. A recent Pew Research survey showed that in America, only 13% of people 65 and older have tried online dating; but among this group of older online daters, 59% report that their experience was at least somewhat positive (Anderson et al., 2020). This suggests that for the older adults who are dating online, the overall outcome may have been pretty good. Future research might explore how older adults' specific relational motives, romantic goals, unique challenges, and perceived risks shape their overall beliefs about and use of online and mobile dating platforms.

Future research on older adults and online dating. In all, online and mobile dating among older adults is a complex, and understudied area. Intergroup effects may be exacerbated by the ways in which older adults are treated by the online dating companies themselves—in an industry that prioritizes youth, older adults risk being separated out or marginalized by the sites and apps, but also by other daters. In fact, a recent analysis of 3,036 couples, Thomas (2020) found that compared to couples who reported meeting offline, couples meeting online were more different than one another in terms of race, religion, and education, but they were likely to be around the same age, compared to those who met offline. From this data, it appears some of this *age assortativity*—that is, romantic partners who are of similar ages—may be due to the ways in which daters themselves use age as a mate selection criterion, but this phenomenon may also be due to the structural segregation and exclusion of older daters by sites and apps. Future work should continue to tease out these various effects and trends, which may change over time as older adults begin to gain comfort with online and mobile dating technology.

Race and Gender in Online and Mobile Dating

Like age, race is another salient quality or category used in impression formation and social categorization among online and mobile daters. But the specifics on how race functions in online dating might surprise you. A recent analysis from Thomas (2020) suggests that compared to daters who met offline "couples who met online have over one and a half times greater odds of being interracial, or an average of 6 percent greater probability [of being interracial]" (p. 1273). Interestingly, couples who report having met online in a space *other* than a dating site or app (i.e., online gaming, social network sites) have an even higher probability of being interracial, at 8.4% on average. This evidence suggests that overall, the Internet can spark more racially diverse connections by simply connecting unacquainted strangers. But while expanding the dating market can create a more diverse pool, that in itself does not guarantee that cross-race interaction will occur. Here we review research regarding patterns of both *intraracial* and *interracial* communication within the relationship initiation stage.

First Contact: Race, Initiation Messages, and Replies in Online Relationship Formation

Although Thomas' findings indicate that online matches tend to be more racially diverse compared to offline couplings, this doesn't necessarily mean that all online daters are eager to partner with someone of a different race than their own. As discussed in Chapter 6, homophily and similarity are key matching criteria online, and they apply to race. To more fully understand Thomas' finding that interracial coupling happens more frequently when partners meet online than off, it is useful to explore how some of these patterns play out in a very large sample of online daters. Some of the most detailed analysis of racial patterns in online message exchange during relationship initiation comes from Lin and Lundquist's (2013) sample of over 900,000 heterosexual online daters. In their study, Lin and Lundquist extracted actual interaction data from a free online dating platform—their initial sample consisted of 200 million messages exchanged between 528,800 heterosexual male and 405,201 heterosexual female daters from November 2003 to October 2010. They note that extracting daters' real messages gave them the chance to analyze real communication behaviors, rather than rely on self-reported survey responses. They identified daters' race from the categories they listed in their personal profiles.

Male-to-female initiation. The men in Lin and Lundquist's (2013) sample initiated contact most often, sending 80% of the first message traffic compared to women (a finding consistent with evolutionary theories of mate selection; see Chapter 6). In examining race within those male-to-female initiation messages,

Lin and Lundquist note that men were much more likely to contact same-race women overall. However, there were some standout patterns with regard to cross-race messaging: First, the experience of Black women was unique as they "receive(d) the lion's share of their messages from Black men, a tiny amount from Latino men, and practically no messages from either Asian or White men" (p. 202). On the other hand, Asian and White women consistently received cross-race initiation messages from men of different races online. In sum, regarding male-to-female initiation, Lin and Lundquist (2013) concluded that overall, men were much more likely to contact same-race women as potential dates; but the data also suggest that Black women were at a unique disadvantage in interracial relationship initiation, in that non-Black men were less likely to send them a first contact message.

Female-to-male initiation. Among the women who initiated contact with men, again same-race pairings prevailed: Asian women were more likely to send messages to Asian men than to Hispanic, White, or Black men. As noted above, Black women were the group least likely to receive cross-race initiation messages from non-Black men, and they themselves showed the "highest levels of homophily" compared to other groups of women. Finally, White women "mostly preferred White men, their second preference is Hispanic men, and they rarely send initial messages to other minority men" (Lin & Lundquist, 2013, p. 202). Thus, regarding female-to-male initiation patterns, it seems that Asian men are at a disadvantage—as a group, they receive far fewer initial messages from women of ethnicities that differ from their own, as compared to Black, Hispanic, and finally White men, who receive more initial cross-race contacts from women.

In sum, the patterns of race seem to differ across male-to-female and female-to-male initiation. While Asian men tended to see the fewest initiation messages from women overall, Asian women received plenty of cross-race initiation messages. Lin and Lundquist (2013) attribute these differential effects to the fact that Asian women are often the recipients of both same-race *and* cross-race initiation messages, while Asian men only receive first contacts from Asian women, and almost no cross-race contacts. Black women suffer a similar exclusion effect to Asian men—while they receive a lot of same-race initiation messages from Black men, they receive almost no cross-race contact from other men online. The disadvantage of Asian men and Black women reported by Lin and Lundquist (2013) also parallels previous findings from Feliciano, Robnette, and Komaie (2009), whose analysis of 6,070 Yahoo! personal ads revealed that White men often exclude Blacks as possible dates, and "White women are much more likely to exclude Asians" (p. 49).

So, what might explain these patterns of racial inclusion and exclusion at the initiation stage? Sociological theorists have suggested that who and what we consider to be attractive has been influenced by decades of various social and cultural forces. In America, the preference for same-race pairings that persists in modern-day online dating may have even been solidified by past institutional laws. For example, just over 50 years ago, when interracial marriages were outlawed, one had no choice but to maintain racial homophily or risk being arrested (Warren & Supreme Court of the United States, 1967). Such laws simply reflected the larger *racial hierarchies* in America that prioritized Whites at the top, Black people and Native Americans at the bottom, and Latinos and Asians somewhere in between. Thus, the notion of "marrying up" would suggest that (a) for all minority ethnic groups, a White mate would help them move up the hierarchy, and (b) Whites would strive to maintain their status by coupling with other Whites to the exclusion of other races (Feliciano et al., 2009; Song, 2006). These structural and cultural legacies, researchers argue, have at least played *some* role in shaping mate selection preferences and attitudes that are still present in today's online and mobile platforms.

Gendered racial formation theories offer a more nuanced picture about how race and gender categories can combine to further influence social judgment and subsequent communication behavior. These theories suggest that certain racial groups are prototyped as more masculine or feminine. Research suggests that in America, Black people are often thought of as prototypically masculine, while Asians are conceived as feminine and exotic (Bem, 1981; Galinsky, Hall, & Cuddy, 2013; Schug, Alt, Lu, Gosin, & Fay, 2017). As such, individuals who are at the *intersection* of two marginalized groups of race and gender (i.e., Black and female; Asian and male) are perceived as being less prototypical of both race *and* gender categories, and are thus more likely to suffer from negative social judgment (see for review Crenshaw, 1991). Specifically, research into these gender and racial categorizations has found that observers classify Asian men as more "feminine, nerdy, subordinate, and 'not sexy'" and Black women as hypermasculine, "unfeminine and aggressive" (Schug et al., 2017, p. 223). These "non-prototypicality" judgments of Asian men and Black women tend to be related to other undesirable effects such as less memorable impression formation (i.e., "invisibility"; Schug et al., 2015) and (as we have already detailed) greater rates of exclusion from others in romantic partner selection and relationship initiation (Feliciano et al., 2009; Lin & Lundquist, 2013).

While racial hierarchies and non-prototypicality are reflected in today's patterns of online romantic relationship initiation, there is nevertheless evidence, as mentioned above, that online and mobile platforms are increasing the overall diversity of the dating pool relative to people's offline networks (Thomas, 2020). Expanded dating pools can help previously unacquainted people find each other and partner up—but only if they are willing to take steps toward cross-race connections by initiating contact and replying to others.

Race, first contact messages, and replies in online dating. Following patterns of initiation messages, evidence also indicates that daters are, on the whole, most likely to reply to messages sent to them by same-race daters (Lewis, 2013; Lin & Lundquist, 2013). However, Lewis's (2013) analysis of OkCupid daters reveals some interesting effects. He analyzed the effect of receiving a cross-race message on the likelihood that an individual would then turn around and initiate contact with another cross-race dater, in other words what was "the average quantity of new cross-race initiations 'created' per person as a consequence of receiving a cross-race message from someone else" (p. 18816)? The idea was to quantify what we call the "cross-race reply bump." It was discovered that, indeed, the 3,918 daters in Lewis's OkCupid sample who *received* a cross-race initiation message were more likely to *send* out new interracial contacts in the following two weeks, compared to a matched control group of daters who didn't receive any cross-race messages. The effect of receiving an interracial message on sending a new interracial message—the cross-race reply bump—was an astounding 37.3%.

When parsed out by each racial group, the cross-race reply bump was most pronounced for Asian women (who showed an increase in cross-race contact of 238%), followed by Asian men (increasing their cross-race contact by 222%), and Black women (who showed an increase of 106%). Some other interesting moderator effects indicated that the bump was stronger if (a) it was an individual's first time receiving a cross-racial message and also (b) if the individual replied to the initial cross-race message sent to them. Notably, the cross-race effect was also specific to the racial background of the initial sender—that is, "if a dating site user receives an interracial message from a member of racial group X, then that recipient is likely to initiate additional exchanges only with other members of group X in the future" (p. 18817). This led Lewis (2013) to conclude that OkCupid daters who receive interracial contact "exhibit greater interracial openness in the short-term future, an effect that also is stronger for certain categories of minorities (e.g., Asian women, Asian men, and Black women) than for Whites" (p. 18817).

Because these are digital trace data, they do not allow for the sort of causal conclusions we might expect from an experimental study. However, one possible explanation for the cross-race reply bump that Lewis (2013) offers is "preemptive discrimination." That is, groups like Asian men and Black women who have experienced effects of past non-prototypicality judgments might then anticipate being excluded by others in online dating. When those expectations are actually *dis*confirmed by receiving an unexpected interracial message from someone on OkCupid, that might trigger them to consider cross-race dating prospects that they might not have otherwise thought possible; this in turn prompts them to send new interracial messages of their own.

Lewis's (2013) argument is reminiscent of Allport's (1954) *contact hypothesis*, which predicts how interpersonal contact with a member of an outgroup can facilitate learning about the outgroup, which, in turn, may ultimately translate into reduced negative social judgments and prejudice against that outgroup as a whole. Notably, the contact hypothesis suggests that intergroup contact must be sustained, cooperative, and interpersonal. Without interpersonal connections and shared goals, ingroup and outgroup members might simply revert back to social categorization and stereotyping. In this way, Allport's contact hypothesis foreshadows Lewis's findings, in that the cross-race reply bump was short-lived, lasting for only about two weeks.

Algorithms that think they know better. Interestingly, a dating app or site's matching algorithm may also push dynamics of race and ethnicity during the matching and partner selection process. Across many popular apps and sites, daters have the option to list their own racial identity within their own profiles, and also to indicate their preferences for the racial identity of potential suitors. Notably, many daters select "no preference" in terms of their potential partners' ethnicity, perhaps thinking that this will prompt the app or site to show them profiles of daters with diverse racial backgrounds. However, that assumption might be incorrect. Notopoulos (2016) reported the case of her friend who used the dating platform Coffee Meets Bagel, which sends each user one "bagel" (i.e., selected match) per day based on that user's stated preferences. The user then has the option to message that bagel, or wait for a new bagel to come in the next 24-hour matching period. Interestingly, Notopoulous's friend listed herself as "Arab" in her Coffee Meets Bagel profile, and although she indicated "no preference" regarding the race of potential mates, kept finding herself seemingly matched with Muslim or Arab men. When Notopoulous's friend inquired into the matter, Coffee Meets Bagel sent her this response:

> Currently, if you have no preference for ethnicity, our system is looking at it like you don't care about ethnicity at all (meaning you disregard this quality alto-gether, even so far as to send you the same everyday). Consequently we will send

you folks who have a high preference for bagels of your own ethnic identity, we do so because our data shows even though users may say they have no preference, they still (subconsciously or otherwise) prefer folks who match their own ethnicity. It does not compute "no ethnic preference" as wanting a diverse preference. I know that distinction may seem silly, but it's how the algorithm works currently. (Notopoulos, 2016)

In a follow-up email message with Notopoulos, the founder of Coffee Meets Bagel—Dawoon Kang—further pressed this point: that often when daters indicate they have "no preference" regarding their partner's ethnicity, they actually *do* have a "very clear preference in ethnicity." If you were to look at the matches they message—"the preference is often their own ethnicity." In an unsubtle (and somewhat infuriating) way, Kang's email suggests designers of the platform are strongly guided by the idea of homophily, so much so that Coffee Meets Bagel has actually programmed its algorithm to ignore users' "no preference" indication.

Such cases may call into question the role of decision making assistance and support that many apps and sites provide daters through their ranking and search algorithms. In guiding mate selection and choice-making, apps and sites say that they are simply using daters' behavioral trace data to "optimize" the selection experience—in essence, giving daters what they think they want. Some algorithms, like Tinder's so-called (and now defunct) "Elo score" ranked daters (in part) based on swipes they receive from others in the larger dating pool (Carr, 2016). Those daters receiving higher numbers of right swipes get a higher ranking and are more likely to be shown to others, compared to those who receive more left swipes. The problem is that such ranking algorithms sustain, or perhaps even amplify, the racial bias that already exists among their daters. Think about it like this: The algorithm relies on daters' judgments of attractiveness and desirability which they signal through their swipe behavior. We already know that Black women and Asian men would be likely to receive more left swipes from others, whereas Asian and White women, and White men enjoy greater numbers of right swipes. Based on such numbers, Black women and Asian men would likely be ranked lower by the algorithm and shown less frequently to others on Tinder. In this way, dating app algorithms trained to optimize daters' preferences might simply reinforce the society-driven, non-prototypical ideals regarding desirability and beauty (McMullan, 2019). This prompts new ethical questions about the ways in which algorithms shape daters' attention in romantic dating, how users' data are being integrated into the algorithm's recommendations, and if such recommendations are distorting daters' mate selection choices (e.g., Tong et al., 2019).

Future issues on race and gender in online and mobile relationship initiation. Overall, the research examining race and ethnicity in online relationship initiation is complex. Evidence suggests that online, intraracial pairings are quite likely (Lewis, 2013; Lin & Lundquist, 2013). Importantly, as Lewis (2013) reports, cross-race interaction can and does occur online, perhaps more so than what would occur offline (Thomas, 2020). Again, though, these data cannot explain exactly why effects like the cross-race reply bump occur. Future work might parse out more specific causal explanations for cross-race pairings, including the individual difference variables that affect people's openness to interracial dating (Herman & Campbell, 2012; Perry, 2013; Qian & Lichter, 2007). Additionally, more work is needed examining the algorithm as an intermediary on daters' mate selection decisions. If cross-race contact is limited by platforms like Coffee Meets Bagel, then the actual odds of daters seeing a potential partner of a race different from their own are greatly decreased. Although from the company's perspective, such algorithms are simply "optimizing" daters' experiences on the platform, the larger effects on romantic matching, as well as their ethical implications, require greater investigation.

One question that interests us enormously is if algorithms did not suppress cross-race (and perhaps religious, cultural, political, and age) contact, would daters have greater opportunities to enjoy interactions with new potential partners and be encouraged to develop relationships that were much more diverse than they would have otherwise experienced? We suppose that it is just tantalizing to imagine a world where the content of our character (or at very least regular old questions of attractiveness and personality) rather than the color of our skin drives our matches. Certainly, the dating industry is bound to prioritize questions of profit. But does this preclude the creation of digital matching systems that help their users to truly engage in sustained contact (Allport, 1954), thus unlocking a world of potential matches? Some technology developers are already exploring this territory; apps like Mingler claim to be facilitating interracial dating. Whether algorithmically encouraging diverse contacts is a panacea or a panopticon is not yet ours to say (cf., Spears & Lea, 1994). However, this is a tantalizing empirical question for future research.

Additionally, most of the results offered here draw on samples from web-based platforms such as OkCupid. It remains to be seen how mobile apps, which rely on geolocation data, affect same-race versus cross-race pairings. Although ethnically mixed neighborhoods have been increasing as a whole since the 1970s, high levels of racial homogeneity are still notable across many neighborhoods in the United States (see Lee, 2016). Given the known importance of physical proximity on relational connections, researchers might examine if and how mobile apps are amplifying, changing, or simply reproducing the effects of geographical proximity on contemporary romantic relationship formation.

A final issue we believe deserves further study in this area resides with the nature of the groups that underlie social categorization. Age, racial, and ethnic groups are often highly visible group memberships. While there are several large-scale studies that have examined the ways that these large category memberships affect the ebbs and flows of online daters' behavior, less research has examined the way that less obvious or less visible category memberships may prove to be important indicators of future relational success.

As an example, as we were on the phone discussing this issue one day, Stephanie said to Brandon, "Yeah, like, might a dating site for lovers of red wine and chocolate provide a better, more consistent match for a partner than matching them according to racial group or religion." A little concerned that such a site might exist, Brandon quickly said, "If that site exists, you have to promise not to tell my wife about it" (Figure 8.1).

While we had a laugh about this, there is some truth—and a fable for researchers—here. Much research concerns the big stuff—similarities and differences of age, race, and religion. But scholars have not yet taken up the mantle of exploring the ways that smaller, seemingly insignificant categories might shape the ways that online daters are truly attracted to one another –despite the fact that the online dating industry has: A few paragraphs ago, we hinted at the lamentable consequences of what's become a ruthlessly capitalist enterprise, but now we must temper those words. The enterprise has recognized a market for specialized *niche dating platforms* like DateMyPet.com (a dating website for pet lovers) or FarmersOnly.com (a dating website for those in the farming or agricultural industry), illustrating that at least some, and perhaps many, people care a great deal more about whether a person is similar in the small stuff. We believe this is a tantalizing question worthy of empirical investigation.

Conclusion

From this review, it is clear that an intergroup perspective on communication can offer great insight into daters' mate selection and interaction behaviors. More work needs to be done to better understand how issues of age, racial hierarchy,

Figure 8.1: Must love chocolate and red wine. Source: Public Domain/Wikimedia. https://commons.wikimedia.org/wiki/File:Red_wine_and_chocolate_pairing.jpg

and gender and race intersectionality influence online and mobile dating. We can see how trends regarding homophily and heterophily shift over time. Changes in daters' demographics and developments in dating technologies will certainly create new patterns that require more in-depth exploration. One such development requiring investigation is the rise of platforms that cater to daters with specific background characteristics such as those discussed above. We have already mentioned dating platforms that focus on daters' age (silversingles.com), love for pets (DateMyPet.com) and agriculture (FarmersOnly.com), but other niche platforms have popped up in the online and mobile dating industry. Some focus on race (Blackpeoplemeet, chispa); others on culture and religion (jdate, Minder, Salaam Swipe). And, of course, some of the longest-standing dating apps were initially focused on sexuality: Grindr is an app designed for men seeking sex with men, and its popularity paved the way for more mainstream dating apps like Tinder and Bumble. How might such niche sites affect dating, mate selection, and interaction?

One of the great (though also troubling) things about the Internet is its ability to gather like-minded people together across time and space. Astute readers might predict that such platforms push homophily to the forefront by matching daters of the same race, culture, sexuality, age, or religion. Interestingly, Thomas (2020) points out that while niche sites may increase endogamy on the particular social characteristic of interest, they could actually create exogamy across other demographic categories. That is, although niche dating pools may consist of people sharing a particular racial, cultural, or religious background, individuals who join a niche dating platform are still likely to vary across other characteristics such as education levels, income, or personality. So, while homophily across a singular social category may be boosted by niche sites, diversity could still be increased overall. More research is needed that examines how patterns of social categorization play out in different dating platforms, and how dating pool diversity and similarity differ across smaller niche platforms and "general" dating platforms, like OkCupid.

References

Adams, M. S., Oye, J., & Parker, T. S. (2003). Sexuality of older adults and the Internet: From sex education to cybersex. *Sexual and Relationship Therapy, 18*, 405–415. https://doi.org/10.1080/1468199031000153991

Allport, G. W. (1954). *The nature of prejudice*. Perseus Books.

Alterovitz, S. S.-R., & Mendelsohn, G. A. (2009). Partner preferences across the life span: Online dating by older adults. *Psychology and Aging, 24*(2), 513–517. https://doi.org/10.1037/a0015897

Anderson, M., Vogels, E. A., & Turner, E. (2020). The virtues and downsides of online dating. *Pew Research Center.* https://www.pewresearch.org/internet/2020/02/06/thevirtues-and-downsides-of-online-dating/

Bem, S. L. (1981). Gender schema theory: A cognitive account of sex typing. *Psychological Review, 88*(4), 354–364. https://doi.org/10.1037/00333-295X.88.4.354

Carr, A. (2016, January). I found out my secret internal Tinder rating and now I wish I hadn't. *Fast Company.* https://www.fastcompany.com/3054871/whats-your-tinder-score-inside-the-apps-internal-ranking-system

Carr, D., & Boerner, K. (2013). Dating after late-life spousal loss: Does it compromise relationships with adult children? *Journal of Aging Studies, 27*(4), 487–498. https://doi.org/ https://doi.org/10.1016/j.jaging.2012.12.009

Crenshaw, K. (1991). Mapping the margins: Intersectionality, identity politics, and violence against women of color. *Stanford Law Review, 43*, 1241–1299. http://dx.doi.org/10.2307/1229039

Crowder, K., & Tolnay, S. (2000). A new marriage squeeze for black women: The role of racial intermarriage by black men. *Journal of Marriage and Family, 62*, 792–807. https://doi.org/10.1111/j.1741-3737.2000.00792.x

Davidson, K. (2002). Gender differences in new partnership choices and constraints for older widows and widowers. *Ageing International, 27*(4), 43–60.

De Jong Gierveld, J. (2004). Remarriage, unmarried cohabitation, living apart together: Partner relationships following bereavement or divorce. *Journal of Marriage and Family, 66*(1), 236–243. https://doi.org/ 10.1111/j.0022-2445.2004.00015.x

Dunaway, J. (2018, Jan 31). Is Tinder Plus' age-based pricing a discount for the young or a surcharge for people over 30? *Slate: Future Tense.* https://slate.com/technology/2018/01/tinder-discriminates-against-older-users-with-higher-fee-court-rules.html

Feliciano, C., Robnett, B., & Komaie, G. (2009). Gendered racial exclusion among white internet daters. *Social Science Research, 38*(1), 39–54. https://doi.org/ 10.1016/j.ssresearch.2008.09.004

Fiske, S. T., & Neuberg, S. L. (1990). A continuum of impression formation, from category-based to individuating processes: Influences of information and motivation on attention and interpretation. In *Advances in experimental social psychology* (Vol. 23, pp. 1–74). Academic Press. https://doi.org/ https://doi.org/10.1016/S0065-2601(08)60317-2

Galinsky, A. D., Hall, E. V., & Cuddy, A. J. (2013). Gendered races: Implications for interracial marriage, leadership selection, and athletic participation. *Psychological Science, 24*(4), 498–506. https://doi.org/ https://doi.org/10.1177/0956797612457783

Granovetter, M. S. (1995). *Getting a job: A study of contacts and careers* (2nd ed). University of Chicago Press.

Herman, M. R., & Campbell, M. E. (2012). I wouldn't, but you can: Attitudes toward interracial relationships. *Social Forces, 41*, 343–358. https://doi.org/10.1016/j.ssresearch.2011.11.007

Lee, D. (2018, Jan 25). Tinder settles age discrimination lawsuit with $11.5 million worth of Super Likes. *The Verge.* https://www.theverge.com/2019/1/25/18197575/tinder-plus-age-discrimination-lawsuit-settlement-super-likes

Lee, K. O. (2016). Temporal dynamics of racial segregation in the United States: An analysis of household residential mobility. *Journal of Urban Affairs.* http://doi.org./10.1111/juaf.12293

Lewis, K. (2013). The limits of racial prejudice. *Proceedings of the National Academy of Sciences, 110*(47), 18814–18819. https://doi.org/10.1073/pnas.1308501110

Lin, K.-H., & Lundquist, J. (2013). Mate selection in cyberspace: The intersection of race, gender, and education. *American Journal of Sociology, 119*, 183–215. https://doi.org/10.1086/673129

Mahay, J., & Lewin, A. (2007). Age and the desire to marry. *Journal of Family Issues, 28*, 706–721. https://doi.org/10.1177/0192513X06297272

Maner, J., Miller, S., Moss, J., Leo, J., & Plant, A. (2012). Motivated social categorization: Fundamental motives enhance people's sensitivity to basic social categories. *Journal of Personality and Social Psychology, 103*, 70–83. https://doi.org/10.1037/a0028172.

McGarty, C. (1999). *The categorization process in social psychology.* Sage.

McMullan, T. (2019, February). Are the algorithms that power dating apps racially biased? *Wired Magazine.* https://www.wired.co.uk/article/racial-bias-dating-apps

McWilliams, S., & Barrett, A. E. (2014). Online dating in middle and later life: Gendered expectations and experiences. *Journal of Family Issues, 35*(3), 411–436. https://doi.org/ https://doi.org/10.1177/0192513X12468437

Moorman, S. M., Booth, A., & Fingerman, K. L. (2006). Women's romantic relationships after widowhood. *Journal of Family Issues, 27*(9), 1281–1304. https://doi.org/10.1177/0192513X06289096

Notopoulos, K. (2014, January 14). The dating app that knows you secretly aren't into guys from other races. *Buzzfeed News.* https://www.buzzfeednews.com/article/katienotopoulos/coffee-meets-bagel-racial-preferences

Perry, S. L. (2013). Religion and whites' attitudes toward interracial marriage with African-Americans, Asians, and Latinos. *Journal for the Scientific Study of Religion, 52*(2), 425–442. https://doi.org/10.1111/jssr.12020

Qian, Z., Lichter, D. T., & Tumin, D. (2018). Divergent pathways to assimilation? Local marriage markets and intermarriage among US Hispanics. *Journal of Marriage and Family, 80*, 271-288. https://doi.org/10.1111/jomf.12423

Roberts, A. W., Ogunwole, S. U., Blakeslee, L., & Rabe, M. A. (2018). The population 65 years and older in the United States: 2016. US Department of Commerce, Economics and Statistics Administration, US Census Bureau. https://www.census.gov/content/dam/Census/library/publications/2018/acs/ACS-38.pdf

Sassler, S. (2010). Partnering across the life course: Sex, relationships, and mate selection. *Journal of Marriage and Family, 72*(3), 557–575. https://doi.org/10.1111/j.1741-3737.2010.00718.x

Schug, J., Alt, N. P., & Klauer, K. C. (2015). Gendered race prototypes: Evidence for the non-prototypicality of Asian men and Black women. *Journal of Experimental Social Psychology, 56*, 121–125. https://doi.org/10.1016/j.jesp.2014.09.012

Schug, J., Alt, N. P., Lu, P. S., Gosin, M., & Fay, J. L. (2017). Gendered race in mass media: Invisibility of Asian men and Black Women in popular magazines. *Psychology of Popular Media Culture, 6* (3), 222–236. https://doi.org/10.1037/ppm0000096

Simmel, G. (1950). *The sociology of Georg Simmel.* Simon and Schuster.

Song, M. (2004). Introduction: Who's at the bottom? Examining claims about racial hierarchy. *Ethnic and Racial Studies, 27*(6), 859–877. https://doi.org/10.1080/0141987042000268503

Spears, R., & Lea, M. (1994). Panacea or panopticon?: The hidden power in computer-mediated communication. *Communication Research, 21*, 427–459. https://doi.org/10.1177/009365094021004001

Tajfel, H. (Ed.) (1978). *Differentiation between social groups: Studies in the social psychology of intergroup relations.* Academic Press.

Thomas, R. J. (2020). Online exogamy reconsidered: Estimating the Internet's effects on racial, educational, religious, political and age assortative mating. *Social Forces, 98*(3), 1257–1286. https://doi.org/ https://doi.org/10.1093/sf/soz060

Tong, S. T., Corriero, E. F., Matheny, R. G., & Hancock, J. T. (2018). Online daters' willingness to use recommender technology for mate selection decisions. In M. de Gemmis, A. Felfernig, P. Lops, J. O' Donovan, G. Semeraro, & M. Willemsen (Eds.), *IntRS'18: Proceedings of* the 5th Joint Workshop on Interfaces and Human Decision Making for Recommender Systems, Vancouver, B. C. (pp. 45–52). Online: CEUR-WS.org. http://ceur-ws.org/Vol-2225/

Warren, E., & Supreme Court of The United States. (1966). U.S. Reports: Loving v. Virginia, 388 U.S. 1. [Periodical]. Library of Congress. https://www.loc.gov/item/usrep388001/.

Wion, R. K., & Loeb, S. J. (2015). Older adults engaging in online dating: What gerontological nurses should know. *Journal of Gerontological Nursing, 41*(10), 25–35. https://doi.org/10.3928/00989134-20150826-67

9

Maintaining Romantic Relationships through Mediated Technologies

Maintenance is not usually something we consciously think about. Maintaining your car, for instance, is a chore—changing the oil, rotating the tires, checking the brake pads. It is not usually something most of us look forward to or enjoy; instead, it is something we feel obligated to do. Most of us perform car maintenance to make sure that our vehicle starts up when we turn the key and runs smoothly so we can drive from place to place. To keep a vehicle in that nice, comfortable, reliable, drivable state requires a little work now and then, which can help us avoid more costly repairs that come from neglect.

Much like our cars, our romantic relationships require maintenance, which includes communication behaviors that couples perform to keep their relationship intact. Trying to keep that relationship in a desirable, satisfactory state requires work. In fact, because romantic relationships are always changing, maintaining them can take quite a bit of effort, and the kind and degree of effort can itself change from time to time. There are things that can threaten the steady state of a couple's relationship—for instance, when one partner begins flirting with a romantic rival. Sometimes, disruption comes from within the relationship itself—such as when one partner begins to feel under-appreciated in the partnership. When these and other kinds of threats and disruptions occur, couples have to put in work to maintain their relationship; otherwise, they may start growing apart and their relationship may begin to dissolve.

We have written about mediated relational maintenance among family members, friends, and couples, previously (see Tong & Walther, 2011); in this chapter, we plan to expand on our prior work by focusing exclusively on mediated maintenance in romantic relationships. We begin by exploring the basic definitions that theorists have used to explicate relational maintenance, as well as what motivates couples to engage in maintenance behaviors. We then review examples of the various maintenance strategies that have been studied in the research literature. After reviewing these background concepts, we then think about the role of technology. What kinds of technology do couples use for maintenance communication? How do those mediated channels affect the performance and achievement of romantic relational maintenance? We conclude the chapter by offering ideas for future work that extend our thinking on mediated maintenance behavior in modern romance.

Definitions, Behaviors, and Motivations of Maintenance

Relational maintenance is a frequently researched topic across communication and psychology, and because of the diversity of study, there is no one, agreed-upon perspective. Dindia (2003) notes that within the long tradition of maintenance research, it is difficult to find a consistent definition. In its most basic form, maintenance can be thought of as simply keeping a relationship in existence (Duck, 1988). In this very general definition, there is no attention paid to each partner's feelings or the nature of the relationship itself. Other theorists offer definitions that account for how partners feel, both about each other and about the relationship. From this perspective, maintenance is about more than just sustaining a relationship; it includes moving toward a "mutually satisfying end state" (Dindia, 2003). Therefore, these definitions add another dimension by suggesting that relationships have to do more than just "exist": Both partners have to feel a certain level of intimacy and satisfaction in order for a relationship to be truly "maintained" (Dindia & Canary, 1993).

Most scholars agree that while maintenance can be enacted at all stages of a relationship, such behaviors are typically enacted when partners feel they have a close, bonded union. In the stage model introduced earlier in the book, this might be when partners feel their relationship move from initiation or experimenting stages into intensifying and integrating, and from there into the bonding stages (Knapp, 1978); and many scholars of relational maintenance suggest that relationships start to unravel and take steps toward dissolution when maintenance is ignored.

Uncovering Maintenance Behaviors

Working from these definitions, communication researchers in the early 1990s embarked on the ambitious task of categorizing the behaviors and strategies that people used to maintain their relationships. For example, Stafford and Canary's (1991) foundational typology featured five maintenance strategies uncovered from romantic couples' responses to questionnaires:

(1) *Positivity:* being cheerful and optimistic
(2) *Openness:* being direct through self-disclosure and discussion of the relationship
(3) *Assurances:* stressing commitment, love, demonstrating faithfulness
(4) *Sharing tasks:* helping equally with tasks facing the couple
(5) *Networks:* time spent with common friends/acquaintances

Later on, the typology was expanded to include *conflict management* (see Chapter 10) and *advice* (Stafford, Dainton, & Haas, 2000). The typology approach suggested that maintenance behaviors were deliberate and enacted consciously by individuals in an effort to sustain positive outcomes like satisfaction and commitment.

Other theorists (Duck, 2005) pointed out that some maintenance processes are not always so deliberate. Couples often engage in *mundane* conversations about ordinary topics, everyday activities, and routine observations. These exchanges may seem banal, but they fulfill multiple communication functions, such as the chance to receive *self-validation* (or confirmation of their own views of themselves and of life events) from a close partner. Self-validation can in turn reduce anxiety and increase trust between partners (North & Swann, 2009; Ogolsky, Monk, Rice, Theisen, & Maniotes, 2017). They also provide a chance for increased *emotional integration* between partners or "ratification for one's own emotional responses to events" (Duck, 2005, p. 2011). By "invit(ing) participation in, concurrence about, or confirmation of an individual's forays into these important psychological processes" couples' exchange of mundane thoughts and interpretations of everyday life can become an important form of maintenance that helps sustain the relationship's existence (Tong & Walther, 2011, p. 113).

Interestingly, social media platforms often facilitate mundane exchanges by prioritizing *phatic communication*—or everyday musings and small talk, "language used in free, aimless, social intercourse" (Malinowski, 1972, p. 142). On Facebook, Twitter, and Instagram, although the message content can be important, more often it is the social function of maintaining one's relationships that is prioritized in the message exchange process (Miller, 2008). Likes, hearts, and upvotes are *paralinguistic digital cues* that serve primarily as phatic communication in social media—"aimless, automatic" responses that may have less to do with liking the actual message content, and more to do with signaling social support to the original poster (Hayes, Carr, & Wohn, 2016, p. 182). It is precisely these mundane exchanges that couples who are separated during a day's work, or across the miles, might otherwise miss in their relationships. Viewing a partner's mundane musings on social media, or having one's musings commented upon, can help fill that void, especially for couples who are in long-distance romantic relationships (Vitak, 2014).

Motivations for Maintenance

Although these behavioral typologies have been extremely useful for cataloging and describing couples' maintenance behaviors, other theorists began to realize that this approach didn't explain *why* couples engaged in these strategies. So, research also began uncovering the motivations behind romantic maintenance behaviors. Many theorists have relied on *social exchange* principles to explain maintenance. Social exchange approaches use an economic metaphor, construing relationships as a complex set of projected costs and benefits calculated by each partner. According to Stafford (2020), within a relationship each partner is not necessarily trying to maximize their personal rewards but is instead motivated by an innate sense of fairness whereby both partners feel like their costs and rewards are equal. When one's relational rewards outweigh the perceived costs, that partner may feel *over-benefited* in the relationship; conversely, when one is putting in greater effort for fewer rewards, they might feel *under-benefited*. Both states create feelings of inequity in the relationship, in which a person's inputs do not match their outputs. This disequilibrium can threaten a partner's desire to continue to maintain the relationship. Not surprisingly, while both kinds of relational inequity can occur, most research findings illustrate that feeling under-benefited is more strongly correlated with a person's relational dissatisfaction and distress (Stafford, 2020).

Apart from the social exchange perspective, Ogolsky et al. (2017) offer two broader classes of motives that drive couples' performance of maintenance behaviors. Strategies motivated by *threat mitigation* are often *reactionary* behaviors that occur in response to some kind of threat presented to the couple's relationship. Partners have to focus on protecting their relationship from *external* forces that can jeopardize its very presence, like romantic rivals, alternative partners, or a partner's sexual or emotional transgressions. Sometimes, threats can be *internal*, such as one partner's feeling of inadequacy, or (as noted above) feeling over-benefited or under-benefited. Threat mitigation behaviors are motivated by couples' desire to sustain the relationship's existence and stability and "minimize lasting harm" (p. 276).

On the other hand, *relationship enhancement* motivations influence couples to create relationship outcomes like satisfaction, intimacy, and commitment. These motives incite *proactive* behaviors that (unlike threat mitigation) are not performed in response to an outside stimulus, but instead come from a desire to "facilitate and sustain positive relational development" (Ogolsky et al., 2017, p. 276). Enhancement behaviors might include things like open relationship talk, social support, humor, or generosity towards one's partner.

In the sections that follow, we survey the kinds of mediated technology that couples could use to execute maintenance behaviors. We borrow Ogolsky et al.'s (2017) motivations, as well as Stafford and Canary's (1991) foundational typology to help situate the kinds of behaviors that romantic partners use in the maintenance process. Finally, we consider how the features of various communication channels that couples use for maintenance could influence the functions and outcomes that they achieve within their relationships.

The Use of Mediated Communication for Relational Maintenance

In Chapter 7, we noted how oftentimes people tend to think of face-to-face as the "gold standard" or ideal form of romantic communication. Obviously, the need to be physically present is essential for the performance of critical physical intimacy maintenance behaviors such as hugging, kissing, or holding hands. However, circumstances often force romantic partners to spend time away from each other, and during those moments, most still find ways to maintain their relationships. Writing letters to each other from a distance is a form of "low-tech" mediated maintenance. Elaborate letters penned by Beethoven, Napoleon, and Frida Kahlo to their respective lovers have become famous examples. Case in point: Ernest Hemingway's steamy love letters to Marlene Dietrich, which Lily Rothman (2014) of *Time Magazine* called an early version of a "sext" message. Later on, the telephone became a popular tool to facilitate maintenance and remains so today (see also Chapter 2).

Research into mediated maintenance has continued into the present, with studies focusing on one of two kinds of relational contexts. The bulk of mediated maintenance research has been conducted on *long-distance romantic partnerships*—or those individuals who live apart and do not engage in frequent FtF communication. Long-distance marriages are relatively common today. In 2000, a US government survey estimated that 2.7 million American adults were living apart from their spouses; by 2017 that number had increased to about 3.9 million (Pinkser, 2019). The greater frequency of long-distance relationships could be driven by changes in employment arrangements, or perhaps other life circumstances like military deployment, incarceration, or personal health (see for example, Maguire et al., 2013; Merolla, 2010). Comparatively less research has explored mediated maintenance among proximate couples, or partners who live together in the same home or in another physically proximate place but are likely to spend a majority of their day at work or school, apart from their partner (e.g., Toma & Choi, 2016). But for both long-distance and geographically-close couples, technology can be an effective means of performing relational maintenance.

Think about the last time a close partner, friend, or family member sent you an "I love you" text message. Perhaps you received it when you were in class, or sitting at your desk at work, or maybe in line at the grocery store. When your phone pinged, that signaled the arrival of a maintenance message. That warm fuzzy feeling, wherever you experienced it, confirms the powerful affordances offered by mediated communication.

When using communication technologies for maintenance, partners can, and often do, spend more time on *message construction* than in typical circumstances. They often think more carefully about what kind of message they want to send and how they want to say it. Moreover, the *documentable* or *recordable* nature of mediated channels and its *asynchronous* nature both provide individuals with greater *availability* and *persistent access* to those messages, giving partners additional time to reread and ruminate on positive maintenance messages. Persistent access can also facilitate *idealization* or *positive illusions* of one's partner. A written text that preserves positive, warm sentiment can be revisited at any time, thus enhancing the likelihood of exaggerated or intensified impressions of one's partner (Walther, 1996). The *portability* of mobile devices also means that partners can take those maintenance messages with them wherever they go, literally holding them in their pocket to view whenever they want. It is hard to imagine doing that with a FtF or phone conversation (unless you take the time to audio record conversations you have with your partner, which seems like a lot of work). If you've ever replayed a voicemail from a loved one or reread a loving text message that someone sent to you, then you know firsthand how these features of mobile communication can combine to keep your relationship in a steady, satisfied state.

In sum, the combination of these features can facilitate relational maintenance outcomes like heightened feelings of closeness by allowing romantic partners to send and receive supportive, reassuring, or positive messages at any time throughout the day. Some individuals even report using their phones and computers to maintain their relationships while they sleep—couples in long-distance relationships, for example, report cueing up their webcams to stream a live feed of themselves sleeping through the night. In this way, they can experience "sleeping next to each other" even if they aren't in the same bed (Cray, 2020). Clearly, mediated maintenance can help sustain feelings of intimacy even when couples aren't physically co-present (or even awake).

Incorporating Mobile and Computing Technology into Relational Maintenance

In thinking about the ways in which mobile and computing technology can facilitate maintenance, a related question you might ask is: What specific channels are couples using? The research literature suggests that couples incorporate many different kinds of platforms into their maintenance communication. Ku, Chu, and Tseng (2013) found that generally, people selected social media, email, and instant messaging (IM) to maintain all kinds of interpersonal connections—including family, friendships, and romantic relationships. Among geographically-close romantic couples, Toma and Choi (2016) found that their sample of 211 college students used text messaging, phone calls, Facebook, and IM most frequently; smaller percentages of their sample reported using Twitter, email, video chat, and gaming.

As reflected in the list generated by Toma and Choi (2016), the different systems that people report using for maintenance include both *private* (i.e., one-to-one) channels like telephone, IM, and texting, and *public* (i.e., one-to-many)

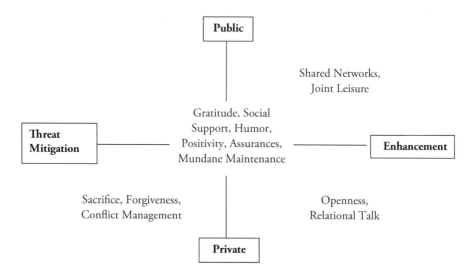

Figure 9.1: Organizing framework of mediated maintenance. Source: Authors

social media channels like Twitter, Facebook, or Snapchat. In the past, maintenance has largely been conceptualized as something performed by couples privately, but as social media platforms blend public and private channels they create a unique environment for the performance of mediated maintenance. As noted by Tong and Walther (2011), the broadcast reach of social media, combined with its participatory nature, provide emerging advantages for the exchange of public maintenance communications between romantic couples. For example, when people post updates about their partners, announce their marriages, and share other important relational milestones online, friends and contacts in their network can comment on these events and offer their support and validation of the relationship as a whole, or of each partner individually.

Given that maintenance can occur privately or publicly, what factors influence people's decisions about which channels to use to perform mediated maintenance? Figure 9.1 shows an organizing framework that consists of two dimensions: (1) the specific maintenance *motivation* or *function* on the horizontal axis (Ogolsky et al., 2017; Stafford & Canary, 1991), and (2) the *public* or *private* *nature* of the mediated channel on the vertical axis. Additionally, in considering how and when individuals choose to use certain channels for specific maintenance functions, we also have to take into account the *social norms* surrounding the disclosure of information (McLaughlin & Vitak, 2012).

Public Displays of Maintenance versus Private Maintenance Moments

If you recall, relational *enhancement* maintenance functions are achieved through performance of proactive behaviors designed to move the relationship toward desirable outcomes such as relational closeness or satisfaction. We define *public-enhancing* maintenance as enhancement behaviors performed in public social media spaces. For example, when you get to know your partner's friends and family by spending time with them, that is often considered an interactive, enhancing maintenance strategy (Stafford & Canary, 1991). Social media platforms help you formally connect with your significant other's friends through Instagram, Facebook, or Twitter. These platforms can facilitate maintenance by literally displaying *shared networks* and evidence of the *joint leisure* time you spend with members of your partner's network. On the other hand, *private-enhancing* maintenance such as *relational talk*—which consists of frank, open discussions about a romantic relationship—can promote heightened trust or intimacy, but such talks are typically less suited for public display. Bazarova (2012) noted that people often see others' public disclosure of intimate information on social media as inappropriate and may judge those who "over-share" on public social media platforms more harshly than those who keep such content to themselves.

Other maintenance behaviors are driven by *threat mitigation* motives. As reactionary behaviors designed to minimize pressures on the relationship, these are often performed privately. For example, couples tend to engage in *conflict management* privately; research has demonstrated that partners who publicly engage in fights, feuds, and name-calling on social media platforms like Facebook risk violating social norms of appropriateness; furthermore, those couples who carry out conflict in full view of their networks risk their friends' social disapproval (McLaughlin & Vitak, 2012). Similarly, displays of *sacrifice* for, or *forgiveness* of, one's partner are best performed in private settings, otherwise people risk similar violations of socially normative expectations. For example, publicly posting to Facebook that you are forgiving your partner for committing a sexual transgression indirectly shames your partner for committing the misdeed, and also indicates that your relationship is not in a particularly stable state. Neither of these disclosures will help *your* public image, either. Clearly, while this is problematic from an individual impression management perspective, such public displays of forgiveness might also not be in the couple's collective interest in terms of overall positive relational outcomes. Note that we are not suggesting that all weaknesses in a romantic relationship must be held in the utmost secrecy; however, public sharing of such weaknesses via social media—where you don't have control (or you appear not to have control)—is likely not in one's best interest.

Brandon has a close friend who told him the story of one of his social media acquaintances who recently went through a messy divorce. She frequently uses Facebook as a place to vent about her former partner. Recently, several of her friends expressed concern that she may be oversharing in a public environment and that her critiques of her partner could be making it back to the children that she and her partner still parent together. She took the time to explain that she very carefully curates the list of who among her acquaintances is able to see her posts about her former partner so as to alleviate the concern that her behavior may be inadvertently harming her children. As most threat mitigation mainte-nance functions tend to be fulfilled through private channels such as texting, telephone, video chat, or IM, you can see that the upper left-hand quadrant of *public-mitigation* maintenance in Figure 9.1 is relatively empty.

As you will also see in Figure 9.1, there are several behaviors sitting right in the middle of both axes. This suggests that they are flexible enough to be commu-nicated publicly *or* privately, depending on the specific behavioral motivation and the media channel each individual decides to use. For example, demonstrating *gratitude* (e.g., being thankful or showing appreciation to one's partner), posting an *assurance* message (e.g., "I love you"), displaying *social support* for one's partner, or just sending a *funny meme* or *mundane status update* can be done both publicly through a social media post, or in a private message. In choosing to perform such maintenance functions publicly, individuals could be exercising a form of (preemptive) threat mitigation, relational enhancement, or both. Indeed, *public maintenance displays* often fulfill several different communication functions at once. In Figure 9.2, imagine Betty tags her boyfriend, Dan, in her Instagram post, captioning it: "I love you more than ice cream!" Betty might be fulfilling an enhancement function, trying to tell Dan how much she loves him, and how committed she is to their relationship. But such public displays of affection, sup-port, or gratitude could also serve more protective maintenance functions. From a threat mitigation standpoint, Betty might be performing a form of *relational "scent marking"*—analogous, in a sense, to animals that use urine or visual marks (e.g., ground scratching) to mark their territory and warn off competitors. Here, she uses social media to signal her relational status to others. Frequently posting on a partner's Facebook wall, liking or favoriting their tweets, or tagging them

Figure 9.2: Betty, Dan, & ice cream. Public displays of maintenance can fulfill multiple communication functions simultaneously. Source: Authors

in Instagram photos can all work as virtual *tie signs* (Tong & Walther, 2011). These are displays of mutual belonging that notify outsiders that two people are connected or in a relationship. In this way, public displays of maintenance can privately reinforce the relationship for the couple, and also remind the larger network of observers who see such displays that they are in love (and also off limits to outside suitors).

The myriad choices that individuals face with regard to mediated maintenance can make for a complex set of decision making processes. In practice, these decisions are not all or nothing—instead, partners often maintain their relationships through multiple forms of media. This practice is known as *mixed-mode* communication (see also Chapter 7), integrating different kinds of mediated channels, as well as FtF interaction (Parks, 2017).

Additional Factors Motivating Maintenance: Individual, Relational, and Technological

In addition to the motivations discussed above, there are other factors that might affect a couple's selection of communication channels when performing maintenance. Below, we explore how individual characteristics, qualities of the relationship, and the features of specific platforms might influence how people integrate technology into relationships with romantic partners.

Individual factors. Past research has shown that our *personality characteristics* or our *attachment styles* might play a role in how we approach maintenance in romantic relationships. According to the original theory (Ainsworth & Bowlby, 1991), the attachment system is formed when we are extremely young. We form initial attachment bonds to the primary caregiver, usually a parent, who provides us with love, protection, and support during infancy. If that initial attachment is secure, the child feels loved and confident, and carries that secure feeling into their social environment when relating with others later on in life. Conversely, if that initial attachment is weak, a child feels neglected, anxious, and insecure. As such the theory predicts that the attachment system that is forged during childhood can affect adult relationships (Hazan & Shaver, 1987).

Both Guerrero and Bachman (2006) and Simon and Baxter (1993) note that individuals with secure attachment styles—characterized as having positive views of themselves and their partners, higher self-esteem, and a comfort level with intimacy—are more likely to engage in prosocial kinds of maintenance, such as positivity, openness, and the expression of assurances. On the other hand, those with dismissive and fearful-avoidant attachment styles hold "negative working models" of their romantic partners and sometimes develop romantic insecurities, such as the fear of getting hurt or rejected. These kinds of attachment styles have been linked to reduced satisfaction in relationships, as well as enactment of negative or destructive maintenance behaviors like avoidance, conflict, or jealousy. Partners might find themselves turning to technology to achieve certain functions—for example, using social media to "check up" on a partner through electronic surveillance or stalking (e.g., Tokunaga, 2016; Vogels & Anderson, 2020; see also, Chapter 11).

Additionally, our feelings about various social computing platforms (and their features) also affect if and how we use them for relational maintenance. The *technology acceptance model* (Davis, 1989) suggests that our perceptions about how easy a specific system is to use, how much we trust the system, and even how enjoyable or "playful" we think a platform is, can all influence our decisions to use it. Take, for instance, *ephemeral* forms of social media, like Snapchat. The playful and visual nature of these platforms do make them attractive options for maintenance, especially among younger users who have taken the time to understand and integrate them into their media use habits. In addition to the playfulness and focus on visual content, ephemeral media like Snapchat offer a unique "self-destructive" feature; messages sent back and forth between partners via ephemeral media are not permanently documented but are instead deleted after a short viewing period (Bayer et al., 2016). The ephemerality of Snapchat can heighten users' feelings of privacy, making them feel more empowered to send messages that might contain more sensitive information (e.g., sexts, self-disclosures, secrets) (Charteris, Gregory, & Masters, 2018). From a maintenance perspective, sending this kind of self-disclosive information can lead to positive outcomes if it fosters more openness, reciprocal exchange, and trust between partners in a relationship. In fact, users of Snapchat note its capacity to strengthen bonds with close relational others (Vaterlaus, Barnett, Roche, & Young, 2016). However, Makki et al. (2018) also found that individuals who do not trust Snapchat—that is, who doubt that their snaps will truly be deleted either by the Snapchat system or others—had a weaker intention to use it for maintenance functions. The case of Snapchat underscores that our perceptions and feelings about technology can affect how we use it for relational communication.

Relational factors. There are also important relational factors that might influence how we appropriate technology for maintenance. One obvious factor is *partner media use.* It is impossible to initiate positivity or send an assurance message via Facebook if that partner is not using Facebook, too. Depending on the *longevity of relationship*, couples may also develop specific media use habits or patterns of maintenance exchange. For example, Stephanie sometimes sends her husband, Daniel, "emoji-texts," which are a series of emojis strung together to form a message (see Figure 9.3). To an outsider, this would look like gibberish, but to Stephanie and Daniel, these are texts that signal that they are thinking of the other partner. Such habitual use might also help define meanings for specific channels used for maintenance purposes.

As an asynchronous channel, text messaging might signal that one's partner can read and respond whenever is convenient; in contrast, a phone call might signal urgency and the need to talk right away. This intimate knowledge of channel significance is learned when partners engage in repeated and habitual mediated maintenance and develop specific and emergent patterns of technology use (Cramer & Jacobs, 2015). Finally, *trust* in one's partner is essential for the exchange of mediated maintenance. In the Snapchat example above, a person

> 🏃 a little late... 🚗 you at 🏠

Figure 9.3: Shared maintenance messages. An example of the kind of emoji text that the author, Stephanie, often exchanges with her partner, Daniel. Although this is a habitual form of maintenance interaction for them, to an outsider it might seem strange. (Can you decipher the message?) Source: Authors.

might feel comfortable sending their partner a sensitive message because they believe their partner will not share it with anyone outside of the relationship. But such openness only works if partners have a sufficient level of trust. Likewise, it can require trust for partners to allow each other access to their computing devices. According to Pew Research (Vogels & Anderson, 2020), it is fairly common for couples to share passwords and login information for their cellphones (75%), email (62%), or social media accounts (42%) with their romantic partners.

Although the above examples indicate how couples integrate mediated technology into their relationships, because CMC and mobile media are such popular tools, there is growing concern that they can be used unethically and ultimately damage a couple's relationship rather than help sustain it (Hales, 2008). As Caughlin and Wang (2020) note, romantic maintenance through mobile media does not always lead to positive outcomes. We explore the "dark side" of dating, romance, and CMC more in Chapter 11, but note here that certain relational factors such as a couple's media use, relational longevity, and trust indicate how both partners must work together in order for mediated maintenance behaviors to contribute to a relationship's continued existence and success.

Technological factors. Up till this point, we have focused primarily on how mediated channels are used by couples as conduits for maintenance. That is, we have discussed how partners use phone calls, text messages, and social media to sustain relationship and bring about greater satisfaction, closeness, and intimacy. But another body of *technoference* literature has focused on how the use of mobile and computing technology in the presence of one's partner can actually be problematic. Evidence from the Pew Research Center (Vogels & Anderson, 2020) suggests that "40% of partnered Americans are bothered by the amount of time their partner spends on their cell phone" (p. 3).

Imagine a couple, Beth and Mike, who have just gotten home from work. Beth is trying to talk to Mike about her stressful day and feels annoyed when Mike picks up his phone during their conversation. There's even an expression for such behavior, *phubbing*, a portmanteau of the words "phone" and "snubbing." The practice has been shown to lead to increased tension and conflict between interactants (Roberts & David, 2016). For some, the mere presence of a mobile phone during a conversation creates a disturbance that can interrupt that feeling of connection with their partner (McDaniel & Coyne, 2016). Interestingly, the very tools that can facilitate open, positive maintenance communication when partners are apart from each other can also cause stress and conflict for partners who are physically co-present.

Conclusion

The culture of social media use often encourages people to share the everyday aspects of their lives, and this includes information about their romantic relationships. According to recent survey data by Pew Research, upwards of 80% of social media users report that they see others in their networks posting details about their romantic relationships (Vogels & Anderson, 2020). In examining specific demographic trends, these data indicate that the practice of publicly sharing private moments is especially prevalent among younger users ages 18–29 (48%), compared to the over-50 crowd (11%). Additionally, LGBTQ individuals (41%) are more likely to have disclosed personal relationship details on social media, compared to heterosexual individuals (27%); and those who are in committed dating relationships (48%) are far more likely than married couples (24%) to post information about their love lives online (Vogels & Anderson, 2020). From these data, it appears that younger users who are involved in committed dating relationships are those most likely to have used social media for public displays of maintenance.

We suggest that, regardless of age group or commitment level, romantic couples are more likely to perform or disclose certain kinds of maintenance functions in public than they are in private. Enhancement behaviors reviewed above, such as the expression of assurances, gratitude, positivity, humor, support, and shared networks are likely to be shared through public social media venues, whereas threat mitigation behaviors such as conflict, sacrifice, and forgiveness are more likely to be performed privately. We hope that future work might delve more deeply into individuals' channel selection decisions, as well as the multiple motives and functions (e.g., threat mitigation, relational enhancement, relational- and self-presentation, relational scent marking) that may be served by the decision to engage in public versus private maintenance. It also seems, as mentioned above, that among younger social media users, public maintenance is a habitual, recognized practice; this suggests that the social norms regarding what information is appropriate to share, when, and with whom might be changing as younger daters begin engaging in public maintenance more frequently. Future research might interrogate those normative perceptions and influences to explore if and how they differ among various cohorts of romantic partners and daters.

Another issue that deserves more investigation is how romantic partners living in the same geographical space use technology to communicate with one another. As we have mentioned elsewhere in this book, CMC scholars have regularly explored the initial stages of relationships, or how people facilitate ongoing relationships over long distances using CMC. In those situations, technology obviously provides an excellent tool. However, even for those partners who live close to or with one another, technologically mediated communication is very regularly employed (in our experiences with our partners, Brandon reports that he regularly texts his partner, Jen, who is sitting only on the other end of the sectional couch; at their home, Stephanie and her husband, Daniel, will often call each other instead of running up and down the stairs to talk FtF—basically using their phones as a modern-day version of the walkie-talkie). Future research ought to explore whether such behaviors are normal (they may well not be), how common they are, and most importantly why they occur. What functions do these mediated maintenance behaviors intend to satisfy, and how successful are these behaviors at accomplishing their aims?

Finally, in examining the Pew Research survey data, we note an interesting discrepancy: Although nearly 80% of social media users in their sample report seeing others' post about their love life, only 28% reported sharing or discussing their relationships online (Vogels & Anderson, 2020). This implies that either (a) there is a small group of people who regularly share details of their relationships online, or (b) people are under-reporting the frequency with which they post about their romantic relationships on social media, or (c) a little bit of both of these explanations is at work. Future work might explore this discrepancy—are there certain kinds of individuals or couples who are more likely to share relational information publicly online? Do people perceive such relational sharing as "inappropriate" and are thus embarrassed to admit that they do so, even though it is (apparently) a large part of their own social media feed? As public maintenance display is still an emerging practice, larger social-level judgments, interpretations, and opinions of the practice are clearly still being formed and remain a topic for future scholarship.

Additionally, as maintenance displays become more common, a related question is what effect they have on the couples' shared networks? If 80% of us report seeing others' relational posts in our social media feeds, how does this impact us, as observers? Does it prompt us to scrutinize our own relationships and contemplate how they measure up to those we see on Instagram or Facebook? Does seeing others' public displays of affection make us feel better or worse about our own relationships in comparison? If our feeds are cluttered with others' public expressions of gratitude and support, do we develop similar expectations of our own partners? Existing work in communication and psychology has explored such *social comparison* effects in Facebook at the individual level, implying that the overly positive content that people craft and display as part of their social media self-image creates an environment that is ripe for increased envy and jealousy; and too much self-comparison can lead to depression (see for review, Appel, Gerlach, & Crusius, 2016). Future work might expand exploration of social comparison effects to the relational level to see if public displays of maintenance have any impact on the larger audience of social media observers in terms of their envy and overall satisfaction with romantic partners and relationships (Vogels & Anderson, 2020).

As hinted at above, mediated maintenance in romantic relationships is not all sweetness and light; there's a "dark side" to maintenance that does not pertain to the protective, proactive, and positive relational outcomes we mainly highlighted in this chapter. Technology can be used unethically for more destructive or dysfunctional purposes that can ultimately lead to relational dissolution or termination. The advantages of mobile communication can quickly become disadvantages. Research shows that couples' over-reliance on texting can lead to misinterpretation and conflict (Brody & Pena, 2015), or heightened expectations for constant availability (Baym, 2015). From the research reviewed in this chapter, it appears that couples who develop shared understanding about how to integrate mediated technology into their relationship fare best. However, because media systems and usage patterns are constantly evolving and changing, it is a safe bet that our relational maintenance behaviors will continue to do so as well.

References

Ainsworth, M. S., & Bowlby, J. (1991). An ethological approach to personality development. *American Psychologist*, *46*(4), 333–341. https://doi.org/10.1037/0003-066X.46.4.333

Appel, H., Gerlach, A. L., & Crusius, J. (2016). The interplay between Facebook use, social comparison, envy, and depression. *Current Opinion in Psychology*, *9*, 44–49. https://doi.org/10.1016/j.copsyc.2015.10.006

Bayer, J. B., Ellison, N. B., Schoenebeck, S. Y., & Falk, E. B. (2016). Sharing the small moments: Ephemeral social interaction on Snapchat. *Information, Communication & Society*, *19*(7), 956–977. https://doi.org/10.1080/1369118X.2015.1084349

Baym, N. K. (2015). *Personal connections in the digital age*. John Wiley & Sons.

Bazarova, N. N. (2012). Public intimacy: Disclosure interpretation and social judgments on Facebook. *Journal of Communication*, *62*(5), 815–832. https://doi.org/10.1111/j.1460-2466.2012.01664.x

Brody, N., & Peña, J. (2015). Equity, relational maintenance, and linguistic features of text messaging. *Computers in Human Behavior*, *49*, 499–506. https://doi.org/10.1016/j.chb.2015.03.037

Caughlin, J. P., & Wang, N. (2020). Relationship maintenance in the age of technology. In B. G. Ogolsky & J. K. Monk (Eds.), *Relationship maintenance: Theory, process, and context*. Cambridge University Press.

Charteris, J., Gregory, S., & Masters, Y. (2018). 'Snapchat', youth subjectivities and sexuality: disappearing media and the discourse of youth innocence. *Gender and Education*, *30*(2), 205–221. https://doi.org/10.1080/09540253.2016.1188198

Cramer, H., & Jacobs, M. L. (2015, April). Couples' communication channels: What, when & why? In *Proceedings of the 33rd annual ACM conference on human factors in computing systems* (pp. 709–712). https://doi.org/10.1145/2702123.2702356

Cray, K. (2020, January). The couples who sleep 'together' over videochat. *The Atlantic*. https://www.theatlantic.com/family/archive/2020/01/couples-who-share-bed-over-videochat/604348/

Davis, F. D. (1989). Perceived usefulness, perceived ease of use, and user acceptance of information technology. *MIS Quarterly*, *13*, 319–340. https://doi.org/10.2307/249008

Dindia, K. (2003). Definitions and perspectives on relational maintenance communication. In D. J. Canary & M. Dainton (Eds.), *Maintaining relationships through communication: Relational, contextual, and cultural variations* (pp. 51–77). Lawrence Erlbaum.

Dindia, K., & Canary, D. J. (1993). Definitions and theoretical perspectives on relational maintenance. *Journal of Social and Personal Relationships*, *10*, 163–173. https://doi.org/10.1177/026540759301000201

Duck, S. (1988). *Relating to others*. Open University Press.

Duck, S. (2005). How do you tell someone you're letting go? *The Psychologist*, *18*(4), 210–213.

Goodboy, A. K., & Bolkan, S. (2011). Attachment and the use of negative relational maintenance behaviors in romantic relationships. *Communication Research Reports*, *28*(4), 327–336. https://doi.org/10.1080/08824096.2011.616244

Guerrero, L. K., & Bachman, G. F. (2006). Associations among relational maintenance behaviors, attachment-style categories, and attachment dimensions. *Communication Studies*, *57*(3), 341–361. https://doi.org/10.1080/10510970600845982

Hales, K. (2008). Ethical issues in relational maintenance via computer-mediated communication. *Journal of Information, Communication, and Ethics in Society*, *7*(1), 9–24. https://doi.org/10.1108/14779960910938061

Hayes, R. A., Carr, C. T., & Wohn, D. Y. (2016). One click, many meanings: Interpreting paralinguistic digital affordances in social media. *Journal of Broadcasting & Electronic Media*, *60*(1), 171–187. https://doi.org/10.1080/08838151.2015.1127248

Hazan, C., & Shaver, P. (1987). Romantic love conceptualized as an attachment process. *Journal of Personality and Social Psychology*, *52*(3), 511–524. https://doi.org/10.1037/0022-3514.52.3.511

Knapp, M. L. (1978). *Social intercourse: From greeting to goodbye*. Allyn and Bacon.

Ku, Y. C., Chu, T. H., & Tseng, C. H. (2013). Gratifications for using CMC technologies: A comparison among SNS, IM, and e-mail. *Computers in Human Behavior*, *29*(1), 226–234. https://doi.org/10.1016/j.chb.2012.08.009

Maguire, K. C., Heinemann-LaFave, D., & Sahlstein, E. (2013). "To be so connected, yet not at all": Relational presence, absence, and maintenance in the context of a wartime deployment. *Western Journal of Communication*, *77*(3), 249–271. https://doi.org/10.1080/10570314.2012.757797

Makki, T. W., DeCook, J. R., Kadylak, T., & Lee, O. J. (2018). The social value of snapchat: An exploration of affiliation motivation, the technology acceptance model, and relational maintenance in snapchat use. *International Journal of Human-Computer Interaction*, *34*(5), 410–420. https://doi.org/10.1080/10447318.2017.1357903

Malinowski, B. (1972). Phatic communion. *Communication in face-to-face interaction*. Penguin Harmondsworth.

McDaniel, B. T., & Coyne, S. M. (2016). "Technoference": The interference of technology in couple relationships and implications for women's personal and relational well-being. *Psychology of Popular Media Culture*, *5*(1), 85–98. https://doi.org/10.1037/ppm0000065

McLaughlin, C., & Vitak, J. (2012). Norm evolution and violation on Facebook. *New Media & Society*, *14*(2), 299–315. https://doi.org/10.1177/1461444811412712

Merolla, A. J. (2010). Relational maintenance during military deployment: Perspectives of wives of deployed US soldiers. *Journal of Applied Communication Research*, *38*(1), 4–26. https://doi.org/10.1080/00909880903483557

Miller, V. (2008). New media, networking and phatic culture. *Convergence*, *14*(4), 387–400. https://doi.org/10.1177/1354856508094659

North, R. J., & Swann Jr., W. B. (2009). Self-verification 360: Illuminating the light and dark sides. *Self and Identity*, *8*(2–3), 131–146. https://doi.org/10.1080/15298860802501516

Ogolsky, B. G., Monk, J. K., Rice, T. M., Theisen, J. C., & Maniotes, C. R. (2017). Relationship maintenance: A review of research on romantic relationships. *Journal of Family Theory & Review*, *9*(3), 275–306. https://doi.org/10.1111/jftr.12205

Parks, M. R. (2017). Embracing the challenges and opportunities of mixed-media relationships. *Human Communication Research*, *43*(4), 505–517. https://doi.org/10.1111/hcre.12125

Pinkser, J. (2019, May). The new long-distance relationship. *The Atlantic* . https://www.theatlantic.com/family/archive/2019/05/long-distance-relationships/589144/

Roberts, J. A., & David, M. E. (2016). My life has become a major distraction from my cell phone: Partner phubbing and relationship satisfaction among romantic partners. *Computers in Human Behavior*, *54*, 134–141. https://doi.org/10.1016/j.chb.2015.07.058

Rothman, L. (2014, March 11). A sext from Ernest Hemingway (sort of). *Time Magazine*. https://time.com/20198/hemingway-dietrich-letter/

Simon, E. P., & Baxter, L. A. (1993). Attachment-style differences in relationship maintenance strategies. *Western Journal of Communication, 57*(4), 416–430. https://doi.org/10.1080/10570319309374465

Stafford, L. (2020). Communal strength, exchange orientation, equity, and relational maintenance. *Journal of Social and Personal Relationships.* https://doi.org/10.1177/0265407520923741

Stafford, L., & Canary, D. J. (1991). Maintenance strategies and romantic relationship type, gender and relational characteristics. *Journal of Social and Personal relationships, 8*(2), 217–242. https://doi.org/10.1177/0265407591082004

Stafford, L., Dainton, M., & Haas, S. (2000). Measuring routine and strategic relational maintenance: Scale revision, sex versus gender roles, and the prediction of relational characteristics. *Communications Monographs, 67*(3), 306–323. https://doi.org/10.1080/03637750009376512

Tokunaga, R. S. (2016). Interpersonal surveillance over social network sites: Applying a theory of negative relational maintenance and the investment model. *Journal of Social and Personal Relationships, 33*(2), 171–190. https://doi.org/10.1177/0265407514568749

Toma, C. L., & Choi, M. (2016, February). Mobile media matters: Media use and relationship satisfaction among geographically close dating couples. In *Proceedings of the 19th ACM conference on computer-supported cooperative work & social computing* (pp. 394–404). ACM Press. https://doi.org/10.1145/2818048.2835204

Tong, S. T., & Walther, J. B. (2011). Relational maintenance and computer-mediated communication. In K. Wright & L. Webb (Eds.), *Computer-mediated communication and personal relationships* (pp. 98–118). Peter Lang Publishing.

Vaterlaus, J. M., Barnett, K., Roche, C., & Young, J. A. (2016). "Snapchat is more personal": An exploratory study on Snapchat behaviors and young adult interpersonal relationships. *Computers in Human Behavior, 62,* 594–601. https://doi.org/10.1016/j.chb.2016.04.029

Vitak, J. (2014, February). Facebook makes the heart grow fonder: Relationship maintenance strategies among geographically dispersed and communication-restricted connections. In *Proceedings of the 17th ACM conference on computer supported cooperative work & social computing* (pp. 842–853). ACM Press. https://doi.org/10.1145/2531602.2531726

Vogels, E. A., & Anderson, M. (2020, May). Dating and relationships in the digital age. *Pew Research Center.* https://www.pewresearch.org/internet/2020/05/08/dating-and-relationships-in-the-digital-age/

Walther, J. B. (1996). Computer-mediated communication: Impersonal, interpersonal, and hyperpersonal interaction. *Communication Research, 23*(1), 3–43. https://doi.org/10.1177/009365096023001001

10

Conflict and CMC in Interpersonal Relationships

When Brandon teaches his undergraduate course on Communication and the Internet, he often asks students on the first day of class to tell him if the Internet is inherently good or bad for social relationships. Their response is predictable. Almost every student will bemoan the stifling effect that the proliferation and now ubiquity of smartphones has had on the traditional institution of the conversation over dinner (the "phubbing" mentioned in Chapter 9 is often irksome to the 18–22 year old set!). They will mourn the presence and prevalence of other peoples' political opinions—once hidden from them, but now shared openly and apparently without shame. Clearly, they will argue, the Internet is killing us slowly from the inside.

The Internet: A Uniquely Alienating, Conflict-Laden Environment?

How does this *social* medium—whose primary use is to connect people and allow them to communicate—have such distinctly *anti-social* outcomes? This was precisely the question Dr. Robert Kraut and his colleagues at Carnegie Mellon University (Kraut, Patterson, Lundmark, Kiesler, Mukophadhyay, & Scherlis,

1998) asked in a classic study that is widely known to scholars as the "Internet Paradox" study. In this piece, the researchers reflected on another popular work of the day, Putnam's (1995) essay (and subsequent book), *Bowling Alone*, and asked whether the Internet was at least partially responsible for driving people away from their local, social connections and increasing physiological deficits, loneliness, and depression.

To answer this question, Kraut and colleagues set out to conduct an ambitious investigation: a longitudinal study designed to provide causal evidence about the impact of Internet use on participants' social involvement. To conduct this study, the researchers enrolled 256 people from 93 families in the greater Pittsburgh, Pennsylvania area. After agreeing to participate, enrollees received a free phone line, a free computer with a modem capable of connecting to the Internet, and free Internet access. In exchange, participants agreed to allow the researchers to monitor their Internet use, participate in an interview, and respond to several questionnaires for the duration of the study. Unsurprisingly, few of those contacted to participate turned down this sweet deal.

There are several fairly specific methodological steps that Kraut et al. (1998) undertake to provide the reader greater confidence that any differences in psychological well-being, depression, and loneliness observed over the course of the longitudinal study were due to Internet use and not something else. We will not go into all of those details here, except to say that although no study is perfect, we trust their results. What Kraut and his colleagues did at the beginning of the study was measure participants' psychological well-being, loneliness, and depression; then, at a later point, they measured their Internet use; and finally they returned to measure participants' psychological well-being, loneliness, and depression again. This allowed them to see changes in their participants' feelings and account for those changes according to how much those participants used the Internet. A smartly-done study in our view.

Their findings rocked the world (or, at least the academic world interested in the societal effects of the Internet)! The researchers concluded that increased Internet use was associated with reductions in FtF interaction among family members in a household, and, overall, that Internet use was related to increased loneliness and depression. Today—nearly 25 years later—journalists still sometimes refer to the original Kraut et al. (1998) study to warn of the socially isolating effects of life online.

One could be forgiven for thinking that Kraut et al.'s first Internet Paradox study is the end of that story. The Internet is socially isolating and that is that. Nonetheless, the landmark 1998 study was not without its critics (for a review of those critiques, see Kraut, Kiesler, Boneva, Cummings, Helgeson, & Crawford, 2002). Scholars offered alternative explanations for the original Internet paradox study's findings. Perhaps, some suggested, the original study needed a control group—households that *did not* have Internet access, to compare to the experimental group who received Internet access. This comparison could help us tell whether declines in social and emotional well-being were due to increased Internet access and use, or whether this group would have shown these effects without the Internet. While Kraut et al. (2002) argued that this was unlikely because the observed deficits in social and emotional well-being were observed in proportion to a participant's Internet use, they too remained curious about their original findings. Specifically, they wondered if the negative effects they observed might diminish over time. They reasoned that the individuals included in the 1998 study had only been recently introduced to using the Internet. Was it possible, then, that such participants' experiences would not generalize to longer periods of Internet use, or to a different group of people?

To address these concerns, Kraut et al. (2002) conducted a follow-up to their original study. They re-contacted participants from their original 1998 study and reassessed their levels of social and emotional well-being. Surprisingly, the results of this work indicated that the negative effects of Internet use had largely dissipated. Specifically, this follow-up study found that although Internet use had been associated with depression and loneliness, these initial effects published in the first study did not persist over the longer three-year period measured in the second study. The results from the follow-up study broadly indicated that Internet use did not result in negative social and emotional effects, but instead was associated, generally, with a range of positive outcomes.

Interestingly, Kraut et al.'s (2002) follow-up study, which challenged the results of the initial 1998 study, garnered significantly less attention from the media or other researchers. The first Internet paradox study from 1998 had a lot going for it: It was carefully conducted; it was well written, persuasive, and maybe most importantly, it confirmed the longstanding belief that technology negatively and pervasively affected American society. The original study probably received more public attention because it furthered popular narratives that still surround technologically-mediated communication: that CMC pales in comparison to FtF; that CMC will always be an impediment to "real" interpersonal interaction; and of course, other, farther reaching ideas like too much screen time will rot your brain! But are these things really the case? It is hard to say conclusively what the Internet does when the follow-up study provides us with conflicting evidence. So what are we to believe? Can the Internet be a conduit for meaningful interpersonal interaction? Or does using it drag us down, producing depression and loneliness? The rest of this chapter visits this seeming contradiction in the context of conflict, and as with many questions related to human communication and technology, the answer is "it depends."

The Nature of Nonverbal Communication and Implications for Conflict

You may be wondering what any of this has to do with conflict. In general, the argument is this: If the Internet cannot support healthy interpersonal communication but results in greater loneliness and depression, then conflict, too, is more likely to arise. Probably the clearest argument about how CMC might inspire elevated levels of interpersonal conflict can be drawn from Argyle and Dean's (1965) *affiliative conflict theory*. This theory proposes that nonverbal behaviors are primarily responsible for establishing intimacy in relationships. Specifically, we adapt our nonverbal behaviors to address a desired level of intimacy in relationships. When we seek to become more intimate, for example, we might reduce the physical distance between ourselves and a partner. In the case of a worldwide pandemic, when we cannot reduce the physical distance between ourselves and a partner safely with a handshake or a hug, we may instead opt for increased eye contact or gestures.

As discussed in other chapters, in the earliest days of CMC research, scholars presumed that text-based interaction was not adequately equipped to allow for intimacy. And when intimacy is stunted (or, potentially, when we have no nonverbal cues to communicate intimacy at a desired level), the assumption is that conflict is more likely to ensue. Holding this set of assumptions, you might expect that CMC would be inherently more conflict-laden than traditional FtF interaction.

There are sound methodological reasons for questioning some of the early pessimism concerning Internet communication and its potential to generate conflict. Walther (1992) argued that many early CMC research studies did not carefully code or analyze the nonverbal behaviors present in FtF conversation, and therefore might well have missed a great deal of the communication that was occurring. Many of those early studies shared the assumption that social information simply could not be transmitted using CMC. For that reason, they often compared a transcript of the verbal behaviors present in FtF conversation to the transcript of CMC interaction. Unsurprisingly, when this comparison was made,

CMC chats occasionally appeared to generate greater conflict; however, Walther argues that these results are a product of an unfair comparison. In CMC, people can adapt to a text-based medium to encode negative social behaviors into their textual messages, but a transcript of a FtF conversation excludes all of the negative nonverbal behaviors like eye-rolls, audible sighs, and the like. For that reason, a record of a CMC transcript might look more conflict-laden only because it represents the whole interaction, compared with only the verbal part of a FtF interaction.

As an example, Brandon has a colleague, of whom he is rather fond, whose behavior in meetings exemplifies the way nonverbals (as significant as they are) tend to be lost in transcription, so to speak. During meetings, this professor tends to sit in the corner of the room closest to the entrance—ostensibly to make the quickest get-away. When discussing important group decisions, sometimes this professor verbally states his or her agreement or disagreement about the group's decisions. However, it is also quite common that this professor says nothing, and instead makes any agreement or disagreement known by way of eyerolls, head shakes, grimaces, audible sighs, vigorous hand-wringing, and the like. If one were simply transcribing the verbal content of a meeting, one might miss entirely the way this faculty member to contributes to an eventual outcome. This is a perfect illustration of Burgoon's (1985) notion that while the nonverbal signals that accompany verbal communication *may* at times reinforce verbal content, these nonverbal signals may also contradict, augment, or invalidate the precise, literal meaning of a verbal message.

Admittedly, a critic may note here that concluding that the Internet constrains social interaction was premature in the nascent days of CMC scholarship does not necessarily rule out the possibility that the Internet of today does exactly that. As the late, great astronomer Carl Sagan once wrote, "absence of evidence is not evidence of absence" (1997, p. 213). So, then, does evidence exist elsewhere that the Internet might *not* be *inherently* socially constraining and also conflict-laden? We believe such evidence does, indeed, exist. As early as 1996, Parks and Floyd demonstrated that close friendships could form on the basis of online newsgroups of Usenet forums, an early platform that functioned like a mashup of online bulletin boards and Reddit forums. While the critic might rightly argue that Usenet newsgroup users in 1990s are not representative of how we use the Internet today, such evidence at least suggests a strong *prima facie* case that the Internet is not inherently incapable of supporting relational communication.

One reason that researchers might fail to see this is that in experimental studies of online interaction, they rarely give people enough time to form connections.

Walther, Anderson, and Park (1994) conducted a meta-analysis of early studies of CMC demonstrating that the time people were allowed to interact online during experimental studies significantly impacted relational development. In short, several early experiments—taken together—showed that when participants had more time to interact with one another they were able to develop personal relationships. Put another way, it wasn't the case that CMC was inherently antisocial, only that social relationships took more time to develop in online spaces.

It is for these reasons that we believe that CMC is capable of supporting interpersonal interaction, and it's not inherently conflict-laden. Conflict and alienation certainly *can* occur online. However, it is not the case that they *must* occur online. Instead, both conflict and resolution exist in online spaces. With respect to the Internet's detractors, perhaps the immortal poet T. Swift has put it best: "Haters gonna hate, hate, hate, hate, hate."

Conflict in Online Relationships

At the outset, it is important to note that relatively few scholars have studied computer-mediated conflict in romantic relationships (Caughlin, Basinger, & Sharabi, 2017). There are likely many reasons for this: Longstanding relationships among the participants that scholars tend to study (undergraduate college students) are not easy for researchers to come by; there are ethical issues with intentionally inciting conflict among existing romantic partners in the laboratory for experimental purposes; and examining instances of conflict is hard work that is particularly onerous, often requiring the sort of lengthy coding and analysis that few scholars want to undertake. Below, we review the research that has informed our understanding of romantic couples' use of mediated technology during conflict and then discuss directions for future research.

Channel Selection & Channel Switching in Romantic Conflict

Frisby and Westerman's (2010) study is one of few to focus on how couples use technology for managing relational conflict. Specifically, they utilized *rational actor theory* (Markus, 1994a, b) to assess the ways that romantic partners chose media channels to express themselves or to avoid conflict in their relationships. Rational actor theory suggests that the communication channel (e.g., email, telephone, FtF, etc.) one opts to use depends on a person's communication goals, the features or affordances of the channel, and the type of message being sent, among other factors. The theory presumes that people make a rational decision about the channel that best meets their needs in light of this constellation of factors.

However, Frisby and Westerman (2010) proposed that people's *conflict styles* (Rahim, 1983) matter as well—that is, that people with different conflict styles would likely seek to satisfy their communication goals using different media. For example, they expected that individuals with an *integrating* conflict style (meaning, having a mutual concern for both self and others), might be more likely to select media that help them attain their communicative goals and provide more control over verbal message construction. However, those with a *dominating* conflict style (that is, people who care much about themselves and little about others) might be more likely to use FtF communication, since dominance is most readily communicated using nonverbal signals. Others, with *avoidant* conflict styles dodge conflict at all costs, making channel selection less of an issue, as conflict avoidant folk seek to evade in conflict using *any* channel (Burgoon, Buller, Hale, & deTurck, 1984; Kayany, Wotring, & Forrest, 1996).

Notably, when Frisby and Westerman (2010) surveyed participants about their media preferences during relational conflict, their conflict styles and channel selections did not match up with what was predicted by rational actor theory. Those participants who reported having an integrating or avoiding conflict style also reported a commensurate reticence to use CMC channels to mediate their relational conflicts; instead, they reported a preference for FtF conflict mediation. Those who reported having a dominating conflict style, on the other hand, reported a desire to use CMC to mediate their conflicts. As Frisby and Westerman point out, findings like these are not uncommon when CMC scholars ask participants about media preferences. What we might take away from these findings is twofold: First, the conventional wisdom that CMC is unsuited to managing relational conflict in healthy ways remains pervasive. Whether that assumption is supported by the evidence, however, is another matter. Interestingly, the researchers also found that approximately two-thirds of their respondents had reported using CMC to mediate a conflict recently. This is seems to represent some level of disconnect between what participants *say* they would do to mediate their conflicts and what they *actually* do.

From a theoretical standpoint, Frisby and Westerman (2010) also reflect on their decision to frame their study using rational actor theory (which broadly falls into the category of media selection theories; Markus, 1994a; see also Carlson &

Zmud, 1999; Daft & Lengel, 1984, 1986), but suggest that perhaps other theories may explain their results. Korzenny's (1978) theory of *electronic propinquity* focuses on people's communication skills and might suggest that these participants were also factoring in their level of competence with various CMC technologies. Perceived skill deficiencies may have altered or amended their media choices. In sum, if one doesn't have the skills (or does not want to spend the time) to manage a complex conflict using CMC, one may not report an intent to do so. Despite the specific reasons, what Frisby and Westerman's results suggest is that one's expressed *intent* to use one medium or another may not necessarily track with what one actually ends up doing.

In a different study, Scissors and Gergle (2013), examined the channel switching during romantic conflict. Specifically, they looked at patterns in the way partners would shift between FtF and mediated communication, together with their motivations for doing so. Twenty-four people were interviewed, all of them between 18 and 30 years old, and in romantic relationships that had lasted anywhere from three to 48 months. Participants reported using all kinds of channels during romantic conflict, including: instant messaging, text messaging, email, video conferencing, and FtF interaction. Sometimes a conflict was confined to a single channel; other times, participants noted that a conflict began in one channel, like FtF, but then resolved later through a mediated channel. In yet another set of reported instances, participants noted that multiple channel switches could take place during a single conflict situation: "the conflict was initiated in one channel, discussed in a second channel, and then resolved/terminated after a final channel switch (either back to the previous channel or to a new channel)" (Scissors & Gergle, 2013, p. 240).

Scissors and Gergle (2013) also reported participants' motivations for channel switching during romantic conflict. Some of these were quite practical. On occasion, partners wanted to work around technical constraints, switching to phone calls or FtF, for example, to save the work of typing. In other cases, logistical issues came into play, prompting a couple to continue a conflict-laden conversation by text message when one partner had to physically leave the FtF conversation to go to work or school.

More interestingly, some participants reported using mediated channels as a way to *avoid conflict escalation*. They preferred using mediated channels to "ease into" a potentially touchy subject, introducing conflict more gradually as opposed to "catching one's partner off guard by bringing it up for the first time FtF and launching into a full discussion" (p. 241). Another motivation was *emotion management*, in which participants reported switching to channels they felt allowed them to better express their feelings. Echoing previous work, many participants felt that mediated channels gave them more control over message composition—several participants' responses highlighted how the text-based nature of mediated channels helped them better express themselves verbally and freed them from having to attend to nonverbals. In this way, we see how text-based CMC may sometimes provide an important advantage in romantic conflict: "use of text-based CMC might support communication that is too *emotionally* hard to conduct FtF" (p. 242).

However, other participants raised the disadvantages present in the use of mediated channels during conflict. Many noted that the increased *response latencies* present in text-based CMC message exchange heightened their anxiety. Waiting around for a response from a partner during a heated argument is never a good experience; and if a response never comes, it can feel like the conflict will never be resolved. Yet some participants noted the silver lining of response latencies during mediated conflict, remarking that they used the increased time between exchanges to think about the problem independently, to come up with new solutions or approaches to the conflict, or to reflect on their own emotions before sending another message.

Scissors and Gergle (2013) note that regarding *romantic conflict resolution*, most participants felt that "some sort of visual or physical contact, like a smile or hug, was required to help them truly feel better and attain closure on a conflict" (p. 244). Yet other times, participants noted that CMC channels were also useful to reiterate apologies that were initially exchanged FtF, or to provide a "final word" that could cast out any "lingering doubts" that remained after a conflict (p. 244). Such responses reflect that age-old idea that richer FtF interaction is still needed to truly resolve conflict that we saw in the Frisby and Westerman study, above. Even though participants noted that CMC channels gave them all kinds of advantages—greater control over message composition, emotional expression, and relational goal attainment—many still reported a preference for FtF when it came to resolution.

While Scissors and Gergle's interviews shed light on the nature of channel switching, there are still limitations to what we can generalize about couples' use of mediated technology during conflict from a set of 24 interviews. But what is striking from their interview results is the duality of people's attitudes present in ideas about mediated conflict. For example, a single feature—like response latency—could be cast as a good thing or a bad thing, depending on how people perceived and treated it during conflict. Another interesting takeaway is the mixed-mode nature of participants' romantic conflicts, or what Scissors and

Gergle refer to as a dynamic "back and forth" between multiple channels, which may provide benefits above and beyond those offered by a single channel. In fact, in the next section, we would like to go deeper into the question of mixed-mode conflict.

Mixed-Mode Conflict: Communication Interdependence & Media Multiplexity

Caughlin and Sharabi (2013) note that very few relationships exist only within a single mode of communication. Most couples who are involved in relationships do not *just* text one another, nor do they *only* chat FtF. As noted in the previous chapter, most relationships are mixed-mode in nature (Parks, 2017)—that is, partners use a variety of platforms to communicate with each other (see also Haythornthwaite, 2005). For example, not too long ago, Brandon was short with his wife, Jen. The argument itself was probably about something dumb— he does not even recall what, exactly. However, it happened in the morning before he went off to work. After a bit more morning coffee, Brandon realized that he needed to apologize and he wanted to do it right away. However, he knew that his wife Jen would be busy at work. Instead of placing a call, he sent a text apologizing. Then he sent an email explaining how much he loved and respected her (he had really not been nice that morning). Close relational partners tend to communicate more frequently and do so using more modes of communication than those who are less close. Even more importantly, as Caughlin and Sharabi suggest, not only do our patterns of communication suggest a greater frequency or "media-diverse" pattern, but that different modes of communication can work particularly well when partners use them together— in an *interdependent* way.

    Caughlin, Basinger, and Sharabi (2017) conducted some of the first research that uses the communication interdependence perspective to understand the ways that technologically-mediated and FtF channels can function together in relational conflict. As with much early pioneering work on any topic, its intent was not to test specific predictions, but instead to map out the basic landscape of the phenomenon. Researchers asked a number of college students how they use technology during conflict, and/or whether they use technology to actively avoid conflict. Just over half of respondents reported about conflicts with a romantic relational partner, while just under half reported about conflicts in other types of relationships (e.g., parents, friends, roommates, siblings). This research sought to identify times that participants reported technology as something that helped (i.e., a "conflict-facilitating factor") and times participants reported technology to be a hindrance (i.e., a "goal-interfering factor"). One particularly interesting finding here was that a substantial number of participants reported that technology was a hinderance in conflict resolution and ought to be avoided; however, at the same time many people—sometimes the very same people—reported *relying* on technology to mediate their conflicts.

Just as we saw with the earlier channel selection studies, Caughlin et al. (2017) found a disconnect between what people *say* they do and what they *actually* do. This research also found a discrepancy between what people reported about their own behavior and how they thought *other people* behaved. Specifically, they found that participants reported using technology to avoid conflict in their own relationships, but those same participants also reported others to be much less likely to use technology to avoid conflict. Unless there was some special sampling error, we would conclude (as the Caughlin et al., 2017 study did too), that there was some bias on the part of respondents.

The Future of Research in Online Relational Conflict

It is difficult to point to what the future of the academic study of online relational conflict might look like. Mostly, that is because there has been precious little of this work conducted to date. With that said, we do have some suggestions about directions researchers might pursue.

Multiple Goals, Mixed Modalities, and Communication Interdependence

First, Caughlin et al. (2017) suggest two main theoretical directions for this work: a *multiple goal directed* theoretical approach and the *communication interdependence* perspective. We agree that both of these approaches are worth pursuing: goal-directed approaches (i.e., Frisby & Westerman, 2010; Scissors & Gergle, 2013) and communication interdependence work (i.e., Caughlin et al., 2017). Both directions offer interesting questions about the ways that technology can affect the process of conflict and its mediation in romantic relationships.

As noted in the earlier parts of this book, multiple goals theories propose that in most any communication encounter there are a variety of end states that communicators seek to achieve (Berger, 2004; Clark & Delia, 1979). In this way, multiple goals perspectives are a close sibling of the functional perspective. Goals are desired places where we hope our communication will take us, and we utilize different functions of communication to achieve those end states. If we hope to deepen our relationship with a partner, we use communication to relate; if we hope to change another person's mind or their behavior, we use communication to exert social influence. In this way, the mediated context is a theoretically interesting environment in which to pursue the study of conflict. Conflict situations bring to the fore multiple, sometimes competing, end states. As Caughlin et al. (2017) suggest, the relative dearth of research that looks at technologically-mediated relational conflict is somewhat surprising given that several technological affordances *ought* to provide some strategic advantages in mediating conflict. For example, selective self-presentation (Walther, 1996) ought to be able to be utilized to carefully manicure our messages and reduce some of the anxiety, stress, and strain that accompany situations wherein managing multiple desired end states (goals) would be challenging in a FtF setting. We believe that scholars could pursue these questions.

Caughlin and Sharabi's (2013) interdependence perspective may be a useful framework for developing theoretically interesting research questions about multimodal conflict processes in relationships. In many ways, the communication interdependence perspective is shaped by theories of multiple goals. By acknowledging that relational partners often use a mix of communication channels (from text, to FtF, to email, to Snapchat, to Facebook, etc.) to relate to one another, Caughlin and Sharabi propose a perspective that allows for multiple relational goals to be addressed in complex ways through mode-diverse communication. In other words, people may well leverage the advantages that technologically-mediated communication can offer to manage the difficult situations that relational life throws at them. We are excited about how this perspective could map onto romantic relationships more specifically.

While the communication interdependence perspective has the capacity to support some immensely complex theoretical work, research that is born out of this perspective need not be complex. We can imagine, for example, that some initial steps might include laboratory experiments simply asking relational partners to resolve a conflict while manipulating the modes (and combinations of modes) of communication available to them. Designs like this might illuminate how media multiplexity affects message content, conflict resolution outcomes, and relational satisfaction.

Is CMC a Useful Conflict Resolution Tool?

There is another simple, but absolutely fundamental question we might ask: Is CMC a more effective tool for the mediation of romantic conflict than FtF? Our read of the available literature is that, incredibly, we do not have definitive evidence to speak to that question...yet! Certainly, we have learned that popular *belief* would tell us that technology is less effective than FtF at mediating conflict and ought to be avoided in relational conflict situations (see Caughlin et al., 2017). On the other hand, there is research from other conflict contexts that might suggest otherwise: Walther et al.'s (2015) work, which examines the ways that CMC can favorably affect interethnic and interreligious conflict, seems to provide some tantalizing reasons to suggest that online communication can ameliorate the stereotypes and prejudice that often provoke conflict. Such findings might even apply to the context of romantic conflict where we would most likely refer to stereotypes and prejudice as unmet or unfair expectations about one's relationship or partner. Moreover, we have learned that people's *beliefs* about what technology is capable of doing and what technology can *actually* do are not necessarily the same thing; this finding emerged in different ways in both Frisby and Westerman's (2010) and Caughlin et al.'s (2017) work.

This suggests that relational conflict research needs to look at more than just participants' perceptions and assumptions regarding technology use. It is important that we expand our investigations to include behavioral conflict resolution measures in some form. For example, are participants more satisfied with their relationships after communicating about their conflicts and disagreements? There are theoretically meaningful reasons to pursue all of these questions, and to date, these research questions are almost completely free for the taking.

Developing a Model of Technologically-Mediated Relational Conflict

We don't have a single, exhaustive model of relational conflict resolution in CMC. While there are reasons we might be optimistic about developing such a model, to date scholars simply have not embraced the challenge of identifying an overarching, unifying structure to pursue. Based on the review you have just read, we wish to propose the beginnings of such a model.

Conflict as multiple goal imbalance. The goals we have as we enter into a relational conflict affect the choices we make about how we communicate, in what

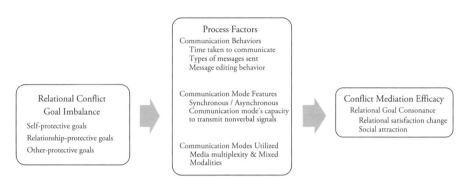

Figure 10.1: A process model of relational conflict. Source: Authors

manner we communicate, and via which modes we communicate. We would propose that there are a few goal categories that are present in most types of conflicts. While we acknowledge that different people have different conflict styles (Rahim, 1983), we suspect that *self-protective goals* and *relationship-protective goals* govern most conflict situations. And a third category of goals that may become operative in romantic conflict (in relative contrast to non-romantic relationships) is *other-protective goals*, that arise from selflessness and a concern for one's relational partner.

For example, imagine that Trevor gets into a fight with his romantic partner, Renee. Trevor knows that he will need to smooth things over at some point in the not-too-distant future. As he thinks about his future communication with Renee, he might think about how he intends to present his side of an argument (self-protective goals) in order to seek a resolution to their fight in a way that their relationship can continue on peacefully after the conflict has been resolved (relationship-protective goals) and do so in a way that doesn't hurt Renee's feelings (other-protective goals).

We propose that conflict in romantic relationships often arises when people sense an imbalance in these three broad goal motivations. Perhaps Trevor and Renee both want to see other people, and perhaps they even both want the other person to have such freedom. However, they have become comfortable in their relationship. They both identify the relationship as a safe space that neither really wants to lose. In this way, there would be a goal imbalance. While Trevor's and Renee's self- and other-protective goals may be in concert, they may experience a discrepancy between these goals and their relationship-protective goals. The multiple and often competing goals that arise in a romantic relationship suggest that couples will have to prioritize certain goals over others, which will often induce conflict. Following Caughlin et al.'s (2017) lead, we believe it could be useful to think about conflict from a multiple-goals perspective.

Process factors affecting mediated romantic conflict negotiation. Recent research has started to explore some of the process factors that ought to affect how romantic partners navigate conflict in their relationships. In a recent study, Kashian and Walther (2020) explored the roles of initial relational satisfaction and platform synchronicity on conflict behaviors and the internal attributions people made about their partners. In short, researchers compared (nearly) instantaneous message exchanges with delayed message exchanges, and examined the effect this temporal difference had on the internal attributions that participants made about their partners' behaviors. The signature finding of this research was that when partners had greater initial satisfaction with their relationship, *less* synchronous CMC resulted in attributing a partner's positive behavior to that person's disposition, rather than the situation. In simpler terms, happy couples who communicated with less synchronous media made more generous interpretations of their partners' behaviors during conflict.

Kashian and Walther's (2020) study is a good example of the type of work that examines the *process* components of mediated conflict. That is, the main focus of this investigation is how technology affects the process of relational conflict. We believe future work that explores message composition in terms of time and editing behavior may also provide unique insights into the relational conflict mediation process. However, keeping in mind the communication interdependence perspective, it is unlikely that feuding couples outside of a laboratory unilaterally restrict themselves to a single synchronous or asynchronous communication modality. Instead, over the span of a romantic relationship, most conflicts are likely navigated across a variety of communication platforms. Although this adds complexity to the role of technology in romantic conflicts, sometimes it is in studying that complexity that some of the most sophisticated findings and principles can become clear.

Conflict mediation efficacy. Finally, if conflict can be thought of as a state of goal imbalance, it is possible to conceptualize resolution as the process by which we use communication to bring those conflicting goals into a state of balance. Defining resolution this way allows for conflict to be "resolved" in relationships, even when the resolution of that conflict results in relational termination. In other words, romantic conflicts do not always have happy endings, and this conceptualization of resolution makes room for that. Still, we expect that the goal and process factors suggested here may meaningfully contribute to romantic partners' *conflict mediation efficacy.*

Conclusion

It should be noted that we have presented a very broad conceptual model. It does not have the explanatory capacity of a carefully articulated theoretical model that clearly spells out the relationships among various constructs, offering specific predictions. Instead, we simply offer an initial framework that specifies some of the variables and processes that research on interpersonal communication and CMC suggest ought to provide theoretically interesting research questions. As such, we think it is important to note that the process variables identified in Figure 10.1 in no way comprise an exhaustive list. Moreover, these variables—people's personalities, conflict styles, and communication skills—may well interact with one another. Additionally, we may need to take into account the nature of the issue involved in a particular romantic conflict. Few researchers have explored how the specific *relational conflict topic* may interact with goals, channel features, and process variables discussed above. While a silly squabble may be easily resolved using a single modality or platform, a much more serious problem—like infidelity or jealousy—may require more effort, ongoing interaction, and multiple channels.

We look forward to the development of research addressing online romantic conflict. There are many interesting questions to be answered. How do our relational goal imbalances affect the ways that we select media to communicate with our partners? Are there people for whom online conflict resolution is a better idea than FtF? If so, why? How does communication modality or the sequence of channel switching affect perceptions of romantic conflict resolution? Why is there a disconnect between how effective people believe technology is as a tool to resolve conflict and how effective technology *actually* is as a tool to resolve conflict? We would encourage researchers to pursue these and many other questions.

References

Allport, G. W. (1954). *The nature of prejudice*. Perseus Books.

Amichai-Hamburger, Y. (2012). Reducing intergroup conflict in the digital age. In H. Giles (Ed.), *The handbook of intergroup communication* (pp. 181–193). Routledge.

Amichai-Hamburger, Y., & McKenna, K. Y. A. (2006). The contact hypothesis reconsidered: Interacting via the Internet. *Journal of Computer-Mediated Communication, 11*, 825–843. http://dx.doi.org/10.1111/j.1083-6101.2006.00037.x

Argyle, M., & Dean J. (1965). Eye contact, distance, and affiliation. *Sociometry, 28*, 289–304. https://doi.org/10.2307/2786027

Berger, C. R. (2004). Communication: A goal-directed, plan-guided process. In D. R. Roskos-Ewoldsen & J. L. Monahan (Eds.), *Communication and social cognition: Theories and methods* (pp. 47–70). Erlbaum.

Burgoon, J. K. (1985). Nonverbal signals. In M. L. Knapp & G. R. Miller (Eds.), *Handbook of interpersonal communication* (pp. 344–392). Sage.

Burgoon, J., Buller, D., Hale, J., & deTurck, M. (1984). Relational messages associated with nonverbal behaviors. *Human Communication Research*, *10*, 351–378. https://doi.org/10.1111/j.1468-2958.1984.tb00023.x

Carlson, J. R., & Zmud, R. W. (1999). Channel expansion theory and the experiential nature of media richness perceptions. *Academy of Management Journal*, *42*, 153–170. https://doi.org/10.5465/257090

Caughlin, J. P., Basinger, E. D., & Sharabi, L. L. (2017). The connections between communication technologies and relational conflict: A multiple goals and communication interdependence perspective. In J. A. Samp (Ed.), *Communicating interpersonal conflict in close relationships: Contexts, challenges and opportunities* (pp. 57–72). Routledge.

Caughlin, J. P., & Sharabi, L. L. (2013). A communicative interdependence perspective of close relationships: The connections between mediated and unmediated interactions matter. *Journal of Communication*, *63*, 873–893. https://doi.org/10.1111/jcom.12046

Clark, R. A., & Delia, J. G. (1979). *Topoi* and rhetorical competence. *Quarterly Journal of Speech*, *65*, 187–206. https://doi.org/10.1080/00335637909383470

Daft, R. L., & Lengel, R. H. (1984). Information richness: A new approach to managerial behavior and organization design. *Research in Organizational Behavior*, *6*, 191–233. https://doi.org/10.21236/ada128980

Daft, R. L., & Lengel, R. H. (1986). Organizational information requirements, media richness and structural design. *Management Science*, *32*(5), 554–571. https://doi.org/10.1287/mnsc.32.5.554

Frisby, B. N., & Westerman, D. K. (2010). Rational actors: Channel selection and rational choices in romantic conflict episodes. *Journal of Social and Personal Relationships*, *27*, 970–981. https://doi.org/10.1177/0265407510378302

Haythornthwaite, C. (2005). Social networks and Internet connectivity effects. *Information, Communication & Society*, *8*, 125–147. https://doi.org/10.1080/13691180500146185

Kashian, N., & Walther, J. B. (2020). The effect of relational satisfaction and media synchronicity on attributions in computer-mediated conflict. *Communication Research*, *47*(5), 647–668. https://doi.org/10.1177/0093650218789581

Kayany, J. M., Wotring, C. E., & Forrest, E. J. (1996). Relational control and interactive media choice in technology-mediated communication situations. *Human Communication Research*, *22*, 399–421. https://doi.org/10.1111/j.1468-2958.1996.tb00373.x

Korzenny, F. (1978). A theory of electronic propinquity: Mediated communications in organizations. *Communication Research*, *5*, 3–24. https://doi.org/10.1177/009365027800500101

Kraut, R., Kiesler, S., Boneva, B., Cummings, J., Helgeson, V., & Crawford, A. (2002). The Internet paradox revisited. *Journal of Social Issues*, *58*, 49–74. https://doi.org/10.1111/1540-4560.00248

Kraut, R., Patterson, M., Lundmark, V., Kiesler, S., Mukophadhyay, T., & Scherlis, W. (1998). Internet paradox: A social technology that reduces social involvement and psychological well-being? *American Psychologist, 53*, 1017–1031. https://doi.org/10.1037/0003-066X.53.9.1017

Markus, M. L. (1994a). Finding a happy medium: Explaining the negative effects of electronic communication on social life at work. *ACM Transactions on Information Systems, 12*, 119–149. https://doi.org/ 10.1145/196734

Markus, M. L. (1994b). Electronic mail as the medium of managerial choice. *Organization Science, 5*, 502–527. https://doi.org/10.1287/orsc.5.4.502

McGinn, K. L., & Keros, A. T. (2002). Improvisation and the logic of exchange in socially embedded transactions. *Administrative Science Quarterly, 47*, 442–473. https://doi.org/10.2307/3094847

Parks, M. R. (2017). Embracing the challenges and opportunities of mixed-media relationships. *Human Communication Research, 43*(4), 505–517. https://doi.org/10.1111/hcre.12125

Parks, M. R., & Floyd, K. (1996). Making friends in cyberspace. *Journal of Computer-Mediated Communication, 1*, 80–97. https://doi.org/10.1111/j.1460-2466.1996.tb01462.x

Putnam, R. (1995). Bowling alone: America's declining social capital. *Journal of Democracy, 6*, 65–78.

Rahim, M. A. (1983). A measure of styles of handling interpersonal conflict. *Academy of Management Journal, 26*, 368–376. https://doi.org/10.2307/255985

Roseth, C. J., Saltarelli, A. J., & Glass, C. R. (2011). Effects of face-to-face and computer- mediated constructive controversy on social interdependence, motivation, and achievement. *Journal of Educational Psychology, 103*, 804–820. https://doi.org/10.1037/a0024213

Sagan, C. (1997). *The Demon-Haunted World: Science as a Candle in the Dark*. Ballantine.

Scissors, L., & Gergle, D. (2013). "Back and forth, back and forth": Channel switching in romantic couple conflict. In *Proceedings the 2013 conference on computer supported cooperative work* (pp. 237–248). https://doi.org/10.1145/2441776.2441804Walther, J. B. (1992). Interpersonal effects in computer-mediated interaction: A relational perspective. *Communication Research, 19*, 52–90. https://doi.org/10.1177/009365092019001003

Walther, J. B. (1996). Computer-mediated communication: Impersonal, interpersonal, and hyperpersonal interaction. *Communication Research, 23*, 3–43. https://doi.org/10.1177/009365096023001001

Walther, J. B., Anderson, J. F., & Park, D. W. (1994). Interpersonal effects in computer-mediated communication: A meta-analysis of social and anti-social communication. *Communication Research, 21*, 460–487. https://doi.org/10.1177/009365094021004002

Walther, J. B., Hoter, E., Ganayem, A., & Shonfeld, M. (2015). Computer-mediated communication and the reduction of prejudice: A controlled longitudinal field experiment among Jews and Arabs in Israel. *Computers in Human Behavior, 52*, 550–558. https://doi.org/10.1016/j.chb.2014.08.004

11

The Dark Side of Online Dating and Romantic Relationships

According to communication theorists Brian Spitzberg and William Cupach (2007), we can use two dimensions of "light" and "dark" to evaluate communication behaviors or processes. We might ask whether the communication behavior is *socially acceptable* or *reprehensible*, and second whether it serves a relationally *supportive* or *destructive* function. Most of the time, discrete communication behaviors are not 100% "light" or "dark"; instead, like most things, they are often somewhere in the middle, partly illuminated and sometimes shadowed (even Darth Vader had his moments).

In this chapter, we organize our analysis of dark side processes according to the same relational stage model that we have been referencing throughout the book. First, we review the dark side of romantic initiation by examining how online and mobile matching platforms can result in overzealous relational pursuit and harassment. We then examine the dark side of mediated technology in relational maintenance processes, exploring how romantic partners sometimes use social media technology in destructive ways and end up sabotaging their own relationships. Finally, we examine relationship termination—a stage we haven't yet discussed. We begin by reviewing functions of mediated communication that can help facilitate a romantic breakup. We then contrast these productive uses of mediated technology with a review of how social media can be used to stalk, monitor, and intrude into the lives of ex-partners.

The Dark Side of Romantic Initiation

As noted in previous chapters, the nature of online and mobile dating has affected mate selection for romantic singles by increasing the size of the dating pool, the number of decisions daters have to make, and also the decision making process itself. But some processes of initiation have remained the same online as they have offline—notably, the *gendered dynamics of initiation*. Following traditional gender scripts, men are much more likely than women to initiate first contacts via online messaging, and women tend to be in a reactive stance, deciding when and how to respond to such overtures (exceptions include platforms like Bumble, which gives women the sole right to make first contact). Interestingly, a recent survey by Pew Research (Vogels, 2020), 57% of men feel they have not received enough messages, whereas only 24% of women report the same thing. Additionally, women (30%) are much more likely than men (6%) to report receiving too many messages from other daters. This evidence only further demonstrates the gendered pattern of initiation interaction.

Feminist theorists have pointed out that initiation practices in online and mobile dating place emphasis on marketplace metaphors like "relationshopping," "catalog searching," and "heterosexual stock market" which are quite popular among daters, who often use them to explain the process of online mate selection (e.g., Cameron, Oskamp, & Sparks, 1977; Heino, Ellison, & Gibbs, 2010; Huang, Hancock, & Tong, 2021). Extending this marketplace metaphor into the "hookup culture" of mobile dating apps, theorists note that men take on the role of "active" consumers who must pursue "passive" women in the competitive marketplace (see Currier, 2013; Hess & Flores, 2018; Thompson, 2018). But (as noted in Chapter 6), the application of evolutionary perspectives on mate selection in online dating suggests that as the "choosier sex," women could actually maintain *more* power than men in the online and mobile dating environment, since they are the ones who selectively attend to men's requests and ultimately deny or reject overwhelming numbers of male suitors. However, feminist scholars point out that the competitive atmosphere of online and mobile dating may foster greater *toxic masculinity*—or a demonstration of sexual dominance and control over women (Currier, 2013). This can lead men to be overly assertive, even belligerent, in their messages—sometimes to the point of outright harassment.

Harassment in online dating. Young women aged 18–34 are the group most likely to report receiving unwanted messages during online and mobile dating initiation; in fact, 60% of women in this age group report having been pursued by another dater after they refused or rejected the initial contact. The kinds of unwanted messages that women report receiving often include sexually explicit content (57%), offensive insults or name-calling (44%), and intimidating threats of physical harm (19%) (Vogels, 2020).

To see specific examples of the unwanted messages that online daters receive, one only needs to look to Instagram accounts @byefelipe and @tindernightmares. These accounts allow daters (mostly female) to submit examples of online and mobile text messages they have received from men, ranging from socially awkward attempts at humor to outright harassment and threats. Most examples come from women who recount the insulting or threatening messages sent to them in response to their avoidance, rejection, or refusal of a man's initial attempts to connect. Perusing these messages provides a glimpse into the darker side of online interaction during the initiation phase: Thompson's (2018) and Hess and Flores' (2018) analysis of posts from Bye Felipe and Tinder Nightmares revealed results consistent with what a Pew Research survey reported in 2020. Key categories that described trends in the dark side of online romantic initiation exchanges included:

(1) "Not hot enough": Most men, it appears, are not terribly creative in their insults to women. The majority of messages in Thompson's (2018) sample denigrated women's physical appearance, with most targeting women's weight and often containing the word "fat." Thompson notes that the attention on physical appearance highlights larger societal linkages between women's sexual desirability and slenderness: "In these examples then, the man labels the woman's body or body part/s as 'fat' in an effort to position her as stigmatized, undesirable, and unattractive, and take back or refute his sexual interest which she has not reciprocated" (p. 77). Although insulting a woman's looks was a common theme in these initiation messages, the level of disgust and profanity that men used to do so varied considerably.

(2) "Groan-inducing" pickup lines that also obfuscate consent: In this category of sexually explicit messages, men communicated overt, hypermasculine demands for casual sex using dirty or crude pickup lines: "Twinkle twinkle little star/Let's have sex inside my car" (Hess & Flores, 2016, p. 1092). In such messages, men frequently described what they wanted

to do to women, displaying a form of *sexual entitlement* without women's consent: "[in] framing it solely about what 'I want', these men show little to no interest in what the woman's desires might be and whether she might even want to engage in such conversations" (Thompson, 2018, p. 81).

(3) "Objectification through consumption": Another common theme was the use of food metaphors by men, which Hess and Flores (2018) argue equates the consumption of food with the consumption of women's bodies or sexuality: "Do you like ramen noodles? Cause I'm gonna be ramen my noodle in ya" (p. 1093). The authors argue that such language figuratively transforms women into food objects that can be easily consumed by men (Hines, 1999), which in turn creates a sense of power over women's bodies.

In conclusion, Thompson (2018) argues that these insults and sexually explicit messages are not intended as "genuine" attempts at relational initiation, rather they are meant to degrade, disgust, and anger any woman who spurns a man's romantic advances during the initiation phase. In this sense, as a function of communication, such messages are aligned more with trolling than with greeting or courting. From these analyses, we can conclude that the dark side of initiation is, therefore, more performative than functional—a way for frustrated male daters to try and exact power over women, who (as the "choosier" sex) are in the unique position of getting to reject or ignore male attention. There is a strange paradox here, in that men are verbally expressing dominance in a situation where they seemingly have none.

Violation of expectations during initiation: The case of the compliment. But not all men are so single-minded in their use of language to denigrate women. A more common (and effective) initiation tactic that some men employ is the *compliment*, which credits someone for some attribute of their appearance, possessions, or some outcome that resulted from their skill or effort (Herbert, 1990). The underlying social functions of a compliment might include the (rather obvious) goal of the speaker expressing admiration to the recipient (Herbert, 1990), or an attempt to create or reinforce solidarity between the speaker and recipient (Wolfson & Manes, 1980). In order to elicit that sense of admiration or solidarity, however, a compliment must be interpreted by the recipient as an *honest* speech act, not simply an attempt to win compliance or influence. Not surprisingly, when offered genuinely, compliments can garner a positive response in online dating as a form of initiation (Khan & Chaudry, 2015).

Recipients' responses to compliments are also highly scripted: Pomerantz (1978) suggests that, typically, speakers expect others to accept a compliment with a gracious "thank you!" that signals agreement; however, in fulfilling this expectation, recipients have several goals that they must attend to. First, they must avoid agreeing with the compliment too eagerly, which would signal arrogance or self-praise, and so reflect poorly on them. To mitigate such arrogance, recipients might offer a *token of appreciation* with their acceptance; in other cases, they might actually politely *refuse* the compliment—disagreeing with the speaker to show modesty.

Clearly, as a communicative exchange, the art of the compliment—both sending and receiving—is fraught with *expectations*. You will recall from Chapter 7 that expectations—defined as "enduring patterns of anticipated behavior"—are based in "societal norms for what is typical and appropriate behavior" (Burgoon, 1993, p. 31). When we talk to others and their behaviors deviate from what we anticipate, our expectancies are *violated*. Burgoon suggests that when others violate our expectancies, it creates *arousal*; we suddenly become more aware of them and start trying to explain and evaluate their odd behavior. Sometimes we judge their strange behavior positively (deviating from the norm in a good way can actually make us like the person even more); but if we judge that behavior negatively, we often end up liking that person less. Our positive or negative judgments of others' expectancy violations are dependent on that person's *characteristics* (more specifically, their "reward valence" or how much we value that person), our *relationship* to them, and the *circumstances* of the situation.

In a recent experiment, DelGreco and Denes (2020) examined the standard pattern of online dating initiation interaction through compliments using a hypothetical text message exchange, in which a man sent an initial text message to a woman that contained the compliment, "Wow! You have gorgeous eyes." DelGreco and Denes then applied Burgoon's (1993) expectancy violations theory to experimentally vary the woman's reply, according to communicative expectations: Positive violations depicted the woman as responding with acknowledgment tempered by gracious self-deprecation, "Thank you, but I don't think so." Negative violations depicted the woman as responding also with agreement and also self-promotion, "Thank you, I know! They are pretty great." In the conformist condition, the woman simply responded with "Thank you!" A total 202 male and 209 female college students participated in this experiment by viewing a hypothetical initiation exchange that contained the opening compliment followed by one of the three kinds of responses. They then rated the female dater and her response along several dimensions including her self-esteem, likability, and conversational appropriateness. They also evaluated the power dynamics of the interaction, rating which dater seemed to have more power in the text message exchange.

Their results indicated that participants judged the negative violations as more powerful than positive violations and less conversationally appropriate than conforming responses. The woman who used negative violations was also judged as less likable than the conforming participant. Additionally, and contrary to expectancy violations theory, compared to the negative violations respondent, the positive violation respondent was judged by participants to be less attractive, less conversationally appropriate, less likable, and someone who had lower self-esteem. Interestingly, the sex of the participant (observer) had no significant effect on these results. DelGreco and Denes (2020) suggested that one weakness of their experiment was the lack of detail their scenarios provided about the female dater, and without such details, participants were unable to evaluate communicator reward valence: "It is possible that because there was no picture provided along with the fictional message exchanges, and no indication of any other characteristics of who the female respondent was or if there is a relational history or future, that participants interpreted the exchange as low-communicator reward value, and they therefore were not positively evaluating the violation as would be expected for a high-communicator reward value (Burgoon, 1993)" (pp. 628–629). As noted in Chapter 5, the visual and verbal information contained in dating profiles is highly salient in online impression formation; trying to evaluate people (and their communication behavior) without it may be difficult.

However, a larger takeaway from this study is that while women who respond with an expectancy violation of outright agreement with another's compliment are seen as more powerful and as having more self-esteem, they are also subject to more negative interpersonal judgments overall, compared to those who offer a more conformist response. Societal expectations regarding women's responses to compliments seem to be alive and well in online dating, although future work may want to examine how other variables (male/female physical attractiveness, male versus female initiator, and recipient roles) might impact how people interpret interactions sent and received during the initiation phase. For now, we note that a silver lining offered by this body of research into the online relational initiation patterns might be that in calling attention to gendered roles, societal expectations, and misogynistic interaction, we might be able to change some of these patterns of expectations in the future.

The Dark Side of Relational Maintenance

As discussed in the previous chapters, romantic couples often use mediated technology in their existing relationships. Several maintenance functions are facilitated by technology—including (re)assurances, positivity, social support, and conflict resolution—and technology can help couples sustain and even enhance their connection and strengthen their bond. Indeed, romantic couples note that their use of mediated maintenance through text messaging (21%) or online conflict resolution (9%) has made them feel closer to their partners (Lenhart & Duggan, 2014). Couples also report using technology jointly—sharing passwords to online accounts, creating joint email addresses, or synching online calendars and social media accounts (Bevan, 2013; Lenhart & Duggan, 2014). Using technology in these ways can help strengthen bonds between partners by signaling mutual trust and facilitating coordination, but research also shows that there is a darker side to mediated relational maintenance in which couples' (mis)use of technology can lead to negative effects that threaten the relationship's existence.

Social media & romantic jealousy. One of the most heavily researched topics in the relational communication literature is the occurrence and experience of romantic jealousy. *Romantic jealousy* can manifest as cognitive thoughts or worries, emotions like anger, sadness, and betrayal, or behavioral processes like communication. Interestingly, Pfeiffer and Wong (1989) demonstrated that each component of jealousy shows unique associations to other relational attributes—for example, while cognitive jealousy is negatively related to love, emotional jealousy is positively related to love. Furthermore, emotional and behavioral jealousy are both negatively associated with happiness. Such relationships show that the effect of jealousy on relationships can be complex, because (like many communicative behaviors), the jealous behaviors that people exhibit can vary widely. Behavioral displays that are *partner-focused* (in which partners openly communicate jealousy or lack of commitment) can be *constructive* when they motivate meaningful discussions about the status of the relationship, but they can also be *destructive* if jealousy prompts deliberate attempts to avoid their partner or directly threaten them. Other displays of jealousy include *rival-focused* communication behaviors that occur when one partner might try to make contact with the other's romantic rival to threaten or derogate them (Guererro, Hannawa, & Babin, 2011). As you might guess, constructive jealousy displays are associated positively with relational satisfaction, while darker destructive and rival-focused displays detract from overall satisfaction.

To be clear, it is not the case that romantic jealousy was created by mediated technology—people were jealous long before Facebook and Snapchat came along, and often express and experience it in offline contexts. Romantic jealousy is often a response to some perceived (or actual) threat to one's relationship or partner (Bevan, 2013), and such threats obviously do occur in the absence of technology. What the research has found, however, is that increased use of mediated technology can incite or worsen cognitive/emotional experiences and behavioral expressions of romantic jealousy.

Bevan (2013) notes that because social network sites (SNSs) like Facebook and Instagram offer permanent, publicly-viewable spaces where romantic couples' romantic histories often collide with messages sent by romantic rivals or ex-partners, there is greater potential for romantic jealousy to develop. Furthermore, reduced-cue environments like SNSs can sometimes lack appropriate communicative context, leading to greater ambiguity and possible misinterpretation (see also Chapter 1). As with most communicative processes, the relationship between romantic jealousy and mediated technology is a "two-way street"—certain affordances and uses of technology, as well as elements of a couple's relationship and each partner's personality can concurrently influence experiences and behavioral manifestations of jealousy.

Some of the earliest work on online romantic jealousy explored how increasing use of SNSs like Facebook could provoke increased jealousy between partners. Muise, Christofides, and Desmarais (2009) found evidence of a "feedback loop" (p. 441), in which people who were already high in trait jealousy (or a general predisposition to jealousy, see Pfeiffer & Wong, 1989) experienced even greater levels of jealous feelings when they used Facebook more frequently. This pattern raises an interesting question about causality: Does Facebook cause jealousy where there would have been none otherwise, or are people's existing tendencies merely focused or intensified by seeing information online?

Imagine that Aliyah is in a relationship with her boyfriend, Marcus. She follows him on Instagram and notices that one of his female co-workers, Kelly, recently followed him too. Scrolling through Marcus' posts, Aliyah notes that Kelly has liked a lot of Marcus' photos and also left several comments. Consider that an analog to this situation could occur offline if Kelly were to encounter Marcus at the office—maybe she stops by his cubicle during the workday, or has an occasional cup of coffee in the breakroom; they talk about what they did over the weekend. However, since Marcus and Kelly's workplace interaction would take place outside of Aliyah's view, she likely would not even know it occurred (unless Marcus decided to mention it to her). Outside of the online context, would Aliyah's jealousy have been sparked at all? Maybe not: out of sight, out of mind. However, because Aliyah *can* see the exchange on Instagram, she can now perceive Kelly as a potential rival, which triggers her romantic jealousy.

In such a case, would we say that Instagram *caused* Aliyah's jealousy? Probably not, if it would have been equally likely that Aliyah would have responded with jealousy had she known about Marcus and Kelly's workplace interaction. Or, maybe so, if Aliyah would not have had jealous thoughts or feelings without having seen Marcus' and Kelly's Instagram exchanges. As such an example illustrates, the direction of such associations is notoriously difficult to disentangle, but notable is how the visibility of SNS interactions spotlights (potentially innocuous) pieces of relational information, renders them open to judgment, and may subsequently spark jealousy in response. Whether or not Instagram can be said to have *caused* Aliyah's jealousy, it is certainly true that by giving us a greater window into our partner's social behavior, social media platforms also open up new opportunities for jealousy, together with all the relational angst it can bring.

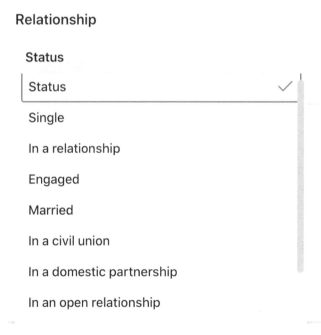

Figure 11.1: Facebook relationship status. The options currently available in the "relationship status" dropdown menu in Facebook. Source: Authors

Other features and practices associated with SNSs have been found to trigger romantic jealousy. One involves going "Facebook official"—that is, when couples officially post that they are "in a relationship," thus broadcasting relational commitment and intimacy (see Figure 11.1). Similarly, when people select a "couples' profile picture" to post on their Facebook pages or create a romantic Instagram Stories reel, this can be another publicly mediated signal of commitment and connection.

Interestingly, depending on how they are used, such SNS customs can strengthen or detract from existing romantic relationships. From a maintenance standpoint, proclaiming one's "official" relationship status via social media can serve a relationally supportive function, a way for couples to communicate publicly to members of their social network about the quality of their relationship. Joint profile pictures, meanwhile, can signal partners' "merged identities," demonstrating how connected partners feel to one another, through visual self-presentation and public disclosure (Saslow, Muise, Impett, & Dubin, 2013).

But all this sunshine can also cast a shadow. The decision of whether, how, and when to disclose one's relationship status, or to post (or not post) joint photos can become a source of tension and friction. Continuing our example above, when Marcus posts his relationship status to Facebook, he might want Aliyah to reciprocate; on the other hand, Aliyah might prefer to craft a more autonomous social media identity (Zhao, Sosik, & Cosley, 2012). This imbalance can leave Marcus feeling less secure or satisfied with the relationship, in turn triggering feelings of romantic jealousy (Emery, Muise, Alpert, & Le, 2015; Papp, Danieleqicz, & Cayemberg, 2012; Saslow et al., 2013).

Other instances of the darker side of mediated maintenance processes abound in the popular press. For example, boyfriends' and girlfriends' captions to the same Instagram picture don't always match. Instagram user Isabella Koval shared how she and her boyfriend captioned the exact same picture differently on their personal Instagram accounts (see Figures 11.2 and 11.3). While she captioned the photo with, "Always a blast with my bff," her boyfriend captioned the same photo with, "Sitting here trying to explain football to this uncultured swine." The difference struck her as humorous, and she then sent out a tweet asking other couples for examples of mismatched captions (and many responded, see Esposito, 2017). Although such examples are often funny, from a communication standpoint, we might also expect such mismatched Instagram captions (and other social media snafus) to produce more deleterious effects if they hint at more drastic misalignment of relational perceptions held by each partner.

Figures 11.2 and 11.3: Two different captions for the same Instagram photo. Source: Esposito, 2017

Interestingly, the effects of social media use on partners' feelings about the relationship and each other may differ depending on their age and how long they have been together. A survey by Pew Research noted that most couples (72%) who are married or in a committed relationship felt that social media "had no real impact" on their relationship; 17% said it had a "minor impact," and only 10% reported a "major impact" (Lenhart & Duggan, 2014). But younger users tended to grant more importance to social media. Forty-five percent of 18–29 year-olds in committed romantic relationships felt that the Internet has had an impact on their relationship compared to just 10% of those 65 and older (Lenhart & Duggan, 2014). These generational differences with respect to media's impact on romantic relationships might be due to the nature and frequency of media use among younger compared to older adults, but if you have ever had a debate over the finer features of Facebook or Instagram with your own partner, regardless of your age, you may know exactly what we're talking about!

Private versus public maintenance communication. In the discussion above, we focus primarily on public exchanges and displays of mediated communication using SNSs like Facebook or Instagram. But as highlighted in Chapter 9, couples often reserve private mediated messages to exchange more sensitive information. Cohen, Bowman, and Borchart (2014) found that knowledge of private messages exchanged between one's romantic partner and another person were more likely to evoke stronger negative emotions than messages shared publicly—moreover, these negative emotions were more likely to spur self-reported behavioral intentions to confront one's partner or one's romantic rival.

In one test of these principles Utz, Muscanell, and Khalid (2015) sought to explore whether platforms that allow private messaging were related to heightened jealousy compared to those platforms whose main mode of communication was public and visible. Specifically, Utz et al. compared Facebook to Snapchat. On Facebook, messaging is fairly public and visible. Additionally, unless messages are intentionally deleted by a message sender or the owner of the space, the messages shared between people are likely to remain public and visible. There are, of course, ways to send more private messages on Facebook; however, by and large the platform is relatively public and messages are reasonably *persistent*—that is, messages don't go anywhere or disappear once they are shared.

Snapchat, on the other hand, is a platform known for the *ephemerality* and privacy of its messages. We suspect that if you are reading this, you are already somewhat familiar with the premise of Snapchat, but we will summarize in case you are not. On Snapchat, users can send messages from one person to another, or from one person to a small group. Typically, the audience a user reaches on Snapchat is smaller than on other social media platforms like Facebook or Instagram, where messages are often cast to a much broader audience. The most distinctive feature of Snapchat is that once a message (a snap) is received by an intended recipient, the message disappears never to be seen again. Again, the messages sent on Snapchat are not persistent, but ephemeral, and this feature seems to grant users a sense of greater privacy and security. One common use of Snapchat is in sexting, or sending/receiving messages with sexual innuendo or other humorous but sexually suggestive material (Roesner, Gill, & Kohno, 2014).

Utz et al. (2015) surveyed respondents to determine whether they reported greater jealousy from one platform or the other. Specifically, participants were asked about their experience of jealousy if a current romantic partner engaged in a variety of messaging behaviors on either Snapchat or Facebook. Utz et al. reported that there is significantly more jealousy aroused from a romantic partner using Snapchat than Facebook. A close look at their results also suggests that this increase in jealousy is most acute when a current romantic partner is actively exchanging snaps with a former romantic partner.

Individual differences in social media jealousy. A variety of research programs have explored the ways that people's personalities and characteristics impact the likelihood that they will experience jealousy from social media interactions. In our own work, we tend to eschew individual difference research, opting instead for theoretical frameworks that operate across individual personality differences or even sexual and gender orientations and identifications, we do recognize that there are some particularly interesting findings with regard to the ways that individual differences seem to impact social media jealousy.

For example, Muise, Christofides, and Desmarais (2014) explore the sex differences that exist in terms of jealousy on social media. Muise et al. argued that one of the central behavioral indicators of jealousy is social/interpersonal monitoring and surveillance (Darvell, Walsh, & White, 2011; Steinfield, Ellison, & Lampe, 2008; Tokunaga, 2011). In other words, when a person feels jealousy, they are substantially more likely to spend time lurking around their partner's (or perceived rival's) Facebook pages to seek information about them. In an experiment, Muise et al. gave (heterosexual) participants one of three hypothetical scenarios. They were asked to look at a Facebook profile page and instructed to imagine that the page was their own. Additionally, participants were asked to look at a picture and imagine it was a photo of their partner with a person of the opposite sex.

The experimental induction in this study was that participants were asked to imagine that their partner was pictured either with (a) an unknown person of the opposite sex, (b) a mutual friend of the opposite sex, or (c) a cousin of the opposite sex. The study measured each participant's reported feelings of jealousy and also the amount of time spent lurking on the hypothetical partner's Facebook page. Women responded that they were significantly less jealous about the hypothetical partner's photograph with a cousin, while men reported fewer feelings of jealousy when a hypothetical partner was pictured with either an unknown other or a cousin of the opposite sex. Interestingly, women's observed lurking behavior was directly in line with their reported feelings of jealousy. They lurked the most when their hypothetical partners were pictured with an unknown other, followed by a mutual friend, and lurked least when their hypothetical partners were pictured with a cousin. Men, on the other hand, displayed lurking behavior that directly contradicted their self-reported feelings of jealousy; although they reported the most jealousy when their hypothetical partner was pictured with a mutual friend of the opposite sex, they lurked least on these occasions, instead lurking most when their hypothetical partner was pictured with an unknown person or a cousin of the opposite sex (although they reported fewer feelings of jealousy in these conditions.) These findings not only suggest potential differences in the ways that men and women report experiencing jealousy, but also how they react to those feelings, behaviorally.

Other research has explored the connection between social media behaviors and some of the Big Five personality characteristics (Seidman, 2019). Many scholars agree that the five-factor model (Funder, 2001; McCrae & Costa, 1994, 1997) is among the best summaries of personality characteristics. It suggests that a constellation of five personality characteristics can adequately capture a large amount of the personality variance between individuals. The five factors include: emotional stability (i.e., neuroticism), extraversion, openness to experience, conscientiousness, and agreeableness (see also Chapter 5). While a broad scope of research has explored the ways these factors are associated with a variety of online behaviors in the context of social networks (see Amichai-Hamburger and Vinitzky [2010] as a good starting point if you are interested in this topic), the personality characteristic that has been linked most closely to jealousy is emotional stability/neuroticism.

Neuroticism was the only one of the Big 5 personality characteristics that Seidman (2019) predicted to be positively associated with maladaptive behaviors and outcomes such as surveillance, jealousy, and conflict. And indeed the results of Seidman's survey revealed that an individual's neuroticism was related to their reported Facebook conflict, jealousy, and—echoing the results of the Muise et al. (2014) study—surveillance. Interestingly, Seidman seeks to go a step farther in this individual difference research, suggesting that surveillance is the *mediating variable* that causes neuroticism to affect both jealousy and conflict online. In other words, a neurotic personality causes more surveillance behavior, directly; and surveillance, in turn, creates more relational conflict and jealousy. Seidman's data were partially consistent with this prediction, allowing her to conclude that a statistically substantial portion of reported differences in conflict were due to neuroticism through the mediating effect of surveillance. However, it should be noted that the relationship between neuroticism and jealousy was even stronger than expected, which means that the mediating effect of surveillance alone could not explain the strength of the direct association between neuroticism and jealousy.

Technologically-Mediated Relational Termination

Most readers probably have a personally-informed sense of what a relational termination looks like. At one point or another, most of us have experienced the end of a romantic relationship. When you think about relational termination or breaking up, you may possibly begin to conjure a visual image or memory of a particular conversation in a particular place. Maybe you were the one who did the breaking up, or maybe you got dumped. In any case, if you are thinking about one of your own relational endings right now, chances are pretty good that you are remembering some hurt feelings. Although technology can affect the ways that relational terminations occur (as you know personally if you've ever dumped someone or been dumped by way of text message!), technology also allows us to observe a former partner's behavior in ways not previously possible.

For the purposes of this chapter (and throughout this book) we find it helpful to think about relational termination not as a one-time thing a couple experiences, or a single conversation or event that a couple engages in to end a relationship, but rather as a *process* that partners go through at the end—and sometimes after—a relationship has begun to fade. After all, if you recall from Chapter 3, the communication experienced in the termination stage can vary widely (Knapp, 1978). If you have ever terminated a romantic relationship, you probably remember that things did not just "go back to normal" after you had had a conversation that officially ended your relationship and you changed your Facebook status back to "single." Rather, if you have experienced the end of a romantic relationship, you had to go through a process with your partner that took some time.

As we have alluded above, romantic relationship termination is complex in even the best of situations. A number of factors influence the situations people encounter after they terminate a romantic relationship: Does the couple have children or pets? Does the couple own shared resources (e.g., a house, joint bank accounts)? How long was the couple together? Was the couple in a formal, legal relationship? How did the relationship end? Is infidelity a cause of the relational termination? Have one or both partners been abused? All of these factors and others can affect the amount of contact and the impact of that contact between partners.

While the main purpose of this chapter is to discuss the ways that technology may encourage the dark side, or more anti-social behaviors, we do think it worth briefly mentioning that there are a variety of ways technology can be used positively to navigate the troubled waters of relationship termination. For example, even after a romantic relationship comes to an end, sometimes ex-romantic partners still desire to maintain an ongoing platonic friendship. Technology can help those individuals to interact while still maintaining appropriate relational boundaries, avoiding unwanted relational escalation or de-escalation. Where children are involved, technology can also assist individuals in keeping up with co-parenting responsibilities. Occasionally, children may be able to observe their parents—although no longer engaged in a romantic relationship—displaying positive behavior of a kind unlikely in FtF settings. Additionally, couples can use the Internet to facilitate more official termination tasks, such as filing for divorce, online mediation (which can help avoid escalation patterns in FtF conflict), or joining "online divorce education programs" to navigate the complex issues involved in co-parenting and partner separation (see, Eichenberg, Huss, & Kusel, 2017). These are only a few examples among many we might name. However, as we have discussed elsewhere, technology is simply a tool, one that can be used in savory, as well as unsavory, ways.

Technologically-aided termination. As we have seen in previous chapters, the nature of much mediated communication means that couples are often integrated into each other's social media spaces. As such, ex-partners often want to "scrub" their profile pages clean or do a "digital detox" by deleting or hiding prior posts, photos, or tags that contain traces of their past relationships. Facebook offers technological features that help users "take a break" from anyone that they may have been friends with previously. And in addition to simply blocking or defriending an ex-partner, users can use the "unfollow" option, which maintains the social tie to their ex, but limits the ex's appearance on their social feed. Those who choose to put their ex-partners on a "restricted list" limit ex-partners' access to personal information, allowing them to see only posts tagged or shared as "public." Helpfully, all of these "take a break" tools pop up when a user edits their relationship status on Facebook.

More recently, new "breakup apps" have emerged that claim to help users facilitate termination processes. KillSwitch is a tool designed to do all the digging on Facebook for you—it claims to identify all the posts containing the [unwanted] target person, and to collect and store these materials in a separate, hidden photo album on the user's Facebook account. The app DrunkMode prohibits users from foolishly contacting ex-partners while under the influence of alcohol, forcing them to pass an online sobriety test before unblocking the ex-partner's contact information. Finally, the Never Liked It Anyway app claims to help its users "shed the stories and the stuff" by offering a marketplace to buy and sell the "breakup baggage" accumulated from past relationships, including old engagement and wedding rings, wedding dresses, or pricey clothes, shoes, and even furniture left behind by ex-partners. All of these technologically-driven mobile apps and website features may sound humorous, but for some, they might actually provide a useful way to facilitate the final stages of relational dissolution.

The Dark Side of Termination: Problematic Internet Use After Breakups

One particularly troubling use of modern technology is its capacity to allow almost anyone to observe what we choose to share online. Many people, ourselves included, have chosen to strike a balance between those things in our personal lives that we are willing to share and those we are not. However, as you will see in Chapter 13, the *privacy paradox* suggests that many users of the modern Internet claim to care a great deal about their privacy while nevertheless sharing a vast amount of personal information to most anyone willing to look. Our willingness to share so much information provides those who want to surveil our lives from the safe, anonymous vantage point of their own laptop a unique opportunity to do so. This often includes online surveillance by a former romantic partner (Fox & Tokunaga, 2015).

Cyberstalking. When online partner surveillance escalates, it often morphs into cyberstalking. Utter this term at a cocktail party filled with communication scholars, and most of them will admit the behavior to be problematic. The challenge is that there are almost as many definitions of cyberstalking as there are scholars who study it. [As we have said before, we are okay with variations in definitions, as long as scholars recognize that findings observed using one definition of cyberstalking cannot be applied to *all* definitions of the concept.]

Spitzberg and Cupach (2007) clearly distinguish between legal and lay definitions of stalking: They underscore the general understanding of stalking as an intentional, unwanted pattern of behaviors that, for a reasonable person, would arouse fear. Spitzberg and Cupach suggest that one challenge with much of the research that explores stalking is that clear conceptual distinctions between true stalking—intentional, unwanted behaviors that arouse fear—and more run-of-the-mill unwanted pursuit of intimacy, termed *obsessive relational intrusion* (ORI; Cupach & Spitzberg, 1998, 2004), are often difficult to make. Spitzberg and Cupach (2007) define ORI as "the repeated and unwanted pursuit of intimacy through violation of physical and/or symbolic privacy" (p. 66). While there is clearly some overlap between ORI and stalking, ORI behaviors tend to be received as annoying, rather than fear-inducing. And while ORI behaviors might be enacted out of romantic attraction or love, a (cyber)stalker is often driven by more sinister motives.

Cyberstalking, then, is defined as the use of the Internet to engage in a targeted, intentional, and unwanted pattern of behavior that evokes fear or distress in the victim. Cavezza and McEwan (2014) examined assessments from individuals who had engaged in "traditional" or "offline" stalking or cyberstalking and were receiving mental health care because of their stalking behavior. Interestingly, the typical length of stalking duration was similar between both offline stalkers and cyberstalkers, and in both groups stalkers predominantly targeted women (though there were male victims in both groups). Although cyberstalking behavior can focus on a wide variety of targets, cyberstalkers were more likely to fixate on former romantic partners than were offline stalkers. This aside, cyberstalkers and offline stalkers shared many of the same behaviors. For instance, at statistically indistinguishable levels, both types of stalkers reported following a victim, loitering or spying on a victim, sending a victim text messages, entering a victim's home, and making explicit threats against a victim. On its face it seems like the biggest difference between cyberstalkers and offline stalkers is not really any particular stalking behavior, but instead what they got caught doing. In other words, people intent on stalking others seem to do so indiscriminately in both online and offline contexts. However, the Internet clearly does affect the tools stalkers have available to find, contact, and interact with a victim. For example, perpetrators can easily take advantage of various technologies that allow messages, posts, and photos to be time-stamped and geo-located. A victim may unwittingly expose themselves to harm simply by posting a picture of a butterfly at a botanical garden without the proper Instagram security settings in place.

The types of problematic behavior that the Internet enables are substantial. The vast audience afforded by many social media platforms and online communities raises concerns about violations of privacy. Consider, for example, the practice of *doxxing*, or the intentional disclosure of private contact information such as physical addresses or phone numbers without a person's consent. Worse still in our view is *revenge porn*, wherein a perpetrator shares sexually explicit pictures or video of the victim with the intent to embarrass or shame them. Again, although both men and women have reported being victimized, women are much more likely to be targets of both forms of harassment (Eckert & Metzger-Riftkin, 2020).

Of course, the very nature of intimate relationships leaves many people exposed to such affronts. In a modern context, many romantic partners share sexually explicit photos, off-color jokes, and other racy materials with one another—albeit typically with the assumption of privacy. Partners also have access to a great deal of information that, while not sexually explicit, is best left private, including social security numbers, financial details, or physical addresses. Unfortunately, in some cases, a former romantic partner can use the affordances of the Internet to broadcast such content publicly.

Conclusion

There has been a great deal of research, then, exploring ways the Internet has been used to facilitate darker sorts of relational behaviors. Much of that research is quite interesting to read and reflect upon. We would caution our astute readers, however, that many studies are limited by the fact they compare one platform's capabilities and effects to another. We would advise temperance as scholars move from such narrowly-conceived work to claims about the state of society, or the effects (broadly speaking) of Internet technology or social media on romantic relationships.

In our view, the most important questions have received proportionally less attention: How does technologically-mediated communication affect the prevalence and severity of dark side communication behaviors between romantic partners? And how do those behaviors—when they are technologically mediated—affect relationships? Admittedly, answering such questions is *really* difficult. One reason is that, if we care about studying romantic relationships as they actually exist, we need to study actual and former partners—and it is becoming increasingly difficult, for obvious reasons, to find adequate control groups among this population that have not, or do not, use technology.

So, yes, doing work in this area is a challenge, but we do have some suggestions for future scholarship. First, we would propose that researchers continue to consider whether the types of dark side behaviors reported in online settings fit the evaluative criteria of being destructive and problematic. The idea of social surveillance behaviors performed in a FtF setting conjure an image of a Peeping Tom trying to inconspicuously observe a current or former romantic partner without that partner's consent. Most people, including us, would consider this to be maladaptive and inappropriate (not to mention illegal) behavior. Yet many social media technologies such as Facebook and Instagram do, in fact, seem to facilitate seemingly parallel behavior; the surveillance of a current or former romantic partner is made much easier via contemporary social media. But in our view, the question of whether such online surveillance is commensurately maladaptive and inappropriate is not so straightforward. On one hand surveillance in a FtF setting seems to violate social norms about *not* hunting down people who do not want to be pursued. Much social surveillance on the Internet, on the other hand, involves observing a person who *chose* to disclose certain information publicly, to a large audience. Whether a lurker who views such information is truly engaging in honest-to-goodness dark side behavior remains an open question. Such questions relate back to Spitzberg and Cupach's definitional criterion of "social acceptance" introduced in the opening paragraphs of this chapter.

Now, while we would suppose this to be an open question, it wouldn't surprise us if it turned out to be true that online romantic surveillance really is not the healthiest or relationally-supportive behavior (which relates back to Spitzberg and Cupach's second definitional criterion). Our point is simply that research ought to demonstrate when such behaviors are unhealthy or destructive, document the ways that online surveillance affects both the individual doing the surveillance and the target, and illustrate the ways that technological developments can impact surveillance behaviors and their effects on both parties. To date, this has been under-studied, and illustrates a place to apply the functional perspective on technology's effects on human relationships. In this case, the functional perspective encourages us to probe more deeply into communication behaviors by asking not just whether people use a technology to do what it was intended to do, but also what the specific social effects of certain off-label uses might be.

References

Amichai-Hamburger, Y., & Vinitzky, G. (2010). Social network use and personality. *Computers in Human Behavior, 26,* 1289–1295. https://doi.org/10.1016/j.chb.2010.03.018

Bevan, J. L. (2013). *The communication of jealousy*. Peter Lang.

Burgoon, J. K. (1993). Interpersonal expectations, expectancy violations, and emotional communication. *Journal of Language and Social Psychology, 12*(1–2), 30–48. https://doi.org/10.1177/0261927X93121003

Cameron, C., Oskamp, S., & Sparks, W. (1977). Courtship American style: Newspaper ads. *Family Coordinator,* 27–30. https://doi.org/10.2307/581857

Cavezza, C., & McEwan, T. E. (2014). Cyberstalking versus off-line stalking in a forensic sample. *Psychology, Crime, & Law, 20,* 955–970.

Cohen, E. L., Bowman, N. D., & Borchert, K. (2014). Private flirts, public friends: Understanding romantic jealousy responses to an ambiguous social network site message as a function of message access exclusivity. *Computers in Human Behavior, 35,* 535–541. https://doi.org/10.1016/j.chb.2014.02.050

Cupach, W. R., & Spitzberg, B. H. (1998). Obsessive relational intrusion and stalking. In B. H. Spitzberg & W.R. Cupach (Eds.), *The dark side of close relationships* (pp. 233–263). Lawrence Erlbaum Associates.

Cupach, W. R., & Spitzberg, B. H. (2004). *The dark side of relationship pursuit: From attraction to obsession and stalking.* Lawrence Erlbaum Associates.

Currier, D. M. (2013) Strategic ambiguity: Protecting emphasized femininity and hegemonic masculinity in the hookup culture. *Gender & Society, 27*(5), 704–727. https://doi.org/ 10.1177/0891243213493960

Darvell, M. J., Walsh, S. P., & White, K. M. (2011). Facebook tells me so: Applying the theory of planned behavior to understand partner-monitoring behavior on Facebook. *CyberPsychology, Behavior, and Social Networking, 14*, 717–722. https://doi.org/10.1089/cyber. 2011.0035

DelGreco, M., & Denes, A. (2020). You are not as cute as you think you are: Emotional responses to expectancy violations in heterosexual online dating interactions. *Sex Roles, 86*, 622–632. https://doi.org/10.1007/s11199-019-01078-0

Eckert, S., & Metzger-Riftkin, J. (2020). Doxxing. *The International Encyclopedia of Gender, Media, and Communication*, 1–5. https://doi.org/10.1002/9781119429128.iegmc009

Eichenberg, C., Huss, J., & Küsel, C. (2017). From online dating to online divorce: An overview of couple and family relationships shaped through digital media. *Contemporary Family Therapy, 39*(4), 249–260. https://doi.org/10.1007/s10591-017-9434-x

Emery, L. F., Muise, A., Alpert, E., & Le, B. (2015). Do we look happy? Perceptions of romantic relationship quality on Facebook. *Personal Relationships, 22*(1), 1–7. https://doi.org/10.1111/ pere.12059

Esposito, B. (2017, October). The girlfriends and boyfriends of Instagram are sharing their different captions. *BuzzFeed News*. https://www.buzzfeed.com/bradesposito/my-post-vs-my-bf

Fox, J., & Tokunaga, R. S. (2015). Romantic partner monitoring after breakups: Attachment, dependence, distress, and post-dissolution online surveillance via social networking sites. *Cyberpsychology, Behavior, and Social Networking, 18*, 491–498. https://doi.org/10.1089/ cyber.2015.0123

Funder, D. C. (2001). Personality. *Annual Review of Psychology, 52*, 197–221. https://doi.org/ 10.1146/ annurev.psych.52.1.197

Guerrero, L. K., Hannawa, A. F., & Babin, E. A. (2011). The communicative responses to jealousy scale: Revision, empirical validation, and associations with relational satisfaction. *Communication Methods and Measures, 5*(3), 223–249. https://doi.org/10.1080/ 19312458.2011.596993

Heino, R. D., Ellison, N. B., & Gibbs, J. L. (2010). Relationshopping: Investigating the market metaphor in online dating. *Journal of Social and Personal Relationships, 27*(4), 427–447. https://doi.org/10.1177/0265407510361614

Herbert, R. K. (1990). Sex-based differences in compliment behavior. *Language in Society*, 201– 224. https://doi.org/10.1017/S0047404500014378

Hess, A., & Flores, C. (2018). Simply more than swiping left: A critical analysis of toxic masculine performances on Tinder Nightmares. *New Media & Society, 20*(3), 1085–1102. https://doi. org/10.1177/1461444816681540

Hines, C. (1999). Rebaking the pie: The woman as dessert metaphor. In: M. Bucholtz, A. C. Liang, & L. A. Sutton (Eds.), *Reinventing identities: The gendered self in discourse* (pp. 145–162). Oxford University Press.

Huang, S., Hancock, J. T., & Tong, S. T. (2021, May). Folk theories of online dating: Exploring people's beliefs about the online dating process and online dating algorithms. [Paper Presentation]. Annual Meeting of the International Communication Association, Online.

Khan, K. S., & Chaudry, S. (2015). An evidence-based approach to an ancient pursuit: Systematic review on converting online contact info into a first date. *British Medical Journal Evidence-Based Medicine, 20*, 445–465. https://doi.org/10.1016/0378-2166(88)900005-7.

Knapp, M. L. (1978). *Social intercourse: From greeting to goodbye.* Allyn and Bacon.

Lenhart, A., & Duggan, M. (2014, February). Couples, the Internet, and Social Media. *Pew Research Center.* https://www.pewresearch.org/internet/2014/02/11/couples-the-internet-and-social-media/

McCrae, R. R., & Costa, P. T. Jr. (1994). The stability of personality: Observations and evaluations. *Current Directions in Psychological Science, 3*, 173–175. https://doi.org/10.1111/1467-8721.ep10770693

McCrae, R. R., & Costa, P. T. Jr. (1997). Personality trait structure as a human universal. *American Psychologist, 52*, 509–516. https://doi.org/10.1037/0003-066X.52.5.509

Muise, A., Christofides, E., & Desmarais, S. (2009). More information than you ever wanted: Does Facebook bring out the green-eyed monster of jealousy? *CyberPsychology & Behavior, 12*(4), 441–444. https://doi.org/ 10.1089/cpb.2008.0263

Muise, A., Christofides, E., & Desmarais, S. (2014). "Creeping" or just information seeking? Gender differences in partner monitoring in response to jealousy on Facebook. *Personal Relationships, 21*, 35–50. https://doi.org/ 10.1111/pere.12014

Papp, L. M., Danielewicz, J., & Cayemberg, C. (2012). "Are we Facebook official?" Implications of dating partners' Facebook use and profiles for intimate relationship satisfaction. *Cyberpsychology, Behavior, and Social Networking, 15*(2), 85–90. https://doi.org/ 10.1089/ cyber.2011.0291

Pfeiffer, S. M., & Wong, P. T. (1989). Multidimensional jealousy. *Journal of Social and Personal Relationships, 6*(2), 181–196. https://doi.org/10.1177/026540758900600203

Pomerantz, A. (1978). Compliment responses: Notes on the co-operation of multiple constraints. In *Studies in the organization of conversational interaction* (pp. 79–112). Academic Press. https://doi.org/ https://doi.org/10.1016/B978-0-12-623550-0.50010-0

Roesner, F., Gill, B. T., & Kohno, T. (2014). Investigating the use of Snapchat's self-destructing messages. *Proceedings of the Financial Cryptography and Data Security Conference,* Christ Church, Barbados, West Indies.

Saslow, L. R., Muise, A., Impett, E. A., & Dubin, M. (2013). Can you see how happy we are? Facebook images and relationship satisfaction. *Social Psychological and Personality Science, 4*(4), 411–418. https://doi.org/10.1177//1948550612460059

Seidman, G. (2019). The Big 5 and relationship maintenance on Facebook. *Journal of Social and Personal Relationships, 36*, 1785-1806. https://doi.org/ 10.11777/0265407518772089

Spitzberg, B. H., & Cupach, W. R. (2007). The state of the art of stalking: Taking stock of the emerging literature. *Aggression and Violent Behavior, 12*, 64–86. https://doi.org/10.1016/j.avb.2006.05.001

Steinfield, C., Ellison, N., & Lampe, C. (2008). Social capital, self-esteem, and use of online social network sites: A longitudinal analysis. *Journal of Applied Developmental Psychology, 29*, 434–445. https://doi.org/10.1016/j.appdev.2008.07.002

Thompson, L. (2018). "I can be your Tinder nightmare": Harassment and misogyny in the online sexual marketplace. *Feminism & Psychology, 28*(1), 69–89. https://doi.org/10.1177/095935351770226

Tokunaga, R. S. (2011). Social networking site or social surveillance site? Understanding the use of interpersonal electronic surveillance in romantic relationships. *Computers in Human Behavior, 27*, 705–713. https://doi.org/10.1016/j.chb.2010.08.014

Utz, S., Muscanell, N., & Khalid, C. (2015). Snapchat elicits more jealousy than Facebook: A comparison of Snapchat and Facebook Use. *Cyberpsychology, Behavior, and Social Networking, 18*, 141–146. https://doi.org/ 10.1089/cyber.2014.0479

Vogels, E. A. (2020, February). "10 facts about Americans and online dating." *Pew Research.* https://www.pewresearch.org/fact-tank/2020/02/06/10-facts-about-americans-and-online-dating/

Wolfson, N., & Manes, J. (1980). The compliment as a social strategy. *Research on Language & Social Interaction, 13*(3), 391–410. https://doi.org/ https://doi.org/10.1080/08351818009370503

Zhao, X., Schwanda Sosik, V., & Cosley, D. (2012, May). It's complicated: How romantic partners use facebook. In *Proceedings of the SIGCHI conference on human factors in computing systems* (pp. 771–780). https://doi.org/10.1145/2207676.2207788

12

The Unbearable Lightness of Dating: Online and Mobile Dating Fatigue

Since taking off in 2015, the online and mobile dating industry has grown 13.3% into a 4-billion-dollar empire in the United States (IBISWorld, 2020). According to recent statistics, "For heterosexual couples in the United States, meeting online has become the most popular way couples meet, eclipsing meeting through friends for the first time around 2013" (Rosenfeld, Thomas, & Hausen, 2019). Clearly, online and mobile dating have moved beyond the initial stigma. Today, dating apps and websites saturate the contemporary dating landscape; in fact, we might argue that they have reached over-saturation. Platforms like OkCupid, Grindr, Bumble, and Tinder have lost some of the original luster and for many are becoming a source of frustration.

Online daters have begun to report feeling jaded, disappointed, and resentful. In 2016, Julie Beck's article in *The Atlantic* discussed the phenomenon of *dating app fatigue* in which daters described feeling completely let down by their use of apps to find romantic love. This sense of fatigue or burnout is often characterized by negative emotional responses like frustration, anger, or disappointment. According to a Pew Research survey, Americans who have tried a dating app within the past year say that their experience "left them feeling more frustrated (45%) than hopeful (28%)" (Anderson, Vogels, & Turner, 2020).

In an effort to cope with these emotions, daters use different strategies. Some curtail or limit their use of apps and websites, while others quit or delete their accounts altogether (Brubaker et al., 2016), and some daters have tried to find "new" ways of dating that don't involve the Internet (Paul, 2018). In this chapter, we begin by first exploring daters' individual experience of fatigue and examine the factors that contribute to it. We then discuss the larger effects of fatigue within the online dating industry, and on the state of dating, courtship, and the romantic imagination in America.

Nine Months on Tinder

In researching this book, we both spoke to a lot of people who engaged in online and mobile dating. But to Stephanie, one interviewee really stood out: Meet Paul, a 34-year-old single man, living in Michigan. He describes himself as an "average guy"—and in many ways, he is totally right. Paul works a 9-to-5 job in Detroit, attends school part-time in pursuit of his Master's degree, and on summer weekends takes his boat out on the lake. After he and his wife divorced, he decided it was time to get back into the dating game. Unfortunately, as he told Stephanie, it all looked so different from when he was single many years ago:

> I don't know. I'm 34, I [was] used to going to the bar and having drinks. So then you meet somebody. But I mean, I just don't have the time and energy to try to go to, say, three bars this week. Or even one for that matter. I just don't want to do that.

So Paul joined Tinder nine months ago hoping it would help him find romance. He had not done any kind of mobile or online dating before, so it was all new to him.

We chose to feature Paul's interview because in many ways, he does represent the "average" Tinder user—single guy getting back into the dating scene in his 30s, work hard/play hard lifestyle, trying to make romantic connections. We also chose to feature Paul because although the attitudes he held were generally representative of other online daters we talked to, he had a great way of phrasing his responses that was truly unique—although waiting for him to open up took patience. When Stephanie would ask him questions, Paul would often reply with one-word answers. But if she waited for a while and asked him a follow-up question, he would give much more detailed (and interesting) answers. Stephanie's interview with Paul started out something like this:

Okay, you've been on Tinder for nine months now. How's your experience been?

"I guess shitty?"

Really? How come?

When Paul elaborated, we found out that in his experience, mobile dating was problematic because of the profile. He used to spend a lot of time on it, trying to stand out and get noticed by women. But now? What's on his profile?

"Nothing."

Really, nothing?

"Nope, I don't even have anything written."

But do you have a picture?

"Well. Yeah. I have a picture. But that's it, really."

Then, it was the swiping. Stephanie asked him, "How do you decide whether to swipe right or left on someone, what's that like?"

"It's weird."

How so?

"I don't know. It feels like you're in elementary school. You're trying to figure out what kind of table to sit at, that kind of thing."

Over time, he said, swiping also made him feel "indifferent." Judging women on their pictures, making selections based on their profiles, all of this was "just something to do." Next, mobile dating was a bad experience because all his in person dates were "*awkward*":

It feels like a bunch of blind dates to me. I mean, even though you're talking and you're chatting and I don't. . .I don't know, it's not real until you meet 'em. So, I mean, it's all bullshit in a box. I'd rather get to know someone slowly...by sitting down with somebody and actually talking to them.

At the end of the interview, Stephanie asked him a final question: "So, in general, after nine months, how has dating on Tinder made you feel?"

"I don't think it's changed anything, I don't know. I mean, my life, like romantically or friend wise, you can say it's like, shitty but um, I don't know. Just maybe a little bit of *hopefulness.*"

Really? hopefulness? because—?

"Oh, maybe I'll meet someone."

Wow, now this Paul sounded like a completely different person. Maybe we misjudged him. Perhaps he is not such a pessimist after all?

"But I don't [ever meet anyone]. But, hey, they build liquor stores for a reason."

Shitty. Nothing. Weird. Indifferent. Awkward. Bullshit in a box. But then, *Hopefulness.* How could Paul be so negative but also optimistic at the same time?

Dating App Fatigue

Daters across America report feeling frustrated and exhausted by all the swiping. When we stop to consider it, the idea that dating would make us feel defeated instead of excited is not entirely counterintuitive. From its distant roots in the 18th century, modern middle-class dating has always brought with it a thicket of sexual, social, and familial anxieties. So why now, when dating seems more in control of the erotically liberated, do we sometimes approach dating as a chore rather than something we enjoy?

The transformation of online and mobile dating from something novel and fun into a form of work has been happening incrementally over time. Moira Weigel (2017) delves into this idea in her book *Labor of Love*, suggesting that dating in general requires not only physical work—grooming, primping—but also increasing investments of time, money, and emotion. In short, romantic dating has become a lot of work.

Applying this idea to online and mobile dating, we can see the time-consuming effort that people have to put in at different stages: *profile development*, which includes writing biographical information, photo curation, answering the match questions of different dating sites and apps, and ongoing revisions; *mate selection*, which consists of reviewing hundreds (sometimes thousands) of other daters' profiles and swipe decisions; and *interaction and discovery*, which might include initiating new flirtations, replying to others' messages in an effort to schedule

FtF dates, and dodging other daters' texts. With all of these tasks to check off the list, managing one's Tinder account can feel like a part-time job rather than full-time fun (and those tasks multiply if you have additional accounts to deal with on Bumble, CoffeeMeetsBagel, Tinder, and OkCupid). Notably, it doesn't seem to matter which apps or sites you are on—since the functions and processes are similar across multiple platforms, all of them create similar feelings of fatigue.

This job-like approach to online and mobile dating may be in part responsible for the disappointment and frustration that daters report. But besides the task-oriented management of dating accounts, what other factors might lead to dating app fatigue? What else may cause this negative emotional response to something that is supposed to be fun and exciting?

What is Causing Dating App Fatigue?

The scholarly research into user fatigue related to technology use has been steadily growing: Most of this work centers on social media and how people manage their fatigue by "taking breaks" from platforms like Facebook (Bright, Kleiser, & Grau, 2015) or Twitter (Schoenbeck, 2014). You might ask why people are motivated to continue using technology (dating apps included) to the point of exhaustion. The answer is that today's most popular social computing and technology platforms are very good at motivating even depleted users to keep going—endlessly swiping, matching, messaging, and scheduling dates.

There are two kinds of motivation that dating apps target: Ryan and Deci (2000) define *extrinsic motivation*, as being driven to do something because it can lead to a discrete, separable outcome or reward; *intrinsic motivation* they define as wanting to do some behavior because it is innately interesting, satisfying, or enjoyable. Dating apps are uniquely suited to prompt continued use because they are capable of pushing their users' extrinsic *and* intrinsic motivation buttons. As long as extrinsic and intrinsic motivation levels stay high, daters will enjoy using their apps. But when motivation levels drop, daters will move into a state of *amotivation* characterized by a lack of intention to act: "amotivation results from not valuing an activity (Ryan, 1995), not feeling competent to do it (Deci, 1975), or not believing it will yield a desired outcome (Seligman, 1975)" (Ryan & Deci, 2000, p. 61).

Below, we examine several intrinsic and extrinsic factors that motivate people to keep using dating apps—*decision making and mate selection, fear of missing out (FOMO) on better dates,* the *semblance of scarcity,* and *guilt over app (in)action.* We then describe how daters can develop app fatigue when these motivational factors decline or run out.

Decision making and mate selection. There are so many potential partners to search through in online and mobile dating platforms that the abundance of choice can feel like a great advantage to finding love and romance. Couple that potential with the novelty of swiping, and daters find themselves *intrinsically motivated* to use their apps. Intrinsic motivation exists "in the nexus between a person and a task" (Ryan & Deci, 2000, p. 58). In other words, if the person finds the task enjoyable, they will gain a sense of reward from performing it and will therefore continue to do it. In the case of contemporary dating, many apps foster intrinsic motivation through *gamification.* Through their design (e.g., features, visual interface, haptic feedback, and rules) dating apps evoke an immersive, "gameful" experience that motivates users toward satisfying specific behavioral outcomes (Deterding et al., 2011; Hamri, Koivisto, & Sarsa, 2014). The act of swiping to make decisions is fun—right swipe/keep, left swipe/reject, up swipe/super-like! Research from cognitive science shows that we generally enjoy the act of choosing; when we make choices, we feel like we are in control of our environment, a feeling that humans tend to crave (Leotti, Iyenger, & Ochsner, 2010). Swiping becomes even more fun when we are rewarded with one of Tinder's "It's a Match!" notifications, popping up when someone we've chosen has chosen us in turn. App notifications can inspire a sense of autonomy and control over their romantic lives that instills the intrinsic motivation needed to continue swiping (see also, Tong et al., 2016).

Additionally, being notified by the system that "It's a Match!" might also feed one's self-esteem. The system notifications that dating apps provide—sending up pings when other daters have viewed your profile, messaged you, or mutually matched with you—all of these notifications serve as direct indications of romantic interest. They provide overt, clear, instant feedback at every stage of the mobile dating process. And that feedback can be addictive: In our own research, we have found that users of the all-male dating app Grindr report that the "ego boost" or self-validation from being liked by other daters was a main motivation to continue using it (Van de Wiele & Tong, 2014). Other research has replicated our results with heterosexual daters, finding similar ego-boost motivations among Tinder users (e.g., Timmermans & De Caluwe, 2017; Ward, 2017).

But at some point, that tingly sensation tied to the "It's a Match!" notification might not be enough of a positive reward for daters to continue swiping. When daters no longer value the ego-boost reward that comes from a match, or feel as though their recent matches were disappointing, they may enter a state of fatigue or amotivation. And although initially, swiping may be enjoyable, over time daters may experience *choice overload*, becoming overwhelmed by the endless profiles and feelings of risk associated with making a poor choice; after a while, selection become demotivating (see Iyengar & Lepper, 2000; Lenton & Francesconi, 2011; Tong et al., 2016, 2018). And once the novelty of swiping wears off, profile review, swiping, and selection are not fun anymore. As Baker (2018) describes it, "All dating apps are relatively the same. They're games of thumb war, your opponent being an endless stream of profiles separated by their bangability. And you lose HOURS of your life doing this. . ."

So in short spurts, dating apps thrill us with a newfound sense of agency over our decision making, but when apps demand that we make too many choices in a single, short period of time, a very different mechanism can kick in: *ego-depletion*, or incremental losses from the part of our brains that governs our feelings of self-control. Ego-depletion can cause feelings of both mental and emotional fatigue, as well as physical tiredness—and to make things worse, ego-depletion and loss of self-control can ripple outwards to affect decisions and behaviors in other areas of our lives. So the effects of all that Tinder use can remain even after we sign out of our accounts (Baumeister & Tiereny, 2012; Vohs et al., 2014). Thus, mate selection, which used to be an intrinsically motivating decision-making task, becomes an ego-depleting and fatiguing chore to be avoided.

FOMO on better dates. Another factor that may initially propel daters' motivation to continue swiping is the overwhelming *fear of missing out* (FOMO) *on better dates*. Dating apps and sites deliberately market their dating pools as being endless, so it can be easy to fall prey to this kind of FOMO. As noted above, daters may intrinsically value the rewards that come from swiping and matching, but the suspense created by the uncertainty that this current match is truly the "best" option is often more than many daters can bear—and so they keep swiping. We note that FOMO wasn't created by dating apps; in fact, it is often touted as the root problem plaguing romantic monogamy in general, immortalized in our romantic imagination by the classic 1955 Marilyn Monroe film, *The Seven-Year Itch* (along with her iconic white skirt scene). So, while it is not a new phenomenon, what *is* novel is how dating apps create and thrive on the atmosphere of FOMO. They intensify our feelings of FOMO by implicitly asking us at all times, "Are you missing out on a hotter, cooler, cuter partner who is just a swipe away? If so, you're wasting your time on this match when you could be on a date with someone better!" They then offer a remedy for that fear by giving us access to a pool filled with hotter, cooler, more attractive partners, just waiting to be found. Fear of missing out on better dates is a common response among Millennials who use dating apps (see for a first-hand account, Toglia, 2017). Oddly enough, this can create a FOMO-feedback-loop: The hunt is exhausting, and the FOMO created by dating apps often ends up ironically making us feel *less* satisfied in our dating choices (D'Angelo & Toma, 2017), thereby leading to more fatigue through continued search.

The semblance of scarcity. Daters may also receive a bump of extrinsic motivation from the notifications sent by the dating apps. Many dating apps employ the *scarcity tactic*—"opportunities seem more valuable to us when their availability is limited" (Cialdini, 1984/2006, p. 180). In doing so, dating apps will push notifications to their users like "See who matched with you before they disappear!" "Someone liked your profile. Find out who NOW!" "Your LAST CHANCE to see the Bagels who liked you!" By using the scarcity principle, dating apps ratchet up the salience of extrinsic rewards (Ryan & Deci, 2000). Daters need to get online *now* to avoid missing out on an opportunity of a lifetime! Some dating systems also deploy the *deadline* tactic, "in which some official time limit is placed on the customer's opportunity to get what the compliance professional is offering" (Ryan & Deci, 2000, p. 181). Instilling the idea that matches will disappear soon makes the dating tasks of swiping and messaging seem much more urgent. Eventually, however, daters will likely become annoyed with these notifications flooding their inboxes. When they realize that scarcity and deadline tactics are bogus attempts by dating app companies to control their behavior, they may stop responding to this contrived sense of urgency and use the app less frequently.

App (in)activity guilt: Feeling bad from taking time off. App (in)activity guilt is a form of extrinsic motivation that Ryan and Deci (2000) call *introjected regulation*, or actions that people are motivated to perform "with a feeling of pressure in order to avoid guilt or anxiety or to attain ego-enhancements or pride" (p. 62). Interestingly, daters report feeling anxious or guilty when they aren't putting in the effort to remain active on an app or site for a period of time. Others report feeling panicked when they don't reply to other daters quickly enough.

Daters' panic and guilt may stem from a *feeling of obligation* to use apps, as something they "have" to do, rather than something they "want" to do. Given the pressure on single adults to find love and intimacy, many experience a commensurate pressure to remain active online, as it is the primary arena for modern dating. And this sense of external obligation then creates guilt when daters stay away from their accounts too long. Daters' guilt may also be compounded by their *fear of being single* (Spielmann et al., 2013), which entails "concern, anxiety, or distress regarding the current or prospective experience of being without a romantic partner" (p. 1049). And this fear can, again, return to feelings of guilt whenever daters take time off from their app accounts. Journalist Rachel Thompson (2016) recounted a memory she had while scrolling through Bumble during a subway ride in London:

> I'd not opened the app in over a week. I'd ignored the notifications that flashed across my screen while I was at work, promising myself that I'd look at them later. But later never came, and my notifications fell by the wayside. As I stared at my reflection in the window before me, an unwelcome thought arrived in my head, "You're going to die alone and it's all your fault!"
>
> It might sound like a ridiculous thing to think, but right there in that Tube carriage, I felt an unpleasant, anxious feeling that I wanted to shake off immediately. As I emerged from the train station, I opened my phone and began swiping hurriedly to make up for lost time. I fired off messages to three guys there and then in an attempt to feel better about the situation. I carried on swiping as I walked home, telling myself to be indiscriminate so that I could maximise [sic] the number of matches.

In this moment, Thompson's fear of being single and guilt from lack of app activity combine, simultaneously igniting her furious swiping and messaging behavior. In the short term, this might keep her engaged. However, even the most dedicated dater may tire of so many negative emotions and to avoid feeling them simply quit dating apps altogether.

The Effects of Dating App Fatigue

Individual response to fatigue: Voluntary "non-use" of dating apps. Although we have come to accept that dating app fatigue may be a part of the online and mobile dating process, we know less about how people respond to it. However, research into Internet and mobile communication technology more generally suggests that people will voluntarily[7] curtail or stop using systems like email,

---

7 We note that our discussion of "voluntary non-use" entails those who deliberately choose to disengage from dating apps in response to a desire "to regain (a sense of) self-control over their own technology use" (Baumer, Ames, Burrell, Brubaker, & Dourish, 2015). This conceptualization of non-use does not include those individuals who would like to use dating app technology, but cannot due to availability, cost, exclusion, or lack of infrastructure.

instant messaging, Twitter, or Facebook for a variety of reasons, including: disenchantment, lack of interest, displacement, desire to reject mainstream technology trends and values, concerns over personal information and privacy, and concerns over their time (Birnholtz, 2010; Luqman, Cao, Ali, Masood, & Yu, 2017; Portwood-Stacer, 2013; Satchell & Dourish, 2009; Schoenebeck, 2014). In her analysis of Twitter non-use, Schoenebeck (2014) studied both break-takers, who give up Twitter use for shorter periods of time, and Twitter quitters, who "seek to make long-term changes in their behavior." Similarly, people's individual response to dating app fatigue might range anywhere from curtailing app use (i.e., reducing the overall amount of time one spends on dating apps), to app "breaks" (i.e., short periods of complete non-use), to quitting apps altogether (i.e., deleting profiles or login information; uninstalling the apps from smartphones).[8]

Case Study: The Development of Fatigue and "Leaving" Grindr

In their study of the dating app Grindr, Brubaker, Ananny, and Crawford (2016) examined how users' fatigue drove them to "leave" the platform. Interestingly, daters' departures from Grindr were not captured in a single moment of deleting the app off of their phones—instead for most daters, leaving Grindr reflected "a relationship to an individual's [unfulfilled] goals and expectations for the app more than its deletion or the running of its code" (p. 9). Just as people report multiple uses for dating apps, they also report multiple reasons for leaving the apps. Brubaker et al. (2016) found that daters' desire to leave Grindr was motivated by several different factors: Some found it to be "a waste of time," or "a distraction," while others mentioned Grindr's failure to live up to its potential to help them "meet the 'right kind of person'" (p. 7).

Their results also pointed to leaving because of the fatigue-inducing overload and the FOMO on better dates that dating apps facilitate. As one of their respondents recounted: "[A]pps like Grindr undermine the creation of fulfilling relationships by promoting 'a gay culture in which we look and always keep looking, because the next best thing is right around the corner'" (Brubaker et al., 2016, p. 8). Over time, some men using Grindr developed a sense of amotivation that

---

8 Notably, deleting the app does not necessarily delete one's actual dating profile or account. In some cases, it can be very difficult to completely remove one's presence from the dating app (see Brubaker et al., 2016).

prompted them to stop. Though some simply curtailed or quit their use of the app, others chose different paths, including anonymizing their profiles with more generic information, deleting their accounts, or uninstalling the app from their phone. These results indicate that fatigue (and ensuing departure) is something that builds gradually over time, with continued app use; and just as the reasons and causes underlying dating app fatigue are multifaceted, so are daters' individual responses to those feelings.

Industry response to fatigue: Outsourcing labor with personal dating assistants. Individual users may choose to curtail their use or voluntarily quit apps altogether in an effort to combat fatigue; however, such coping strategies are at odds with the dating app industry itself. Rather than having their users opt-out, dating apps and websites would prefer that daters remain active, paying customers. To do so, however, requires that the industry provide other ways to boost daters' motivation, helping them cope with the anxiety, fatigue, and frustration.

One recent response to daters' increased app fatigue is the "personal dating assistant." This cottage industry has gained popularity in recent years, and can be found across the United States, Canada, Europe, and Australia (see www.vidaselect.com; www.personaldatingassistants.com; www.prodatingassistant.com). Daters feeling fatigued can pay to outsource the labor associated with mobile and online dating. These self-described "done- for-you online dating" companies will help their clients with a variety of services. To better understand the business, we conducted a study of people who currently work as *online dating assistants* (ODAs). Specifically, we relied on a phenomenological approach to communication to gain insight into the lived experiences of ODA workers. We conducted in-depth interviews with six people who were currently working as ODAs or had in the past. Because the ODA industry is so new, getting access to the sample of workers was difficult—so we relied on a method called *snowball sampling*, in which we asked our participants to nominate other acquaintances, friends, or coworkers whom they knew who would (a) fit our sampling criteria and (b) might consent to be interviewed.

Our results indicated that those who worked as ODAs had a variety of roles corresponding to different stages of the online dating process. *Profile writers* are essentially ghostwriters. After the company conducts extensive interviews with its clients, profile writers use that information to compose content for their clients' profile bios and helps them select and curate photographs and other profile content. Other ODAs work as *matchmakers* whose job was to learn the romantic preferences of their clients and then screen dating sites and apps for possible dates. Finally, those who work as *closers* are tasked with digital interaction and message exchange, which was perhaps the most lucrative form of ODA labor. *Closers* impersonate their clients by logging in to their dating app accounts to exchange messages with other daters in an effort to obtain others' phone numbers and arrange FtF dates on behalf of their clients (see Rochadiat, Tong, Hancock, & Stuart-Ullin, 2020; Stuart-Ullin, 2018).

In some ways, the services that modern-day ODAs offer can be compared to those of matchmakers from the past. Both aid in daters' search for love and shape the larger romantic imagination that there is a "soulmate" to be found. Although one very important difference is that when daters use a matchmaking service to find a date, *both partners know they are using that service.* In the current case of ODAs, only those clients who paid for ODA services know they are outsourcing their profile writing, matchmaking, and messaging; their potential (unsuspecting) partners remain in the dark. In this sense, it's reminiscent of the 1897 play *Cyrano D'Bergerac* (minus the big nose and French poetry). But the ODA industry is not make-believe: Online daters are paying real money for *relational outsourcing.*

We found that ODAs' personal attitudes toward the deceptive nature of their work varied widely—on one end, some ODAs thought their work was inherently dishonest, inauthentic, and deliberately manipulative, and these feelings sometimes made it difficult for them to perform their jobs. Yet other ODAs thought of their work as no different than any other copywriting job in marketing or advertising—except in this case, the copy they were writing was for personal dating profiles, and the products they were selling were people. Some even described their work as a "sales challenge" in which they had to work harder to sell "less desirable" clients and drum up business for them in a competitive marketplace (Rochadiat et al., 2020).

Our study also found that most ODAs worked remotely from home, rather than commuting to a physical office. As part of the rising "gig economy," ODAs functioned as "online freelancers": "[T]he execution of traditional working activities . . .[and] also forms of clerical work, is channeled through apps managed by firms that also intervene in setting minimum quality standards of service and in the selection and management of the workforce" (De Stefano, 2015). When we consider that so many other forms of on-demand gig labor exist, individuals' willingness to pay someone else do the dirty work of dating is not all that surprising. There are obviously other forms of gig labor where customers contract workers for specific, discrete services like transportation (Uber and Lyft), food delivery (DoorDash), or dog-walking (Rover.com). Yet what is surprising is that the services proffered by ODAs imply that customers are also willing to pay someone else to complete very "human-based" tasks of personal interaction, message exchange, and mate selection. The outsourcing of relational tasks might seem strange, but it is simply an extension of the sharing economy that uses digital platforms to manage and organize work (Scholz, 2017).

Conclusion

In summary, the underlying causes of online dating fatigue are complex and multiple. It is not just one factor that fuels daters' feelings of frustration—many elements create amotivation and leave people struggling for solutions. The ODA gig industry is just one more indicator of the way that romantic relationship initiation is changing in our modern times. Of course, such changes bring about all kinds of questions—what kinds of daters hire ODAs? At what point in their online and mobile dating experience do people feel fatigue and consider outsourcing to be a good idea? How might other, unsuspecting daters feel if they found out that they were messaging with a professional dating assistant, instead of a genuine dater? Would they feel betrayed or deceived? Do those daters who hire ODAs ever disclose that fact to their partners, assuming they begin a committed relationship?

All of these questions remain unanswered for the moment. The ODA industry is too new to know exactly how it will impact relational initiation processes in the long-term and the larger contemporary romantic imagination. But in the meantime, it remains an option for daters like Paul whose intrinsic and extrinsic motivation levels are sinking fast, but whose steadfast bit of hope that they might meet somebody keeps them swiping on Tinder.

References

Anderson, M., Vogels, E. A., & Turner, E. (2020, Feb). The virtues and downsides of online dating. *Pew Research Center: Internet & Technology.* https://www.pewresearch.org/internet/2020/02/06/the-virtues-and-downsides-of-online-dating/

Baker, E.-R. (2018, November). I tried Facebooks' new dating app and it was exhausting. *Vice.* https://www.vice.com/en_au/article/nep3v7/i-tried-facebooks-new-dating-app-and-it-was-exhausting

Baumeister, R. F., & Tierney, J. (2012). *Willpower: Rediscovering the greatest human strength.* Penguin Press.

Baumer, E. P., Burrell, J., Ames, M. G., Brubaker, J. R., & Dourish, P. (2015). On the importance and implications of studying technology non-use. *Interactions, 22*(2), 52–56. https://doi.org/10.1145/2723667

Beck, J. (2016, October). The rise of dating-app fatigue. *The Atlantic Online.* https://www.theatlantic.com/health/archive/2016/10/the-unbearable-exhaustion-of-dating-apps/505184/

Birnholtz, J. (2010). Adopt, adapt, abandon: Understanding why some young adults start, and then stop, using instant messaging. *Computers in Human Behavior, 26*(6), 1427–1433. https://doi.org/10.1016/j.chb.2010.04.021

Bright, L. F., Kleiser, S. B., & Grau, S. L. (2015). Too much Facebook? An exploratory examination of social media fatigue. *Computers in Human Behavior, 44*, 148–155. https://doi.org/10.1016/j.chb.2014.11.048

Brubaker, J. R., Ananny, M., & Crawford, K. (2016). Departing glances: A sociotechnical account of 'leaving' Grindr. *New Media & Society, 18*(3), 373–390. https://doi.org/10.1177/1461444814542311

Cialdini, R. (1984/2006). *Influence: The psychology of persuasion.* William Morrow and Company, Inc.

D'Angelo, J. D., & Toma, C. L. (2017). There are plenty of fish in the sea: The effects of choice overload and reversibility on online daters' satisfaction with selected partners. *Media Psychology, 20*(1), 1–27. https://doi.org/10.1080/15213269.2015.1121827

Deci, E. L. (1976). Notes on the theory and metatheory of intrinsic motivation. *Organizational Behavior and Human Performance, 15*(1), 130–145.

De Stefano, V. (2015). The rise of the just-in-time workforce: On-demand work, crowdwork, and labor protection in the gig-economy. *Comparative Labor Law & Policy Journal, 37*, 471–503. https://doi.org/10.2139/ssrn.2682602

Deterding, S., Sicart, M., Lennart, N., O'Hara, K., & Dixon, D. (2011). Gamification: Using game-design elements in non-gaming contexts. In *CHI'11 extended abstracts on human factors in computing systems* (pp. 2425–2428). ACM Press.

Hamari, J., Koivisto, J., & Sarsa, H. (2014, January). Does gamification work? A literature review of empirical studies on gamification. In *HICSS* (Vol. 14, No. 2014, pp. 3025–3034). https://doi.org/ 10.1109/HICSS.2014.377

Huotari, K., & Hamari, J. (2012, October). Defining gamification: A service marketing perspective. In *Proceedings of the 16th international academic MindTrek conference* (pp. 17–22). ACM Press.

IBISWorld. (2020, April). Dating services industry in the U.S. https://www.ibisworld.com/united-states/market-research-reports/dating-services-industry/

Iyengar, S. S., & Lepper, M. R. (2000). When choice is demotivating: Can one desire too much of a good thing? *Journal of Personality and Social Psychology, 79*(6), 995–1006. https://doi.org/10.1037/0022-3514.79.6.995

Lenton, A. P., & Francesconi, M. (2011). Too much of a good thing? Variety is confusing in mate choice. *Biology Letters, 7*(4), 528–531. https://doi.org/ 10.1098/rsbl.2011.0098

Leotti, L. A., Iyengar, S. S., & Ochsner, K. N. (2010). Born to choose: The origins and value of the need for control. *Trends in Cognitive Sciences, 14*(10), 457–463. https://doi.org/10.1016/j.tics.2010.08.001

Luqman, A., Cao, X., Ali, A., Masood, A., & Yu, L. (2017). Empirical investigation of Facebook discontinues usage intentions based on SOR paradigm. *Computers in Human Behavior, 70*, 544–555. https://doi.org/ 10.1016/j.chb.2017.01.020

Matyszczyk, C. (2014, April 24). Why all men should have someone else do their online dating for them. https://www.cnet.com/news/why-all-men-should-have-someone-else-do-their-online-dating-for-them/

Paul, K. (2018, August 28). Tired of swiping right, some singles try slow dating. *The Wall Street Journal.* https://www.wsj.com/articles/tired-of-swiping-right-some-singles-try-slow-dating-1535468479

Portwood-Stacer, L. (2013). Media refusal and conspicuous non-consumption: The performative and political dimensions of Facebook abstention. *New Media & Society, 15*(7), 1041–1057. https://doi.org/ 10.1177/1461444812465139

Rochadiat, A. M. P., Tong, S. T., Hancock, J. T., & Stuart-Ulin, C. R. (2020). The outsourcing of online dating: Investigating the lived experiences of online dating assistants working in the contemporary gig economy. *Social Media + Society.* https://doi.org/10.1177/ 2056305120957290

Rosenfeld, M. J., Thomas, R. J., & Hausen, S. (2019). Disintermediating your friends: How online dating in the United States displaces other ways of meeting. *Proceedings of the National Academy of Science, USA, 116*(36), 17753–17758. https://doi.org/10.1073/pnas.1908630116

Ryan, R. M., & Deci, E. L. (2000). Intrinsic and extrinsic motivations: Classic definitions and new directions. *Contemporary Educational Psychology, 25*(1), 54–67. https://doi.org/10.1006/ ceps.1999.1020

Satchell, C., & Dourish, P. (2009). Beyond the user: Use and non-use in HCI. *Human-Computer Interaction, 366*(7), 9–16. https://doi.org/ 10.1145/1738826.1738829

Schoenebeck, S. Y. (2014, April). Giving up Twitter for Lent: how and why we take breaks from social media. In *Proceedings of the SIGCHI conference on human factors in computing systems* (pp. 773–782). https://doi.org/10.1145/2556288.2556983

Scholz, T. (2016). *Uberworked and underpaid: How workers are disrupting the digital economy.* Polity Press.

Spielmann, S. S., MacDonald, G., Maxwell, J. A., Joel, S., Peragine, D., Muise, A., & Impett, E. A. (2013). Settling for less out of fear of being single. *Journal of Personality and Social Psychology, 105*(6), 1049–1073. https://doi.org/10.1037/a0034628

Stuart-Ulin, C. R. (2018, April). You could be flirting on dating apps with paid impersonators. *Quartz.* https://qz.com/1247382/online-dating-is-so-awful-that-people-are-paying-virtual-dating-assistants-to-impersonate-them/

Thompson, R. (2016, October 9). Online dating FOMO is ruining my chances of finding a date. *Mashable.* https://mashable.com/2016/10/09/online-dating-fomo/

Timmermans, E., & De Caluwé, E. (2017). Development and validation of the Tinder motives scale (TMS). *Computers in Human Behavior, 70*, 341–350. https://doi.org/10.1016/ j.chb.2017.01.028

Toglia, M. (2017, April 21). The hardest part about deleting my dating apps is also the scariest. *Bustle.* https://www.bustle.com/p/the-hardest-part-about-deleting-my-dating-apps-is-also-the-scariest-52114

Tong, S. T., Corriero, E. F., Matheny, R. G., & Hancock, J. T. (2018). Online daters' willingness to use recommender technology for mate selection decisions. In M. de Gemmis, A. Felfernig, P. Lops, J. O' Donovan, G. Semeraro, & M. Willemsen (Eds.), *IntRS'18: Proceedings of* the 5th Joint workshop on interfaces and human decision making for recommender systems. Vancouver, B. C. (pp. 45–52). Online: CEUR-WS.org. http://ceur-ws.org/Vol-2225/

Tong, S. T., Hancock, J. T., & Slatcher, R. B. (2016). Online dating system design and relational decision making: Choice, algorithms, and control. *Personal Relationships, 23*(4), 645–662. https://doi.org/ 10.1111/pere.12158

Van De Wiele, C., & Tong, S. T. (2014, September). Breaking boundaries: The uses & gratifications of Grindr. In *Proceedings of the 2014 ACM international joint conference on pervasive and ubiquitous computing* (pp. 619–630). ACM.

Vohs, K. D., Baumeister, R. F., Schmeichel, B. J., Twenge, J. M., Nelson, N. M., & Tice, D. M. (2014). Making choices impairs subsequent self-control: A limited-resource account of decision making, self-regulation, and active initiative. *Motivation Science, 1*, 19–42. https://doi. org/ 10.1037/2333-8113.1.S.19

Ward, J. (2017). What are you doing on Tinder? Impression management on a matchmaking mobile app. *Information, Communication & Society, 20*(11), 1644–1659. https://doi.org/ 10.1080/1369118X.2016.1252412

Weigel, M. (2017). *Labor of love: The invention of dating.* Farrar, Straus and Giroux.

13

Strange Bedfellows: Data Collection, Data Use, and Personal Privacy in Online and Mobile Dating

Although we have spent the majority of this book examining the effects of online and mobile technology on romantic relationships, one issue we haven't yet explored is individual privacy. At their core, all popular dating platforms are founded upon a confounding paradox: daters are paying dating companies to publicly blast out some of their most sensitive personal information: "online dating profiles may be simultaneously *more public* (e.g., accessible to a wider audience since users often aim to connect with people *outside* their social networks) and contain *more sensitive information* than profiles on other social media" (Cobb & Kohno, 2017, p. 1). Daters have to populate their profiles with personal information about their lives. Dating platforms often ask very intimate questions about daters' sexual preferences, religious beliefs, political attitudes, past and current drug use, even their health (i.e., sexually transmitted infections, HIV status). Although daters typically reveal such information voluntarily, they may not always be aware of the ways in which their data are being bought, sold, and used by people and companies outside of the dating platform, or the privacy risks they are being exposed to.

As the legions of online and mobile daters grow, other concerns about data production, data collection, and users' privacy are also growing. Communication scholars have been theorizing about the role of websites and mobile apps as conduits for romantic connections, but other topics—about the collection and use of daters' private information, the potential risks to daters' privacy, and the effects of these things on other (non-relational) aspects of daters' lives—are also being examined. The chapter is organized into four sections, focusing on (1) data production and data collection in online and mobile dating; (2) privacy theory; (3) the application of information privacy theory to online and mobile dating; (4) and an examination of online dating privacy threats, both interpersonal and institutional.

Data Production in Dating Platforms

As discussed in Chapter 2, at a minimum most daters are required to provide basic demographic information and a photo for their dating profiles. Some platforms like OkCupid also urge users to answer more detailed questions about their personality, mate preferences, and past relationships. Many mobile apps like Tinder, Hinge, and The League require users to authenticate their dating profiles by linking them to their existing social media accounts (Facebook, LinkedIn, etc.), which contain lists of friends and contacts, personal photographs, interests, employment and work history, education, and other sensitive information about their lifestyle. Apps like Tinder and Grindr also collect users' approximate geographic location and publicly display it to others. Clearly, at the center of the online and mobile dating experience is *personal information and data*; after all, getting to know about one another is the central activity of the early stages of online dating. Online dating companies stockpile all of this information, ostensibly for "primary use" in their proprietary matching algorithms—but, as we will examine later, daters' information is sometimes used for secondary and tertiary purposes.

Albury, Burgess, Light, Race, and Wilken (2017) analyze such practices in light of the *culture of data production*: "the institutionalized routines, habits and knowledge practices of the app publishers with respect to data in dating apps" (p. 2). Those of you who have used a dating app know that your information (and others' information) is the lifeblood of the entire system. If you chose not to provide your information, Tinder would not let you use the app. That is because Tinder, and other platforms like it, need your information in order to function. This dependency on users' information reveals another oddity about the online and mobile dating industry, in which a customer serves as both the *creator* and the *consumer* of its product. Dating apps and sites are selling a service—the ability to connect with other daters—and yet sustaining that service depends on their users' willingness to interact with others on their app: "customers are actively engaged in the co-creation of the service. . .the platform provider merely acts as a value facilitator" (Dechant, Spann, & Becker, 2019, p. 92). That is, platforms like Tinder, Grindr, and Bumble really aren't creating anything "new." They are merely hosts for information exchange, while sometimes providing a mechanism or interface to put in front of daters the kind of information they want to see.

This dependence on users' personal data also allows online dating platforms to thrive on the so-called "freemium" business model[9] so common in the digital economy. Companies that implement freemium models will allow their customers to experience basic services without paying money first; however, if a customer wants to obtain access to premium features or additional services, then fees are charged (Rietveld, 2018). For example, OkCupid's "A-List" allows you to see who has viewed your profile recently (that information is hidden for non-paying users) and to "boost" your profile to get seen by more potential partners; "Tinder Gold" provides access to features such as Unlimited Likes (non-paying Tinder users are limited to 100 likes per every 12 hour period), Passport (swipe anywhere in the world), and Rewind (a feature that allows you to review profiles you have previously swiped). (For more on these features and lightweight communication cues, see also Chapter 2). Obviously, dating sites and apps didn't invent the freemium model—it had already been made popular by social media sites like Facebook, content sharing platforms like YouTube, and other service providers like the antivirus company Avast (Molla, 2020). Just like these companies, dating sites and apps lure in customers with the boast their service is free of charge. Technically, they are correct—most daters are not paying online dating companies with cold, hard cash. But it would be more accurate to say that daters are paying companies in the form of *personal information*.

The Online Dating Business Model: A "Perverse Incentive"?

Fundamentally, almost all online dating companies state that their goal is to help customers realize their dreams and romantic imaginations by assisting them on the search for love, sex, and relationships. On the surface this makes

---

9 We are using the term business model in a relatively simplistic way. From the company's point of view a business model is basically their plan to make money. While that plan might raise other kinds of questions, such as "Who is our customer?" and "What do they value?" we do not delve into those issues.

sense; the apps and sites want their users to fulfill their desires for intimacy and romance. But scholars like Eli Finkel and his colleagues (2012) note the "perverse incentive" implicitly embedded in the business model of many online dating companies:

> The incentive structure for most sites is inconsistent with their stated aims; because dating sites lose two paying customers (or potential advertising revenue) when they facilitate the formation of a romantic relationship, dating sites have a perverse incentive to keep users single (although they presumably also have an incentive for at least some of their users to develop romantic relationships, to foster positive word-of-mouth). (p. 49)

The dater who keeps actively swiping and messaging is one who will continue to produce data, contribute to the site's or app's dating pool, and pay their subscription fees. So, the dirty secret of the online dating business model is that apps and sites don't *really* want their users to fulfill their goals, because the minute two people find each other and form a committed partnership, they will delete their profiles, drop off the app, and stop supplying their data and their money. Instead, dating apps and sites are best served, financially speaking, by making their customers *believe* that they are one swipe away from love, but never actually leading them to a lasting relationship.

Interestingly, at the root of this perverse incentive lies an economic force that all service-based companies must contend with, called *customer churn*. In business and marketing research, *customer churn* describes what happens when a customer terminates a company's services. For instance, let's say you are a customer of AT&T Wireless. You've been with them for two years, paying them a monthly fee for your cell phone service. But recently they have begun to raise your rates and your reception has been terrible. Dissatisfied, you decide to leave AT&T and sign with Verizon, a direct competitor. *Negative churn* describes that scenario—you were not satisfied with AT&T's services, so you left. For other reasons we discussed in Chapter 12, negative churn can occur with online dating as well: When daters become disillusioned with the platform or feel like it isn't helping them fulfill their romantic, relational, or sexual goals, they will leave. In this circumstance, they might turn to a different app or site, or simply leave the online dating space altogether.

But unlike AT&T, online and mobile dating companies also have to guard against *positive churn*, which happens when customers whose needs *are* fulfilled still quit using the company's service for very different reasons. Dechant, Spann and Becker (2019) note that positive churn is also present in service industries like healthcare and weight loss. When a company delivers a cure, facilitates weight loss, or (in the case of online dating) helps someone find a romantic partner, positive churn will likely occur because the customer no longer needs the service. Positive churn creates another strange paradox in the online dating world. At the same time that online dating companies attempt to guard against it, they also actually *need* some amount of positive churn as a way to demonstrate that their service works—or at least this is probably the most efficient way to make customers *believe* that their service works. In fact, most of the popular dating platforms will highlight positive churn as "success stories," featuring them as part of their marketing and advertising strategy.

When couples write to online and mobile dating companies to express their gratitude for having met each other on the site or app, or to share their engagements and upcoming weddings, marketing teams spring into action. Bumble has staff members whose job is to recognize couples' upcoming nuptials by sending them presents from their wedding registries; OkCupid offers its congratulations by sending framed copies of the first messages the happy couple exchanged on their site; Tinder has invited couples to propose (and pose for photos) at the company headquarters, and even "gave" one couple $100,000 for their "dream wedding"—which Tinder of course photographed, publicized, and splashed all over the Internet (see Fielding, 2017; Krueger, 2018). All three platforms maintain public relations blogs where they feature such couples. Bumble's blog, *The Buzz*, asks couples to pen their "Success Stories," OkCupid has a similar Success Story page, and Tinder's *Swipe Life* blog asks couples to "submit your story." Some positive churn is the cost of doing business, but rest assured, the online dating companies will find a way to turn that revenue loss into advertising gain.

So, even when daters pair up and shut down their dating accounts, companies do their best to incorporate that positive churn into their advertising strategy. But even so, online dating companies do take a revenue hit when they lose romantically-satisfied customers. Dechant et al. (2019) ask if the loss of revenue from swiping singles might motivate online dating companies to actively discourage their customers from fulfilling their romantic goals: "Since it seems economically rational to adapt the service levels and postpone purpose fulfillment until later, it would be worthwhile to investigate the ramifications of this ethically questionable behavior" (p. 96). In other words, do online and mobile apps deliberately "postpone" realization of the very romantic goals they promise to facilitate? How much does Tinder impede, and how much does it help, daters? To what extent can we trust online dating companies to truly deliver the service that customers think they are paying for?

That, in itself, is a frightening question to ask: *Are customers of online dating sites and mobile apps really getting what they pay for?* In some ways, the answer is "yes"—daters are gaining access to larger pools of potential partners, but foolishly or not, many are also paying with the expectation that the app's proprietary algorithms can match them with their soulmate. Of course, as we have already discussed, money is not the only form of currency accepted by online dating platforms. Dating sites and apps are also asking us to pay with our personal information and private data. So maybe another question that online daters should be asking is: "Are we getting our *data's* worth?"

Privacy in Online and Mobile Dating

As we reviewed above, the freemium model highlights how daters exchange their personal information and privacy for access to basic dating services. This might seem like a strange idea—is one's privacy and personal information something that can be exchanged, bought, and sold? In order to think through the concept of personal information as a form of currency, it is useful to review briefly the different theoretical approaches to privacy used in past research.

A Brief History of Privacy

Conceptual definitions of privacy have been offered by theorists across nearly all social science disciplines from communication, law, political science, sociology, and psychology. Early on, many scholars adopted a classical *value-based* approach to privacy, considering it to be an intrinsic human right. This view is often attributed to Warren and Brandeis's (1890) definition of general privacy as "the right to be left alone." Notably, early conceptualizations of privacy were set squarely in the realm of *physical privacy*, or a person's right to control their physical surroundings and space. Later, scholars began to interrogate other aspects of privacy, such as Burgoon's (1982) four dimensions that include *physical privacy*, as well as *social privacy* (to foster closeness among some individuals while simultaneously creating distance from others), *psychological privacy* (control over affective and cognitive inputs and outputs), and *informational privacy* (the control over processing and transfer of personal information). Burgoon further notes that this final dimension of privacy is "closely allied to psychological privacy, but its legalistic and technological implications, coupled with its significance beyond the individual to the society as a whole, warrant treating it separately" (p. 228—see also, Nissenbaum, 2010). Issues of *informational privacy* are intrinsic to online and mobile dating, as individuals' personal information keeps the entire industry afloat.

One development that began to draw theorists' attention toward information privacy was the increasing amount of *personal data collection*. Although we are all familiar with our information being recorded in things like income tax records and medical histories, deeper contemplation of information privacy became necessary when people's personal data began to be collected by other institutions, like credit card companies cataloging our purchase data and video rental stores like Blockbuster compiling our recently rented DVD titles.[10] As companies in the private sector began gathering more of people's private information, thinking about personal privacy as a human right became more complex.

Smith, Dinev, and Xu (2011) argue that in the context of modern consumer behavior, the idea of privacy as a distinct human right began to change. They note how—under certain conditions—people voluntarily disclose their personal information in exchange for goods or services: "Thus, the notion of *privacy as commodity* was conceptualized. … . Under the commodity view, privacy is still an individual and societal value, but it is not absolute, as it can be assigned an economic value and be considered in a cost-benefit calculation at both individual and societal levels" (p. 993). As privacy began to become commodified, our thinking shifted—privacy is something that each person possesses, but that person can sell it and others can purchase it. Often, we do not buy and sell our privacy with conventional money; instead we use our privacy as a form of capital unto itself. In other words, privacy is not thought of purely as a civil liberty, but as a product that can be priced and sold in the marketplace—often in exchange for convenience.

As Internet technology became more popular, it became clear that individuals were not just disclosing their personal information, but began to "cooperate in the online gathering of data about themselves as economic subjects" (Smith et al., 2011, p. 994). While such a statement might refer to the information that people

---

10 Fun fact: The Video Privacy Protection Act (VPPA) of 1988 prevents the "wrongful disclosure of video tape rental or sale records (or similar audio/visual materials such as video games and future DVD format)"—in other words, video rental retailers are "prohibited from disclosing video rental records to anyone without a court order or the renter's personal consent" (Laudon, 1996). Seems antiquated, doesn't it? But in the 1980s, this was the kind personal data acquisition that people were worried about! Perhaps it should be updated?

voluntarily and intentionally disclose, several Internet companies also began collecting people's *behavioral trace data.* Also called *digital trace data,* the "traces" refer to information we produce when using digital devices and Internet technologies (Lampe, 2013; Newell & Marabelli, 2015). People leave behind all kinds of trace data online, such as web search histories, clicks and likes on social media, and online purchases, just to name a few. Online behavioral trace data is often collected and acquired through various (inconspicuous) methods (e.g., scraping, accessing via an API, or through company server logs; see Lampe, 2013). The invisible nature of such data collection methods raised questions as to whether individuals were even aware that their online behavior was being surveilled or their behavioral trace data collected. Moreover, even if users were *generally* aware that they were being surveilled, many users did not have the technological proficiency to understand exactly how closely they were being watched and the kinds of private data that were being collected. With the popularity of online services and digital devices, privacy scholars now had to integrate behavioral trace data into their thinking about information privacy (Westin, 2003).

To summarize, this brief history reveals that before the Internet, definitions of privacy were rooted primarily in the idea of physical boundaries. That is, theorists simply applied former definitions of physical privacy onto the context of information privacy, without realizing that there might be some slippage: "In the initial period of this transition, physical privacy concepts and definitions were directly and seamlessly applied to information privacy, without reported contradictions" (Smith et al., 2011, p. 990). But as Internet revealed other privacy issues, early definitions became strained, generating a host of social, political, and legal problems. With the increasing amount of data collection and the popularity of Internet technologies, informational privacy grew into a distinct area of research, separate from physical privacy.

Issues of Information Privacy in Online Dating

In 1982, Judee Burgoon laid down the theoretical foundation for subsequent study concerning people's perceptions about information privacy. In her view, "The key consideration is whether the individual perceives any threat to his or her privacy. That experience should depend on several factors, which may be regarded as the isolates defining the degree of informational privacy" (p. 230). Ultimately, she identified five crucial factors, centered around three broad areas of information content, control, and access:

(1) *Content of the information*: Innocuous details like your age, gender, race, occupation, and relationship status—maybe these do not require such careful protection. If you were to meet a person walking down the street, we would not be surprised if that person were able to make pretty good guesses about all those things. But what about your physical home address? Your childhood home address? Your social security number? Somehow, that information feels a lot more private, possibly because if you were to meet a person FtF, you wouldn't assume that they knew such details. When someone gets a hold of information like this without your consent, it can feel a lot more threatening.

(2) *Degree of information control:* Control in this sense is "not only over the initial release of the information but also over its subsequent distribution and use." Do you really maintain control over the data that Tinder or OkCupid or Facebook collect about you? This factor is rooted in the idea that our private information belongs to us—it is valuable. It is ours, and we decide whether to share it or not. When someone whom we have given access to our private information shares it publicly, we presume that they follow *our rules* for sharing that information (Petronio, 1991) whether we're right in that presumption or not.

(3) *Number of people who have access to that information:* "Even a few trivial facts, if spread to many others, create more of a sense of risk because of the possibility of their distortion or misuse." While you may deliberately share your profile information with other Tinder users, what if some of them forward your information on to other people?

(4) *Actual amount of information in the hands of others*: This is closely related to the previous factors—if you cannot control the number of people who can access your information, then you can never be completely sure about the actual amount of information that others possess about you. The fact that someone knows your name, age, and occupation might not seem especially troubling; but what if someone knew *everything* about you—your driver's license number, your shoe size, the name of your childhood cat, or your personal battle with anxiety disorder and panic attacks? Suddenly, in a world where identity theft, online impersonation, and Internet stalking are ever-present possibilities, this becomes more worrisome.

(5) *Your relationship with those who possess the information*: When and how you disclose personal information usually depends on who you're disclosing it to and how you're related. Consider your boss, your best friend,

and your neighbor—you probably share different amounts and kinds of personal information with each one. In short, how we feel about others' possession of our personal information often depends on who those others are.

Writing in 1982, Burgoon's five factors of information privacy seem eerily prescient! Using these factors as a framework, below we explore privacy threats in online and mobile dating.

Factor 1: Content of Information—What Data Are Dating Platforms Gathering about Me?

One news story that really exposed the ubiquity of personal data collection in dating apps was Judith Duportail's (2017) report published in the *Guardian*. Duportail had been using Tinder for approximately four years before she teamed up with a privacy activist[11] and a human rights lawyer to request access to her entire personal Tinder data set. As a citizen of the European Union (EU), Duportail invoked the EU's data protection law. What she received astounded her (and many other Tinder users):

> Some 800 pages came back containing information such as my Facebook "likes," links to where my Instagram photos would have been had I not previously deleted the associated account, my education, the age-rank of men I was interested in, how many Facebook friends I had, when and where every online conversation with every single one of my matches happened. . .the list goes on.

---

11 In a follow-up report, that privacy activist—Paul-Oliver Dehaye—explained how difficult it was for Duportail to obtain information from Tinder. Notably, because Duportail was a citizen of the EU and Tinder is based in the USA, this created loopholes that Tinder readily exploited: "The Dallas-based company is, at least for now, untouchable from a legal standpoint: in most cases, a European citizen simply has no meaningful access to scores computed about them in the US" (Dehaye, 2018). At the time of that report, Tinder was not required to comply with certain aspects of the EU's data protection law; however since then, the EU has passed the General Data Protection Regulation, which is more stringent with respect to US-based companies. Notably, the USA has no real comparison to the GDPR when it comes to Americans' information privacy.

In a different kind of investigation, Farnden, Martini, and Choo (2015) used "forensic techniques" to see what kind of data they could recover from dating apps being run on the Android system. Specifically, they set up their experiment by first replicating how daters would likely use their smartphones to fill out dating profiles, swipe and decide on potential dates, and message others on the apps. They then examined the data that accumulated on the individual smartphone devices from that replicated app use to determine what kind of privacy risks such information collection might pose for the user. Across the different apps Farnden et al. (2015) analyzed—Badoo, Grindr, Skout, Tinder, Meet Me, Jaumo, FullCircule, and MiuMeet—all but one of them stored users' physical location[12] (some with exact longitude and latitude coordinates); and in half of the apps, researchers were able to recover messages sent and received through the app, along with the specific date and time. Regarding images, FullCircle stored all image files that daters attached to their messages; and Grindr stored the profile pictures of any dater that a user viewed, along with corresponding personal information including those individuals' email addresses and time of last login.

So, the answer to the question "what kind of personal information are dating apps collecting about their users" is simple: they are collecting *everything*. This includes the information daters voluntarily provide in their profiles and messages, all behavioral trace data such as mate selection and swipes, viewed profiles, and geolocation data, and linked data such as social media photographs, posts and comments, friends and contacts, and other information tags. If you're curious about requesting and obtaining the full copy of your personal dating data from apps like Tinder, see more in Figure 13.1.

Factor 2: Control Over Information—Awareness, Knowledge, and Concerns Over Privacy

Another factor that influences whether online daters feel their information privacy is being threatened is the degree of control that they maintain over their personal data. Notably, in order for daters to exercise that control, they have to be fully aware of what their rights and abilities are—but most dating platforms

---

12 Oddly enough, though, we have come back full circle—geolocation data collected through daters' smartphones now threatens both their information privacy *and* their physical privacy.

Tinder > A Guide To Tinder > Profile and Account Settings

How do I request a copy of my personal data?

At Tinder, we are committed to protecting your data and privacy as well as providing you access to the information you have provided us.

If you would like to request a copy of your personal data, please visit https://account.gotinder.com/data

The information you will receive through our Download My Data tool is largely already available to you through the app and may vary, depending on the way you have used Tinder.

If you have deleted your Tinder account, you will not be able to access the Download My Data portal, as you no longer have an account on Tinder. After you have deleted your account, your data is disposed of in accordance with our privacy policy.

Figure 13.1: Requesting Tinder data. Interested in obtaining your own Tinder data? Go to this website: https://www.help.tinder.com/hc/en-us/articles/115005626726-How-do-I-request-a-copy-of-my-personal-data-. Source: Authors

make this difficult. Most mobile apps (dating apps included) often make privacy awareness the users' problem. Several dating apps abide by the "notice and consent" approach to online privacy in which a lengthy (often horribly difficult, boring, undecipherable) terms of service (TOS) document is flashed up for the user to read prior to downloading the app. In order to download the app on their devices, users are required to click an "I agree" button which indicates their consent. Clearly the notice and consent approach is flawed for many reasons, but mainly because most people do not actually read TOS documents. Generally, the decision to download and try out a dating app occurs before the user sees the TOS documents, and because of this clicking "I agree" is simply one last hurdle to cross before downloading the application in the early registration phase. Even if users did read the TOS document, it is (a) unlikely that they would have the expertise or experience required to understand what their user rights are, (b) unlikely that they would know how to exercise any control over their data, and (c) would likely have to "agree" to their data being collected anyway in order to use the app (Liu, 2014).

Overall, people generally report a poor understanding of the data collection practices and data use permissions of the mobile apps they routinely use

(Brandtzaeg, Pultier, & Moen, 2019). And it's not just app users: App developers also admit that they do not fully understand exactly what kinds of data their apps collect from their users. After surveying 228 app developers, Balebako, Marsh, Lin, Hong, and Cranor (2014) concluded: "Our results indicate that many developers lack awareness of privacy measures and make decisions in an ad hoc manner" (p. 9). If dating app developers don't even know, it is not a big surprise that individual users don't know either.

For the many who are at least aware of such concerns, their incomplete knowledge about information collection and an absence of personal control over the situation can create real uneasiness. *Privacy concerns*, or the "negatively valenced emotional attitude that people feel when personal rights, information, or behaviors are being regressed by others" (Dienlien & Trepte, 2015) describe how worried and anxious people can become about the amount of data that mobile apps and websites are collecting from their users. A survey conducted by the Pew Internet Project in 2020 indicated that 57% of American online daters reported feeling "somewhat" or "very" concerned over how much of their data dating sites and apps are collecting about them; interestingly, those privacy concerns tended to be related to age, with older users expressing greater worry compared to younger ones (Turner & Anderson, 2020).

Factors 3, 4, & 5: Information Access—How Many People Have Access to My Information? How Much Information Might They Actually Have about Me? Who Are These People Anyway?!

The last three factors all center around issues of *information access*. Who might have access to your online dating information, how much of your personal data could others actually have, and who are these people who crave my information so badly? Obviously, daters who are using the platform will get access to your profile information, but other (sometimes unintended) parties could also access these data. Online information is easily recordable and can be quickly disseminated to others, or stored for other purposes that are unrelated to romantic dating. Within the online dating industry, collecting and selling daters' information to third-party companies who re-purpose it for things like targeted advertising is another way that dating platforms generate revenue. In this section, we examine how issues of unauthorized information access—by both individual daters and companies—can threaten daters' privacy.

Typically, most daters probably think that the people whom they intend to allow to see their profiles—other daters who are also on the app or site—are the only ones who are accessing their personal information. And so, a dater's intention would be to openly share their profile information with potential partners on the platform. However, the written and visual nature of profile information can be easily accessed and shared by others who are not on the platform at all, often without daters' knowledge. For example, the Tinder daters in Cobb and Kohno's (2017) study reported taking screenshots of others' profiles to document "especially funny, weird, offensive, or strange content," to "share with friends," or to "post screenshots on social media" such as Facebook or Reddit (p. 7). Screenshots can become an even worse violation of information privacy if a dater's profile is published online (check out WhyTheyreSingle.com), posted on Instagram (@overheardbumble), or featured in a Buzzfeed story titled "*17 Internet Dating Profiles that will probably put you off of Internet dating*" (Parker, 2018). (Astute readers will note a separate issue that arises here, namely that daters' information privacy is being violated for entertainment value. Is this ethical? Probably not, in our view.) In thinking about Burgoon's information privacy factors, once someone screenshots your profile and posts it online, all of that information is now completely out of your control. Additionally, the sheer number of people who have access to your profile info has grown dramatically. . . .. It is now accessible by anyone with an Internet connection (so billions of people, potentially?) Part of what makes this scenario feel so incredibly threatening is that your profile has been made public for complete strangers (who are not potential dates) to view.

What if your dating profile was accessed and used out of context? Imagine that you are applying for a new job. After reading your resume and conducting your interview, what if the hiring manager accessed your dating profile as another part of your job application? Would the access and use of your dating profile for a professional purpose not feel like a violation of your information privacy? Among Cobb and Kohno's (2017) sample, 65% of their respondents felt that businesses or employers who looked at dating profiles to make employment decisions were violating daters' privacy; as an interesting comparison, only 36% felt the same way about Facebook profiles. This suggests that perhaps the specific romantic purpose of dating platforms somehow make them more "private" spaces compared to the more social nature of platforms like Facebook. Yet access to both could be just a few clicks away.

Again though, how we feel about others' possession of our information often depends on who those others are. Burgoon (1982) cites Lewin (1936), who explained that invasions of information privacy can feel more or less threatening depending on the nature of our relationship with the person who has our information. When "another gains access to facts more personal than the intimacy of the interpersonal relationship itself" we often have heightened concerns over our privacy (Burgoon, 1982, p. 231). In the context of online dating, individuals often report feeling most threatened when complete strangers use information from dating profiles to access and gather other, more detailed, personal data. As an example, Cobb and Kohno (2017) analyzed the "findability" of daters' identity from their Tinder data. A dater was classified as being "findable" if Cobb and Kohno could use their profile data to (a) find out the dater's last name, (b) find additional social media accounts or pages with more personal information, and (c) if they could be certain it was the same person in all linked accounts. Using these criteria, they "found" 188 out of 400 daters in their sample. From an access standpoint, if complete strangers are able to gather data to piece together a composite of our identity, this could make a lot of daters very nervous.

All of the above examples focus on how freely disclosed dating profile information can be accessed to threaten privacy. But what about behavioral trace data—the activity data that dating companies often invisibly collect from their users? This kind of information is often far outside daters' control. Although most daters are generally aware that companies collect such data, as we noted above, most have no real knowledge of what it consists of or who has access to it. Brandtzaeg et al. (2019) investigated two popular dating apps, Tinder and Happn, to find out not only what kind of trace data were being collected, but also the "dataflow," or where apps were sending it. Both apps tracked users' real-time GPS location along with personal identifiers (e.g., Facebook ID, age, names, birthdays, jobs, gender), which is no big surprise. However, Brandtzaeg et al. (2019) found that Happn actually accessed and sent all of that user trace data to Upsight, "a major third-party tracking company" that uses such information for customer advertising and marketing (p. 476). Oddly enough, accessing and selling their users' trace data violated Happn's own company charter and TOS.

Such practices raise questions about information access and user control. Once daters' information is sold to a third party like Upsight, that company can do whatever it likes with it. Recent cases like the Cambridge Analytica scandal (c.f., Confessore, 2018) have opened the public's eyes to issues of information privacy—but somehow, such issues do not seem to be influencing us to demand much change from social media or dating platforms, many of which still deploy the notice-and-consent model of privacy complete with ridiculous, incomprehensible TOS agreements. Another fun fact about those TOSs: if you ever did take the time to read the fine print, most of them basically give companies complete control over your information. Brandtzaeg et al. (2019) point out the unreasonable tenor of Tinder's TOS: "according to the terms of use and privacy policies, users risked losing control of their images and other user-generated content 'perpetually' and 'irrevocably.' Tinder could change its terms of use at any time without notifying users, and could exclude and delete user accounts without justification" (p. 482). Most TOS wordings clearly have one central goal, which is to strengthen the company's control over individuals' information. The more opaque and far-reaching the privacy policy, the less control daters have over their own information, and the more likely the company is to be able to access, store, and sell users' personal data off to the highest bidder.

Risky Business: The Multifaceted Nature of Privacy Threats in Online Dating

In the above examples, it is easy to imagine how another Tinder dater with access to your profile might also be able to gain access to additional information through your linked social media accounts or a thorough Google search. They could use that information to leverage multiple communication channels, sending you inappropriate or unwanted messages through the dating app, pester you on Instagram, or call you on your cell phone. Such a breach would not only threaten your *information privacy*—your right to "appropriate the flow of personal information" (Nissenbaum, 2010, p. 127)—but would also threaten your *social privacy*—or your right to "manage your interactions with others" (Burgoon, 1982, p. 218). Sometimes, information access breaches can also create physical privacy risks. For the most extreme example, look no further than Bruce McArthur, a serial killer who murdered seven men between 2010 and 2017. All of McArthur's victims were part of the gay community in Toronto, Canada, and he reportedly used mobile dating apps to connect with them, inviting them to his home where he would restrain and kill them (Brammer, 2018). Threats to physical privacy are, of course, the most dangerous kind of outcome that can result from information privacy breaches in dating platforms. But electronic surveillance and cyber harassment are also potential risks. To combat such threats, new apps like Bsafe (https://getbsafe.com/) and Kitestring (https://www.kitestring.io/) have launched as tools to help daters feel safer in their physical surroundings.

Despite the lingering social and physical privacy threats, most online and mobile daters are still mostly concerned about *informational privacy*. Lutz and Ranzini (2017) surveyed almost 500 Tinder daters regarding their privacy concerns. Like the Pew survey cited above, they found that among the Tinder daters in their sample the issue that prompted the greatest degree of concern over privacy[13] was "Tinder selling personal data to third parties," although this worry was, again, more pronounced among older daters. Younger Tinder daters seemed to be more concerned with social privacy breaches—like other daters stalking them or forwarding their personal information to others without their consent.

Another potential threat to informational privacy comes from the (in)security of the data gathered and stored on the app or site itself. Gallagher (2019) published a report in *Ars Technica* detailing how the all-male dating app Jack'd "left images posted by users and marked as 'private' in daters' chat sessions open to browsing on the Internet, potentially exposing the privacy of thousands of users." The images, along with geolocation and other data, were uploaded onto servers over an unsecured Web connection that were publicly accessible: "The result was that intimate, private images—including pictures of genitalia and photos that revealed information about users' identity and location—were exposed to public view." Initially, when security researcher Oliver Hough reached out to Jack'd's CEO, Mark Girolamo, about the privacy breach, he did not respond very quickly. It was only after *Ars Technica* notified Girolamo that Gallagher's story would be published that the issue was fixed—a full year after Hough initially spotted and notified Girolamo of the issue. Similar issues have been reported with the all-male apps Grindr and Hornet, whose information security problems have resulted in the "outing" of some users as queer, gay, or bisexual in countries where homosexuality is either stigmatized or even illegal (Shamas, 2018). Although we characterize these cybersecurity issues as threats to information privacy, they are also tied to *psychological privacy*, in that such security problems encroach on daters' capacity to regulate "their own self-identity and relational definitions with others" (Burgoon, 1982, p. 224).

Conclusion

After this discussion about the nature of data privacy, you might presume that, from a functional communication perspective, privacy concerns drive, or at least affect, a large number of behaviors and outcomes on online dating apps and

13 It should be noted that compared to the Pew survey, Lutz and Ranzini's (2017) sample of Tinder users were not as concerned about their privacy. The highest concern score was only a three out of five, suggesting only "moderate concerns" over institutional privacy.

websites. However, there is one last wrinkle in the privacy picture. Privacy breaches can occur in any kind of online or mobile communication platform: Indeed, the very personal nature of romantic and sexual interaction that takes place on dating apps and sites may make such security breaches even more risky for individual privacy. Yet, despite daters' heightened awareness and concerns about information privacy, it doesn't appear that users are leaving dating platforms in droves. If anything, most dating apps and sites still enjoy a robust following, and users share information—often wantonly. So, in yet another apparent contradiction, we see that although daters report distinct concerns about their privacy in dating platforms, they still continue to use them and knowingly or unknowingly share lots of private data. This *privacy paradox* (Barnes, 2006) occurs when people who claim to be concerned about their personal privacy will, at the same time, freely disclose their personal information in order to use the online services of social media or dating platforms. The privacy paradox has become a familiar phenomenon in online privacy research more broadly, wherein people's "concerns toward privacy are unrelated to the privacy behaviors" (Dienlin & Trepte, 2015, p. 285).

The implications of that paradox for online and mobile daters remain largely unexplored to date. Furthermore, as we can see, the issues that arise in online and mobile dating are often very complex because they affect multiple dimensions at the same time, including social, psychological, and physical privacy. Finally, another potential paradox exists in that daters seem both aware of and very concerned with their information privacy, but possess very little knowledge about what data companies tend to collect, what their own user rights are, and when companies are in breach of their own privacy policies. Future research might examine the extent to which awareness of the privacy "problem" correlates with actual knowledge about the "problem," and work to educate daters on how to take control of their information. We hesitate to take a position on what a user *should* do to protect their data. However, we would propose that *if* dating apps and websites see our data as a commodity to be sold, we should be informed consumers with an accurate sense of what our data can buy. In short, if we're going to be using online dating platforms, we would very much like to be getting our data's worth.

References

Albury, K., Burgess, J., Light, B., Race, K., & Wilken, R. (2017). Data cultures of mobile dating and hook-up apps: Emerging issues for critical social science research. *Big Data & Society, 4*, 1-11. https://doi.org/10.1177/2053951717720950

Balebako, R., Marsh, A., Lin, J., Hong, J. I., & Cranor, L. F. (2014, April). The privacy and security behaviors of smartphone app developers. *Network and Distributed System Security Symposium (NDSS'14)*. San Diego, CA. https://doi.org/10.14722/usec.2014.23006

Barnes, S. B. (2006). A privacy paradox: Social networking in the United States. *First Monday*. https://doi.org/ 10.5210/fm.v11i9.1394

Brammer, J. P. (2018, April). Toronto's alleged 'Gay Village' serial killer facing 7th murder charge. *NBC News*. https://www.nbcnews.com/feature/nbc-out/toronto-s-alleged-gay-village-serial-killer-facing-7th-murder-n865071

Brandtzaeg, P. B., Pultier, A., & Moen, G. M. (2019). Losing control to data-hungry apps: A mixed-methods approach to mobile app privacy. *Social Science Computer Review, 37*, 466–488. https://doi.org/ 10.177/0894439318777706

Bsafe. (n.d.). https://getbsafe.com/

Burgoon, J. K. (1982). Privacy and communication. In M. Burgoon (Ed.), *Communication yearbook 6* (pp. 206–249). Sage.

Cobb, C., & Kohno, T. (2017). How public is my private life? Privacy in online dating. *Proceedings of international world wide web conference committee (IW3C2)*, Perth, Australia. ACM. https://doi.org/ 10.11145/3038912.3052592

Confessore, N. (2018, April 4). Cambridge Analytica and Facebook: The scandal and fallout so far. *New York Times*. https://www.nytimes.com/2018/04/04/us/politics/cambridge-analytica-scandal-fallout.html

Dechant, A., Spann, M., & Becker, J. U. (2019). Positive customer churn: An application to online dating. *Journal of Service Research, 22*, 90-100. https://doi.org/10.1177/1094670518795054

Dehaye, P.-O. (2019, May). Getting your data out of Tinder is really hard—but it shouldn't be. *The Guardian*. https://www.theguardian.com/technology/2017/sep/27/tinder-data-privacy-tech-eu-general-data-protection-regulation

Dienlin, T., & Trepte, S. (2015). Is the privacy paradox a relic of the past? An in-depth analysis of privacy attitudes and privacy behaviors. *European Journal of Social Psychology, 45*(3), 285–297. https://doi.org/10.1002/ejsp.2049

Duportail, J. (2017, September). I asked Tinder for my data. It sent me 800 pages of my deepest, darkest secrets. *The Guardian*. https://www.theguardian.com/technology/2017/sep/26/tinder-personal-data-dating-app-messages-hacked-sold

Farnden, J., Martini, B., & Choo, K. K. R. (2015). Privacy risks in mobile dating apps. *arXiv preprint arXiv:1505.02906*. https://arxiv.org/pdf/1505.02906.pdf

Fielding, S. (2017, July). Tinder is giving this couple a $100k dream wedding after hearing their love story. *Bustle*. https://www.bustle.com/p/tinder-is-giving-this-couple-a-100000-dream-wedding-after-hearing-their-dating-app-success-story-69550

Finkel, E. J., Eastwick, P. W., Karney, B. R., Reis, H. T., & Sprecher, S. (2012). Online dating: A critical analysis from the perspective of psychological science. *Psychological Science in the Public interest, 13*, 3-66. https://doi.org/10.1177/1529100612436522

Gallagher, S. (2019, February). Indecent exposure: Gay dating app left 'private' images, data exposed to Web. *Ars Technica*. https://arstechnica.com/information-technology/2019/02/indecent-disclosure-gay-dating-app-left-private-exposed-to-web/?comments=1

Kitestring. (n.d.). https://www.kitestring.io/

Krueger, A. (2018, July 3). A Tinder moment, a gift from OkCupid and a Bumble officiant. *New York Times*. https://www.nytimes.com/2018/07/03/fashion/weddings/a-tinder-moment-a-gift-from-okcupid-and-a-bumble-officiant.html

Lampe, C. (2013). Behavioral trace data for analyzing online communities. *The SAGE Handbook of Digital Technology Research, 236*. https://doi.org/10.4135/9781446282229.n17

Lutz, C., & Ranzini, G. (2017). Where dating meets data: Investigating social and institutional privacy concerns on Tinder. *Social Media + Society, 3*. https://doi.org/10.1177/2056305117697735

Molla, R. (2020, January 29). Why your free software is never free. *Vox: Recode*. https://www.vox.com/recode/2020/1/29/21111848/free-software-privacy-alternative-data

Newell, S., & Marabelli, M. (2015). Strategic opportunities (and challenges) of algorithmic decision-making: A call for action on the long-term societal effects of "datification". *The Journal of Strategic Information Systems, 24*, 3-14. https://doi.org/10.1016/j.jsis.2015.02.001

Nissenbaum, H. (2011). A contextual approach to privacy online. *Daedalus, 140*, 32-48. https://doi.org/10.1162/DAED_a_00113

Parker, S. (2018, May 8). 17 Internet dating profiles that will probably put you off Internet dating. *Buzzfeed*. https://www.buzzfeed.com/samjparker/weird-dating-profiles

Petronio, S. (1991). Communication boundary management: A theoretical model of managing disclosure of private information between married couples. *Communication Theory, 1*, 311–335. https://doi.org/ 10.1111/j.1468-2885.1991.tb00023.x

Rietveld, J. (2018). Creating and capturing value from freemium business models: A demand-side perspective. *Strategic Entrepreneurship Journal, 12*(2), 171–193.

Shamas, N. (2018). Queer dating apps need to protect their users better. *Slate.com* . https://slate.com/technology/2018/02/queer-dating-apps-need-to-protect-their-users-better.html

Sloan, R. H., & Warner, R. (2014). Beyond notice and choice: Privacy, norms, and consent. *Journal of High Technology Law, 14*, 370–414.

Smith, H. J., Dinev, T., & Xu, H. (2011). Information privacy research: an interdisciplinary review. *MIS quarterly, 35*, 989-1015. https://doi.org/10.2307/41409970

Sorell, T., & Whitty, M. (2019). Online romance scams and victimhood. *Security Journal, 32*(3), 342–361. https://doi.org/10.1057/s41284-019-00166-w

Turner, E., & Anderson, A. (2020, May). Roughly six-in-ten online daters in the U.S. are concerned about data collection. *Pew Research Center*. https://www.pewresearch.org/fact-tank/2020/05/29/roughly-six-in-ten-online-daters-in-the-u-s-are-concerned-about-data-collection/

Warren, S. D., & Brandeis, L. D. (1890). The right to privacy. *Harvard Law Review, 4*(5), 193–220. https://doi.org/ https://doi.org/10.2307/1321160

Westin, A. F. (2003). Social and political dimensions of privacy. *Journal of Social Issues, 59*(2), 431–453. https://doi.org/ 10.1111/1540-4560.00072

14

Concluding Thoughts, New Ideas

If you have stayed with us all the way to this concluding chapter, you know that throughout this book, we have explored numerous ways in which communication and technology function within romantic dating and close relationships. As the Internet, alongside computing and mobile technologies, has developed and diffused into society, they have expanded our collective romantic imagination by changing, augmenting, and sometimes challenging, how we initiate, maintain, make up, and break up our romantic relationships. As you have already read, many of the discoveries that we've made about romantic communication and daters' technology use comes from research.

Over the course of many chapters, we have reviewed, examined, and critiqued much of this research, as conducted by scholars in diverse disciplinary fields such as communication, psychology, human-computer interaction, economics, and law to name a few. Standing on these scholars' shoulders has given us a great view of how the landscape of dating and romance has changed in contemporary times. In this final chapter, we offer some concluding thoughts about this body of scholarship (from which we have drawn so much knowledge) and offer some ideas about future of inquiry into these topics.

How Is the Research Done?

One overarching consideration stems from the methods that scholars commonly select to address questions about the effects of communication technologies on romantic relational processes. We do not wish to issue broad condemnation of any particular methodological approach; however, we would caution all researchers working in this arena to carefully consider whether the *method* they select can legitimately help them with the inferences that they hope to make.

For example, researchers often employ *surveys* and/or *interviews* which query one partner within a romantic relationship or one suitor about their perspectives concerning relationships or dating experiences. From these survey or interview data, inferences are made about the effects of technology on ongoing romantic relationships or relationship initiation choices. Often these are the same methods that scholars of interpersonal communication use to address FtF relationships. This can be a strength that scholars whose original interests lie outside of technology bring with them. Often, their fresh perspectives highlight issues that scholars trained in technology proper may not have uncovered. It is also true, though, that scholars whose interests drift to the effects of technology on human relationships sometimes walk unknowingly into debates or questions that have long been discussed and studied among technology researchers. For example, scholars of technology know that research participants' self-reported *perceptions* about the effects of technology on human relationships and behaviors are regularly inconsistent with the ways that technology has been demonstrated to *actually* affect relationships and behavior.

For this reason, some scholars in those fields will prefer behavioral methods to recall methodologies. There are real compromises involved in relying on individuals' recollections about relationships, as opposed to data based in the careful laboratory manipulation of technological factors. Scholars are likely to accept such compromises insofar as they value data that are ecologically and externally valid—we often prefer work that applies to large portions of the relationship lifecycle and population. Our perspective is that this sort of work certainly ought to continue, but with it we would advise more research that seeks to address the smaller, more nuanced processes that govern technologically-mediated romance. We argue that simply because these processes are more granular (or address only specific moments in romantic relationships), they ought not to be of less interest to scholars. Instead, a careful small-step approach to accumulating knowledge about technology's larger effects on human relationships can illuminate vistas that larger-scale efforts may find impossible to capture.

With that said, a more granular, incremental approach is not without its challenges. A complete commitment to such an approach may lead to research that is more narrow in scope with findings that are more situated than generalizable. In the end, we would neither advocate that any single study ought to *try* to address an entire understanding of the impact of technology on romantic relationships, nor would we suggest that a raft of disconnected, one-off experiments addressing only minute components become the norm. Instead, we would advocate *programmatic research* that combines several of these more narrow studies to generate a more comprehensive theoretical understanding. And, the findings of these research programs ought to stand the test of larger-scale environmentally, ecologically, and externally valid replications.

In keeping with this more granular approach, one popular method that researchers have relied upon is the *experiment*, in which specific conditions—reflecting one dating platform's design or interface, or aspects of a (hypothetical) interpersonal interaction, flirtatious exchange, or relationship—are systematically manipulated and then compared to another. These carefully constructed experimental comparisons allow researchers to explore if and how subtle differences in technology design, platform use, or interpersonal interaction might influence daters' romantic thoughts, feelings, or reactions.

As researchers who have used experiments ourselves, we strive (and hope others will too) to design experiments that are thoughtful about key points of comparison. As an example: Imagine you are investigating whether using Facebook tends to exacerbate romantic partners' experience of jealousy. To address your research question, you conduct a survey that measures people's reported Facebook use, and how jealous and angry they are.[14] Suppose that the outcome of this survey study demonstrates a strong correlation: The more often romantic partners report using Facebook, the more jealousy they experience. After collecting data, the analysis suggests that your observed correlation is significantly different from zero; hooray! results that a journal might be interested in publishing![15] Given your data, you are careful to avoid drawing causal conclusions; you presume no order of effect, and you even suggest the possibility that Facebook use and jealousy are only spuriously correlated. Methodologically and analytically you are on solid

---

14 For the purposes of illustration, let us also assume that all these measures are valid and reliable, and the statistical findings of the work are sound!

15 Let us also set aside scientific journals' bias toward publishing statistically significant results—others have commented on this thoughtfully, so we will not belabor the point here; see Levine, Asada, and Carpenter, 2009.

ground, but is it possible that your study, and other studies of this variety, have missed the point in important ways?

It is not that there is anything wrong with the study itself (indeed, we have occasionally conducted similar ones!), but from our perspective—the functional perspective—it is difficult to know whether increased Facebook use is the thing that is really focal here. Perhaps Facebook use is simply a proxy or tool for watching other people communicate with one's partner. Sure, people happen to be watching their partners communicate with other people in an online setting, but maybe this effect would have emerged regardless of *where* that person was watching his or her partner around others—on Facebook, at work, in a café, at the gym; FtF or online. In short, because the study does not provide a meaningful comparison point, it is difficult to isolate the genesis of its correlation. As scholars who care deeply about understanding the effects of technology on social behavior, it is our view that this sort of work—while interesting—does not push theoretical understanding of technology and romantic relationships forward as much as it could.

Of course, experiments are also popular because they offer many advantages. Above all is *precision*—the degree of control that experiments afford researchers gives them the ability to isolate specific causes, processes, and effects embedded within daters' online and mobile feelings, behaviors, and interactions. Yet for all the advantages, there will always be problems with experimental studies that do not (and probably never will) approximate the dating world outside of the lab. In short, we know that experiments will never be truly reflective of circumstances beyond the laboratory, which fundamentally limits the generalizability of their results. As discussed above, some researchers (us included) are comfortable with gaining experimental control and precision, while sacrificing decreased generalizability of results—but given that romance is something that takes place outside of the lab (and fairly rarely inside of the lab)—such a tradeoff will always be a nagging problem.

One way we would recommend that scholars begin to expand the scope of their research is to expand the pool of dependent variables they use. We understand that such a suggestion may be met with skepticism—and for good reason. First, dependent variables ought to be derived from the theories that inspire the research itself, and so, this logic might dictate, new dependent variables mean new theories. "Yes" would be our response. However, we would hasten to say that adding a slew of "new" theories to the communication discipline isn't the point. What matters, rather, is that we continue to adapt and expand existing theories into new domains.

Take for example social information processing theory (SIPT; Walther, 1992), which suggests that processes and functions surrounding relational communication and interpersonal impression development ought to vary according to the ways that people use technology. However, scholars who use SIPT now recognize that key variables absent from the original theory (e.g., social or physical attraction) are consistent with its tenets. Though early work exploring impression formation on Facebook utilized SIPT as a guiding framework, it excluded the sorts of extended interaction between perceiver and target that was proposed in SIPT (see Walther, Van Der Heide, Kim, Westerman, & Tong, 2008). Instead, this research explored whether observing the interactions that people have with their friends through their Facebook comments, could affect how we judge them. That we could make such interpersonal judgments without ever directly interacting with the profile's owner with was a novel finding that pushed SIPT beyond its initial boundaries of long-term online group interaction and also showed its utility in predicting impression formation on social media. Understanding that the original theory was less of a dogma to be worked within and more of a springboard to be worked from has allowed scholars a much more nuanced understanding of the theory itself and its boundaries.

Of course, another complaint against expanding dependent variables is that it makes it more difficult to compare findings, particularly when multiple studies have focused on different outcomes. This is a valid concern. One real benefit to new research that utilizes the same "goal posts" as past research is that it can help us pinpoint whether new methodologies and/or causal variables affect the "usual" dependent variables in novel ways. But while we acknowledge this challenge, we would simply suggest that when it is warranted by theory, scholars *eventually must* break new ground. For example, as you've read about previously, warranting theory (Walther & Parks, 2002) was initially composed as a way to understand the process of interpersonal impression formation in a media-rich networked environment, and as such, scholars explored how different variables affected the ways that interpersonal impressions formed on Facebook (Walther, Van Der Heide, Hamel, & Shulman, 2009). However, it did not take long for scholars to realize that this theory may be useful far beyond the online interpersonal impression domain. For instance, the application of warranting to the credibility of online product reviews has helped us to understand how people make e-commerce decisions (see for review DeAndrea, 2014). The upshot here is that when theories are applied to new domains, they often exceed their authors' original expectations. If we are careful and treat those theories appropriately, the expansion of our dependent variable pool can help us craft and refine theoretical boundaries in ways that even the original authors of those theories could not have envisioned.

Finally, drawing on theory to illuminate the expansion of outcome variables may not be the only strategy. Another potential way forward is to observe people's *actual behaviors*. As noted above, because we are not always privy to our own motivations, goals, or interactions with technology (or those of our relational partners), we might not be able to report accurately on our own behavior. As a result, one way to examine the effects of technology on relational behavior is not to ask people what they do, but rather watch what they actually do. If—through systematic observation—we can identity how people are using technology to achieve certain relational functions, then we can be better positioned to identify and examine the factors that affect those behaviors. In doing so, key dependent variables may be integrated into our theories, further expanding their overall explanatory and predictive power.

It is important to highlight that our point here is not to critique the research process itself. Ultimately, seeking to understand the effects of technology on social behavior, and separating out things that are not technological effects but communicative or psychological ones (and vice versa), means we must carefully consider the comparison points which will allow us to make the precise theoretical claims we want to, but on the basis of our data.

What Might We Examine in the Future?

Because of their popularity and seeming ubiquity, online and mobile dating—and the broader topic of technology's role within contemporary romantic relationships—is a topic that interests scholars and students alike. The up-and-coming student who is searching for a thesis or dissertation idea often draws on their personal interests, which might include their own use of dating platforms, personal romantic imagination, or past romantic relationship experiences. Seasoned researchers interested in technology are often inquisitive about the latest, newest niche dating app to hit the market.

Don't be fooled by shiny objects. Dating apps and sites are certainly great at sparking new interests. When students discuss their ideas for research projects about online or mobile dating or romantic relationships, they often come to our office hours saying, "I really want to do a study about Tinder" or "Have you heard about The League? I'd like to investigate how it works!" Such curiosity is a wonderful starting point—but studies examining a single platform like Tinder or The League last only as long as the platform does. What happens when Tinder is no longer the most popular platform? Will the study be obsolete? Remember

MySpace? Or Friendster? Or Xanga?! (If you're too young to remember these, go Google them). When those platforms became obsolete, the studies that explored them and only them also lost relevance. However, research that focuses on how certain broader *features* or *affordances* affect *human communication* transcend any particular platform, and thus are likely to live on well after the lights go out at Match.com, Tinder, or eHarmony.

And too, investigations motivated by more than a narrow curiosity about this or that platform are more likely to yield greater understanding into contemporary courtship processes and dating practices. Studies that provide insight into how broader dimensions of dating platforms impact or reinforce patterns of communication behavior are much more likely to stand the test of time and make real, lasting contributions to theory and research. Furthermore, this approach can be adapted as new features and dimensions are added to the online and mobile dating ecosystem. Currently, the two most popular mobile dating apps—Tinder and Bumble—feature mutuality in their platform design (Statista.com, 2019), but that might not always be the case. We argue that an approach focused on shared platform dimensions, as opposed to a specific platform all by itself, can help researchers maintain empirical flexibility, while achieving theoretical longevity.

Rather than focusing in on the newest or most popular dating app of the day, another useful approach might be to focus on the *communicative aspects* of the research topic—phenomena like impression formation, mate selection, or interpersonal conflict are unlikely to go away, as long as humans continue to desire and forge romantic connections. Our advice is that focusing on that side of the topic—the human side—will ensure that your study stays relevant long after the hype over the latest app has died down. So, while it is fine to be inspired by the shine of an app, when developing your research topic, don't forget to look beyond the screen.

Consider multiple modalities. Thus far, little research has addressed the ways that mixed-mode communication affects people in romantic relationships. From its conception, the study of mixed-mode communication (Walther & Parks, 2002) has not progressed as quickly as other areas of inquiry. This is partially because the past research has fallen into two distinct camps: Research that explores mixed-mode relationships as conceived by Walther and Parks (2002) focuses on those relationships that begin in mediated spaces and then make a singular shift toward offline contexts (see Chapter 7, which concerns modality shifting). Alternatively, other researchers have explored the effects of modalities on romantic relationships, but their exploration is more focused on relational theory than considering the role of technology.

Future research work might expand upon mixed modality work more meaningfully. Walther and Parks' (2002) conceptualization of mixed-mode relationships has helped contemporary scholars realize that mixed-mode relationships are not a unidirectional phenomenon—that is, they don't only happen when people meet online and then move offline. We now know that mixed-mode connections also occur when people who met one another offline but fell out of contact use technology to reconnect online, and also when partners in well-developed (offline) relationships interact with each other regularly using multiple online channels. Each of these directional shifts (online-to-offline, from offline-to-online, and simultaneous on-and-offline communication) is likely to raise important theoretical issues.

In addition to understanding how mixed modalities affect human relationships by thinking about the "directionality" of the modality shift, it will also be important that scholars understand how these modality shifts operate throughout the lifespan of relationships, not just their beginnings. For reasons that are fairly obvious, the lion's share of research that has explored the effects of modality shifts has examined a single direction of modality shift (from online initiation to offline development) at a single relational stage (relationship formation). Given that this is the most common form of modality shift, it is not surprising that this work is well represented in the social science literature. However, when we consider the full gamut of relational issues and the larger set of relational stages, it becomes clear maintaining a romantic relationship requires *constantly* weaving between mediated and FtF messaging.

For example, Brandon regularly texts examples of products he would like to buy to his wife. Verbally describing these things would be time consuming and would require a great degree of explanation, whereas sending her a link to Amazon makes it very clear what product he wants to buy. Moreover, using technology to communicate allows Jen to read Brandon's message when (and sometimes *if*) she wishes, without Brandon having to bother her with his minute-to-minute machinations. Later, the two can meaningfully converse about the prospective product purchase, with a shared understanding of what value that product might bring to their household.

These sorts of mixed-mode interactions were not necessarily the sort that Walther and Parks envisioned when they coined the term; however, they have become increasingly common within long-term romantic relationships. Despite their relative frequency, scholars have few comprehensive answers about how partners conduct mixed-mode interactions, whether such interactions have positive or negative effects, or even if they are of any overall use to partners in romantic relationships. And this invites the question whether CMC functions differently in mature relationships than in emerging ones, about which we have more established findings.

A Final Invitation

At the end of a book like this one, it may sound a bit strange that we do not have any particular pronouncement about a direction in which the scholars who study the effects of technology on romantic relationships ought to move. Instead, we would invite scholars—new and experienced, from all disciplines—to join us as we uncover how technology affects the functions of human communication. If you have read this far, you have probably already begun to imagine the ways that you might implement some discussion of technology's effects on human relationships in your own work. All we would say to you at this point is: "Welcome to the club!" And (unlike Fight Club) the first rule of this club is that you have to talk about your research. The members of this club will promise to listen—skeptically, to some extent, but also thoughtfully and graciously. Science is a public endeavor that thrives on open discussion, debate, and exchange. Communicating what we know is how we stay *up to date*. We look forward to hearing from you!

References

DeAndrea, D. C. (2014). Advancing warranting theory. *Communication Theory, 24*, 186–204. https://doi.org/10.1111/comt.12033

Levine, T., Asada, K. J., & Carpenter, C. (2009). Sample sizes and effect sizes are negatively correlated in meta-analyses: Evidence and implication of publication bias against nonsignificant findings. *Communication Monographs, 76*, 286–302. https://doi.org/10.1080/03637750903074685

Statista.com (2019). *Most popular online dating apps in the United States as of September 2019, by audience size.* https://www.statista.com/statistics/826778/most-popular-dating-apps-by-audience-size-usa/

Walther, J. B. (1992). Interpersonal effects in computer-mediated interaction: A relational perspective. *Communication Research, 19*, 52–90. https://doi.org/10.1177/009365092019001003

Walther, J. B., & Parks, M. R. (2002). Cues filtered out, cues filtered in: Computer-mediated communication and relationships. In M. L. Knapp & J. A. Daly (Eds.), *The handbook of interpersonal communication* (3rd ed., pp. 529–563). Sage.

Walther, J. B, Van Der Heide, B., Hamel, L., & Shulman, H. C. (2009). Self-generated versus other-generated statements and impressions in computer-mediated communication: A test of warranting theory using Facebook. *Communication Research, 36,* 229–253. https://doi.org/ 10.1177/0093650208330251

Walther, J. B., Van Der Heide, B., Kim, S.-Y., Westerman, D., & Tong, S. T. (2008). The role of friends' appearance and behavior on evaluations of individuals on Facebook: Are we known by the company we keep? *Human Communication Research, 34,* 28–49. https://doi.org/ 10.1111/j.1468-2958.2007.00312.x

Index

Howard Giles

GENERAL EDITOR

This series explores new and exciting advances in the ways in which language both reflects and fashions social reality—and thereby constitutes critical means of social action. As well as these being central foci in face-to-face interactions across different cultures, they also assume significance in the ways that language functions in the mass media, new technologies, organizations, and social institutions. Language as Social Action does not uphold apartheid against any particular methodological and/or ideological position, but, rather, promotes (wherever possible) cross-fertilization of ideas and empirical data across the many, all-too-contrastive, social scientific approaches to language and communication. Contributors to the series will also accord due attention to the historical, political, and economic forces that contextually bound the ways in which language patterns are analyzed, produced, and received. The series will also provide an important platform for theory-driven works that have profound, and often times provocative, implications for social policy.

For further information about the series and submitting manuscripts, please contact:

Howard Giles
Department of Communication
University of California at Santa Barbara
Santa Barbara, CA 93106-4020
HowieGiles@cox.net

To order other books in this series, please contact our Customer Service Department at:

peterlang@presswarehouse.com (within the U.S.)
orders@peterlang.com (outside the U.S.)

Or browse online by series at:

www.peterlang.com